THE LIFE OF SIMON LORD LOVAT

WRITTEN BY HIMSELF, IN THE
FRENCH LANGUAGE, AND NOW
FIRST TRANSLATED FROM THE
ORIGINAL MANUSCRIPT

NEW EDITION
EDITED BY HUGH KEITH FRASER

PRIVATELY PRINTED BY
ARTHUR L. HUMPHREYS, 187 PICCADILLY, LONDON
1902

THE GENUINE AND REMARKABLE HISTORY OR MANIFESTO OF SIMON LORD FRASER, OR FREZEL OF LOVAT

One of the most ancient Peers of Scotland, and Head of the Clan of the FRASERS, so celebrated in the North, and in the Highlands of Scotland

IN TWO PARTS

The FIRST, treating of the cruel Injustice of the Family of Athol, and the other Enemies of that Nobleman.

The SECOND, relating the unexampled Persecution employed against him by the Court of St. Germains, for the Space of twelve Years, after he had abandoned his Estates and his Clan as a Prey to his Enemies, to go into France, to tender his Services to that unfortunate Court.

PREFACE.

THERE are no materials of history more valuable, and indeed few departments of historical composition more interesting and instructive than those details of important facts, which have been committed to writing by the persons principally concerned in conducting them.

Of this nature are the following sheets, originally written in French, by Lord Lovat, who was certainly no common personage. As his Lordship wrote them with a view to their being made public in due time, and the reasons which retarded the publication of these Memoirs no longer existing, the public are now put in possession of them, faithfully translated; without any further liberty being taken with the original work, than dividing it into sections, and adding the marginal dates and notes, by the Translator; who has to remark, that the genius of the Author may be clearly traced in the panegyric on the Intendant Rogeault, and the story of the Abbé Pouget, towards the conclusion of the work.

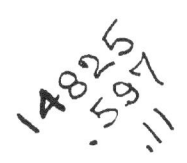

INTRODUCTION.

AS Lord Lovat engages to advance nothing in this manifesto which shall not be indisputably true, and which he will not be ready to prove before any prince or court of judicature in Europe, he most humbly intreats all candid persons to read his work in an unprejudiced manner, in order that they may do justice to his character, as well as to the treachery and ill faith of his persecutors. Since however the first part relates only to his quarrel with the family of Athol, and may appear tedious to the reader, Lord Lovat begs of him, if he be fond of intrigues of State, to bestow a perusal upon the second part, which explains the transactions of Great Britain and France, in relation to the Court of St. Germains. In the mean time there will not fail to occur, even in the first part, some interesting passages relative to State affairs.

MEMOIRS OF THE LIFE OF LORD LOVAT

PART THE FIRST.

'Nona ætas agitur, pejoraque secula ferri
Temporibus; quorum sceleri non invenit ipsa
Nomen, et à nullo posuit Natura metallo.

'Adspicimus populos, quorum non sufficit ira
Occidisse aliquem, sed pectora, brachia, vultum
Crediderint genus esse cibi.'
JUVENAL, Sat. 13, 15.

SIMON LORD LOVAT was descended from ancestors, both by the father and mother's side, who had always been celebrated for fidelity to their sovereigns: he was himself of a warm and active constitution. His father was the twenty-second person who had enjoyed the title of Lovat in lineal descent; they were uniform in their adherence to their country and their kings. His mother was Dame Sybilla Macleod, daughter of the chief of the clan of the Macleods, so famous for its inviolable loyalty to its princes.* These dispositions, as well general as individual, induced Simon Lord Lovat to display a

---

* The children of Thomas Fraser and Sybilla his wife were Alexander, Simon the hero of the present memoirs, and John, all of whom are mentioned in this history, and one daughter.

violent attachment to the ruined cause of the late King James of pious memory from his earliest youth.

He bore at that time the title of Laird of Beaufort, by which he was distinguished during the life of his cousin-german Hugh Lord Lovat. By the death of Hugh Lord Lovat without issue male, Thomas, father of Simon, and uncle of Hugh, had an incontestible claim to the honours and estates of Hugh Lord Lovat his nephew, and Hugh Lord Lovat his father, of whom Thomas was the younger son* by Dame Isabella Wemys, daughter of the Earl of Wemys, ancient peer of Scotland. Thomas therefore took possession without opposition of the honours and estates of his father and his nephew, and enjoyed them till his death.

Simon his son was, at the time of his father's accession to the title, by a most extraordinary stroke of Providence a captain in the regiment of the Earl of Tullibardin, now Lord Athol.

1694 This nobleman, who was then known by the title of Lord Murray, had received the commission of Colonel to raise a regiment of infantry for the service of William the Third, the reigning King of England. He presently found, however, that he was incapable of enlisting so much as a single company for his new

---

* According to Douglas's Peerage Hugh the father of Thomas of Beaufort was great-grandfather to the Hugh here mentioned. Of consequence Thomas of Beaufort was brother to his grandfather and Simon Lord Lovat at the same distance from the original stock as his father.

regiment, which he had promised King William to complete in a short time. This arose from the alienation of the Stewarts and the Robinsons of Athol, who were always much attached to the interests of King James, and who, regarding Lord Murray as their tyrant, were never willing to admit his claims of vassalage and obedience. On the contrary, they carefully sought all occasions to desert and affront him. Lord Murray sometimes had his revenge. He put the Laird of Balleahan, chief of the Stewarts of Athol, together with his brother Alexander Stewart, a man of high courage, in prison at Edinburgh, for having, in opposition to his orders, joined the expedition of Lord Viscount Dundee: there Simon Lord Lovat saw them in want of bread, and assisted them with his purse.

Lord Murray, being thus embarrassed in the affair of his regiment, conceived the idea of gaining over the confidence of Hugh Lord Lovat, who had married his sister, and persuading him to accept a company in his regiment, confident, that, by means of his clan of the Frasers, he would contribute much to render his regiment complete. Convinced, however, that Lord Lovat was much attached to King James, and the farthest in the world from an idea of entering into the service of William, he engaged in the execution of his project the Laird of Glengary, chief of a branch of the clan of Macdonalds, and an inveterate enemy of the Frasers, though at that time married to the sister of Hugh Lord Lovat, and nearly related by the Macdonalds to the Laird of Beaufort.

The Laird of Glengary, the hireling sycophant of Lord Murray, by whose means he received a pension from King William, at the very time that he appeared zealously engaged in the service of King James, having received his instructions, came to Beaufort, the seat where Lord Lovat then resided. He persuaded him that King James would infallibly arrive in Scotland in a short time, and that Lord Murray had accepted the regiment merely for the service of the King. He therefore conjured Lord Lovat to accept a company in the regiment, declaring to him, that it was impossible to render a more important service to King James, to whom he was so much attached.

Lord Lovat, who was known for a man of a feeble understanding, gave into the snare, and accepted the infamous commission that Lord Murray tendered him; though in the beginning of the reign of King William he had refused the offers of that prince to give him a regiment either of horse or foot, or to make him lord sheriff, or grand justiciary of his province during life. These offers had been conveyed to him by General Mackay his relation, who well knew that Lord Lovat, at the head of his clan of the Frasers, is the laird, of all the north the most capable of promoting or disturbing the commencement of a government, not yet well established, and this as well by the advantage of his situation, as by the known valour of his clan.

The Laird of Glengary, however, by the subtlety of his wit, and the insinuation of his manners, induced Lord Lovat to accept this infamous company, after having refused such valuable offers. By this means Glengary rendered the most important service to Lord Murray his patron, who, not daring to attack the Frasers in an open and decisive manner, endeavoured to tarnish their reputation by ruining that of their chief. Perhaps, too, he flattered himself, that, in case King James should be restored, he would obtain the confiscation of the lands of Lord Lovat, which he has usurped for so many years, under the pretence of indemnification for a debt that was never contracted. For Glengary, it will scarcely be wondered at that he should endeavour to ruin the Frasers, as it is notorious to the whole Scottish nation, that he set out with ruining his own clan in a manner the most unjust and detestable, and that he is properly regarded by his nearest relations, less as their laird and chief, than as their oppressor and tyrant.

Lord Lovat was soon convinced that every gentleman of his clan was in the highest degree scandalised at the affront he had put upon them in accepting this infamous commission. He therefore wrote to his cousin Simon of Beaufort, who was at that time at the royal university of Aberdeen, intreating him to quit his studies, though

1694 he had just taken his degree of master of arts, and was entering upon the science of civil law. Lord Lovat declared in the most solemn manner that he would ever regard him as his son and the representative of his house, and that with these views he had just accepted a commission in the regiment of his brother-in-law, Lord Murray, that he might bestow it upon him, and thus bring him forward most advantageously in the world.

Simon was animated with the most vigorous zeal for the interests of King James; he had already discovered this disposition under the command of General Thomas Buchan, and he had been three times thrown into prison for his exertions in the royal cause before he attained the age of sixteen years. He accordingly wrote a letter to his cousin full of the bitterest invectives, telling him that he had for ever lost his honour and his loyalty, and that possibly he would one day lose his estates, in consequence of the infamous step he had taken: that for himself, he was so far from consenting to accept a commission in the regiment of that traitor, Lord Murray, that he would immediately go home to his clan, and prevent any one man from enlisting into it.

Simon of Beaufort was as good as his word, and, being regarded by the whole clan as the heir apparent of his family, and their chief after the death of his cousin, he was able to exert so successful an influence, that Lord Lovat could not raise three men for his new

company. His lordship accordingly began to be ex- 1694
tremely ashamed of his engagement; he swore to the
Laird of Beaufort that it was Glengary that had persuaded him to do it for the service of King James; in
consequence of this confession Simon thought himself
obliged to talk in a very round manner to Glengary.

The old Marquis of Athol was the first man in
Scotland that had declared against King James; but,
having been dissatisfied with the recompences bestowed
upon him by King William, he changed sides again,
and displayed upon all occasions a violent zeal for the
interests of the unfortunate prince. This nobleman
professed the highest esteem for the Laird of Beaufort
for his late conduct. There had for some time subsisted a complete estrangement between him and Lord
Murray, his eldest son, to whom his father would not
so much as speak; calling him a traitor to his sovereign,
for having accepted a regiment from King William.
The old Marquis therefore remonstrated with Lord
Lovat, his son-in-law, in a very sharp style, praising at
the same time the loyalty of Simon of Beaufort, and
engaging him to pass the winter in the city of Perth
with his son Lord Mungo Murray in the study of the
mathematics.

Huntingtour, the seat of Lord Murray, was about 1695
three miles from Perth, and, as he saw himself still very
much embarrassed in the business of completing his
regiment, he conceived the idea of inviting Lord

1695 Mungo and Simon of Beaufort to come and spend a few days at his house. They accepted the invitation, and were very politely received. After some time had elapsed in general conversation, Lord Murray thought proper to blame the Laird of Beaufort for having refused so advantageous a commission, from which he might have derived a considerable income, at the same time following his studies wherever he pleased, and leaving to his lieutenant the management of his company. Simon thanked him very much, but added, that he could never accept any commission contrary to the interest of King James, to whom he was so much attached, and that he was extremely sorry that his cousin Lord Lovat had accepted it contrary to the dictates of his honour and his conscience.

Lord Murray, observing the inviolable loyalty of the Laird of Beaufort to King James, and knowing at the same time of what consequence it would be to gain him over in the business of recruiting his regiment, intimated that he was desirous of speaking to him in his closet. There he swore to the laird, that his design in accepting the regiment from King William, was that he might have a regiment well trained and accoutered to join King James in a descent he had promised to make in the ensuing summer. Lord Murray added, that he dared not discover his design to the old Marquis, his father, as he was apprehensive that his secret would not be safe in his hands; but he swore

that King James had not a more loyal subject in all 1695
Scotland, and that, since the Laird of Beaufort was so
zealous for his cause, he could not render him a more
valuable service than by accepting a company in the
regiment of Murray, at the same time conjuring him
in all events to preserve his secret.

Simon, after so many protestations of loyalty, gave
into the snare that was spread for him, and returned to
his clan to raise recruits. The old Marquis of Athol,
who did not know upon what foot the Laird of Beaufort
had entered into engagements with his son, reproached
him in the bitterest manner, for having suffered himself
to be inveigled into disloyalty by the insinuating
discourses of Lord Murray. Simon had no sooner
engaged in this regiment, than he led to it a complete
company, almost entirely made up of the young gentlemen of his clan. Murray, however, broke his word
with him in the affair of the company, and obliged him
to sit down for some time with a commission of
lieutenant of grenadiers. In a word, Simon did not
obtain a company in the regiment till after having
brought to it three hundred recruits, and was then
obliged to make a compensation in money to the
captain who made room for him. He did not fail to
be extremely disgusted at having suffered himself to
be over-reached by Lord Murray, whose treachery he
conceived to be of a very infamous nature.

The year following, his lordship being appointed 1696

principal Secretary of State for Scottish affairs, he devoted himself in so high a degree to the interests of King William, that he was continually torturing his invention for means to display the ardour of his zeal for his new master. As he knew that his regiment was filled with persons well affected to the service of King James, he in the first place gave it the appointment of guard to the royal palace of Edinburgh. He then assembled his officers, represented to them that they were regarded by the common men in the light of Jacobites, and added, that, to demonstrate how little foundation there was for this idea, he was obliged to tender them the oath of abjuration against King James, and the pretended Prince of Wales. Many of the officers replied, that this oath had never been tendered to the officers of the Scottish army, and therefore intreated that their regiment might not be the first that should be called upon to take it. Lord Murray alleged, that he could not be dispensed with from giving this mark of his zeal for King William, and that therefore it was necessary to submit or to quit the regiment. Accordingly, officers, highly attached to King James, were forced to sign the oath of abjuration, in order to preserve to themselves the means of subsistence.

As Lord Murray recollected upon what principle the Laird of Beaufort had entered into his regiment, and well knew that he was firm and intrepid in the interests of King James, he sent for him to his closet, and besought him to sign the oath of abjuration. Simon told him, that he did not well understand this demand, after all the promises he had made in behalf of King James. The Colonel upon this acknowledged, that he had been at that time very much inclined to King James's party; but that since, he had been much enlightened upon the subject, and that it was his regard to the welfare of the Protestant religion that induced him to be faithful to King William. Simon replied without any circumlocution, that what induced him to be faithful to King William was the appointment of Secretary of State: adding, that, if he pressed him a moment longer upon this subject, he would declare to all the world that Lord Murray had engaged him in his regiment for the service of James.

Thus it was that this nobleman, now Lord Athol, and who is at this hour the favourite hero and the grand pillar of the Court of St. Germains, was the first and the only man who obliged the officers of the Scottish army to take the oath of abjuration against King James.

The following incident, however, will make it sufficiently evident that the zeal of the Colonel for King William did not alter the inclinations of some of the officers of his regiment. At the time that an invasion was so much apprehended in the years 1696 and 1697, the castle of Edinburgh being in a very defenceless state and almost without a garrison, the Earl of Leven, at that time a zealous adherent of King William, and Governor of the place, obtained an order for a company of the regiment of Lord Murray, which was stationed as a guard to the royal palace of Edinburgh, to do duty at the castle, in conjunction with the half of the garrison, which scarcely exceeded an hundred men.

The Earl Marishal of Scotland had been committed prisoner to the castle, together with Lord Drummond, his brother-in-law, son of the Earl of Perth, and many other lords, for their attachment to King James. Lord Marishal was the intimate friend of the Laird of Beaufort, at that time a captain in the regiment of Lord Murray, and who mounted guard at the castle in his turn. This nobleman, therefore, proposed to Simon, that, as soon as the King should arrive in Scotland, or they should even receive advice of his departure from France upon an expedition either against England or Scotland, he should contrive to mount guard at the castle, in conjunction with another captain of the same regiment, distinguished for his attachment to King James, but whom I do not here name, because he is still in the service of the English Government: that, when they should be upon the parade in order to relieve the guard, and consequently when both their companies were present, they should make themselves masters by a *coup de main* of the

LIFE OF LORD LOVAT.

unarmed garrison, and shut the gates: that they should 1696 then declare for King James, appoint Earl Marishal governor, and commit the Earl of Leven prisoner in his turn.

The other captain and the Laird of Beaufort engaged upon oath, together with Lord Marishal and other lords, who, as they are yet living, shall also be nameless, to preserve an inviolable fidelity to this design. The scheme, indeed, was infallible, had not the navy of France been so irretrievably ruined by the decisive defeat of La Hogue.* The Court of St. *1692 Germains, which was informed of this project by Lord Marishal, made warm acknowledgements for his share in it to the Laird of Beaufort, though she has since recompensed all these services by an unexampled persecution.

The friends of Lord Lovat exclaimed bitterly against Lord Murray, that he did not resign his regiment in favour of his brother-in-law; there having been no example of a Secretary of State retaining his appointment of Colonel to a regiment after being raised to that office. Lord Murray at length promised his regiment to Lord Lovat; and, being desirous to display to King William his power among the Highlanders of Scotland, whose importance William well knew, by presenting to him one of their greatest lords, he sent three expresses one after the other, to intreat Lord Lovat to set out immediately for London to

1696 take upon him the command of the regiment. His Lordship accordingly took post, and as he had an extreme affection for the Laird of Beaufort, his cousin, he took him with him to London. Lord Murray received them very politely; and, without saying a word of the regiment, carried Lord Lovat to Kensington, and presented him to King William, saying, that he was his brother-in-law, one of the most ancient peers of Scotland, and head of one of the bravest clans in the Highlands, that therefore he could venture to assure his majesty of their fidelity. King William accosted Lord Lovat in a very gracious manner, telling him that he knew the antiquity of his house and the importance of his clan, and that he might depend upon his providing for him.

Lord Murray, who was obliged to set out for Scotland in two days, and who was not willing to leave to Lord Lovat an opportunity of speaking to the King, whispered him, that it was proper for him to fall upon one knee and take leave of his majesty. Lord Lovat, who, as we have already seen, was of a contracted understanding, and who had never been at Court before, did as he was directed.

When, however, he had left the presence chamber, and parted with Lord Murray, his cousin, Simon of Beaufort, told him that that nobleman had caused him to take leave of the King in order to deprive him of all opportunity of obtaining a fresh audience, and soliciting a regiment. Simon, meantime, obliged him the next day to demand of Lord Murray for what reason he had caused him to come to London at so enormous an expense. Lord Murray replied, that it was his design to have resigned to him the command of his regiment, but that the King had obliged him to keep it in his own hands till the fears of an invasion should be blown over, when he certainly would surrender his command to Lord Lovat.

Lord Lovat was much displeased with this answer; and, having spent the evening with his cousins, Lord Tarbat,* and Colonel Alexander Mackenzie, son to the Earl of Seaforth, and at this time an officer in the Guards, they showed him very plainly that Lord Murray made a jest of him, and had brought him to London in order to make his court to King William at Lord Lovat's expense; at the same time advising him to break with him.

Lord Lovat, being by this time convinced how much he had been deceived, and how ill he had been treated by the family of Athol, took their advice, sent back his commissions of captain and of lieutenant-colonel to Lord Murray, his colonel; expressing at the same time in very strong language his resentment of Lord Murray's treachery, and protesting that he would never see him more, nor any individual of his

---

* Afterwards Earl of Cromarty.

family, except his sister, whom, as being his wife, he was obliged to retain.

Lord Murray was better pleased to retain a salary of four thousand pounds in his own hands by keeping his regiment, than to preserve the friendship of Lord Lovat, as there was no further advantage to be derived from him. He also turned to account the resignation of Lord Lovat, though it was made in favour of the Laird of Beaufort, his cousin, as he gave the company to Lord James Murray, apologizing to Simon that Lord James had a wife and a family, without having bread to eat. It is proper to remark in this place that Lord James, who accepted this company, was the most violent partisan the exiled family had in Scotland, and that he could not bear to hear so much as the name of King William, down to the very moment that he received the appointment of captain in his service.

Lord Lovat was so deeply impressed with the treachery of the family of Athol, as well respecting him, as respecting the Kings William and James, that, intreating his cousin Simon to return with him to his own seat of Lovat, he swore that he would never see the Marquis of Athol, nor any of the young lords, his children, whom he had hitherto supported from year to year, they not having so much as a maintenance in their own family.

Impressed at the same time with the tender affection

of the Laird of Beaufort, and the resolution he manifested never to abandon him, Lord Lovat declared, that he regarded him as his own son. And as Lord Athol had urged him to execute some papers at his marriage, which might perhaps be prejudicial to the claims of Simon as his male heir, he obliged the young laird to send for an attorney, and made an universal bequest to him of all his estates in case he died without issue male, leaving the ordinary dowries to his daughters, and annulling and abjuring whatever he might at any time have done, in opposition to the ancient claims of his house in favour of the male heirs. Simon expressed the most grateful sense of the affectionate conduct of Lord Lovat, and protested that he would ever consider him as his father.

Lord Lovat fell sick at London, his chagrin and disappointment having induced him to frequent too much the taverns of the metropolis, where he contracted his distemper. But his health at length being restored, he set out upon his return for Scotland with his cousin, the Laird of Beaufort, who quitted him neither day nor night during the whole period of his misfortune.

When he arrived at Edinburgh, the family of Athol, having understood that he was resolved to go immediately to Lovat, without passing by Athol, or so much as seeing any of the family, persuaded his wife to come to Dunkeld, a seat of Lord Athol, from whence she

1696 wrote to her husband an affectionate letter, telling him that she waited his arrival at the house of the Marquis, her father.

Lord Lovat was resolute not to go thither to meet her; but the Laird of Beaufort, who had much influence over him, fearing that Lord Murray, who had just been created by King William, Earl of Tullibardin, and appointed High Commissioner to the Scottish Parliament, should attribute to him the actions of Lord Lovat, and employ his influence as his commanding officer to ruin him, advised his cousin to go to Dunkeld to conduct his wife to Lovat, but not to consent to make any stay with Lord Athol. Lord Lovat yielded to the persuasions of Simon, shedding many tears upon parting with him, and crying, 'We shall never see each other more; this savage family of Athol will certainly kill me.'

In reality he had been only two days at Dunkeld, when he fell sick, and the Athols, not willing to be troubled with the care of an invalid, or for some other reasons, sent him to an inn in the city of Perth, hard by the house of Doctor James Murray, a physician, the relation and the creature of the Marquis of Athol, upon whom the care of Lord Lovat's person was devolved.

The moment the Laird of Beaufort heard the news that Lord Lovat had been conducted very ill to the town of Perth, he set out without delay to his assistance. But before his arrival, in consequence of the

violent remedies that had been administered to him, 1696
he lost the use of his reason, and lay in his bed, in
a manner incapable of motion, abandoned by his wife
and the whole family of Athol, who waited for his
dissolution in great tranquillity at the house of Doctor
Murray, their relation.

Lord Lovat, however, recollected his cousin, and
embracing him, said: 'Did not I tell you, my dear
Simon, that these devils would certainly kill me? See
in what a condition I am!' Simon could not refrain
from tears at this melancholy spectacle. He threw
himself upon the bed beside Lord Lovat, and did not
quit him for a single moment till he died the next
morning in his arms. Meanwhile, not an individual
of the family of Athol entered his apartment, after
having once seen him in the desperate condition in
which he had been found by the Laird of Beaufort.

Simon reproached in a very undisguised manner
the whole Athol family with the death of his cousin;
and, after very high words on both sides, he set out
to join his regiment, then attending their Colonel, the
Earl of Tullibardin, formerly Lord Murray, who represented the person of King William in the Parliament
of the present year.

Thomas of Beaufort, father of Simon, and uncle
of the deceased Hugh, now took possession of the
honours and property of his nephew, who had died
without male children. The rights of the house of

1696 Lovat, and indeed of almost all the heads of clans, had been for time immemorial always in favour of the male heirs in exclusion of the female. The claim of Thomas, now Lord Lovat, being therefore considered as incontestible, not a man in all the north of Scotland dreamed that the Marquis of Athol would endeavour to disturb his possession. In consequence of this event Simon quitted the title of Laird of Beaufort, and took that of Master of Lovat.

The apparent security, however, of Thomas Lord Lovat was quickly seen not to be entirely well founded. The Earl of Tullibardin had at that time five sons without having fortunes to bestow upon them. He saw himself Secretary of State, Viceroy of Scotland for King William, and of consequence master of the Privy Council and of the Scottish army. In this situation he conceived a design of causing the eldest daughter of Hugh Lord Lovat to be declared heiress to the estates of her father, and to bestow her upon one of his sons in marriage; persuaded that his sister, the dowager Lady Lovat, would be pleased with the idea of thus aggrandising her paternal house.

Simon, Master of Lovat, being informed of this design, previously to his communicating it to Lord Lovat, his father, consulted the most able lawyers in the kingdom upon the subject. The unanimous opinion of these lawyers was, that Lord Tullibardin had no more power to make his niece heiress of Lovat than to

put her in possession of the kingdom of Scotland; that 1696
the right of Thomas of Beaufort to the honours and
property of Lovat was incontrovertible; and that the
King himself could not deprive him of them, without
incurring the guilt of high treason.

The Master of Lovat, delighted with the issue of
this consultation, dispatched an express to his father,
beseeching him not to make himself uneasy about the
reports raised by the family of Athol; that his rights
were incontestible, and that he had nothing to do but
to defend them. Lord Lovat replied, that he knew
this as well as all the lawyers in the kingdom, and
that nothing gave him any pain upon the subject, but
the continuance of the Master in the regiment of a
tyrant, who was capable of contriving his assassination.

Lord Lovat was not in the wrong, to fear as he did,
the pernicious designs of the Earl of Tullibardin. This
nobleman, having learned that the Master had consulted
the ablest lawyers in the kingdom, and had transmitted
their favourable opinions to Lord Lovat, his father, sent
for him one evening, when it was his turn to mount
guard for the defence of the person of the Viceroy,
his Colonel. As the Master of Lovat entered the
apartment of Lord Tullibardin, he saw the two centinels,
who were placed in the antichamber according to
custom, and he found with the Lord Commissioner an
attorney and a barrister. His lordship received the
Master in a very gracious manner, telling him that he

1696 must have been already convinced that Lord Tullibardin entertained an extreme friendship for him, and that he had now formed a project for making his fortune. Simon thanked him for his good intentions.

'But,' cried my Lord Commissioner, 'I am told you have assumed the title of Master of Lovat, and that you have sent opinions of counsel to your father, recommending to him to take possession of the property of my late brother-in-law.' Simon replied, that his father had taken possession of the honours and estates of his nephew immediately upon his death, and long before it was in his power to have sent him such a consultation as my Lord Commissioner mentioned.

Lord Tullibardin answered, that he had also had a consultation upon this affair; that he was conscious nobody could hinder Thomas of Beaufort from taking the title of Lord Lovat, he had a right to it; but that for the property of the deceased, it belonged to his eldest daughter and heiress; adding, that if Simon would consent to renounce his pretensions to the property and honours of Lovat, he would give him a regiment, and an income that should make him easy for life. Simon rejoined, that he had either a just right to the succession of Lovat, or he had not; if he had no right, it was to little purpose to renounce his claim; but if he had a right, he would not renounce it for the revenues of Scotland.

To this the Lord Commissioner answered, that he had

sent for the lawyer and attorney then present to draw
up his renunciation; that if he would execute it he
would make his fortune, but if he refused he would
not fail to ruin him. Simon replied, that it was idle to
have sent for an attorney and a barrister in this business,
that he had consulted the first lawyers in the kingdom,
that his claim was legitimate and incontestible, and that
all the power and all the riches of Scotland should
never prevail upon him to surrender it.

This firmness and spirit threw the Lord Commissioner
into a violent passion. He exclaimed with a furious
tone: 'I have always known you for an obstinate,
insolent rascal. I do not know what should hinder
me from cutting off your ears, or from throwing you
into a dungeon, and bringing you to the gallows, as
your treasons against the government so richly deserve.'
Simon, having never before been accustomed to such
language, immediately stuck his hat upon his head, and
laying his hand upon the hilt of his sword, was upon
the point of drawing it, when he observed that Lord
Tullibardin had no sword. Upon this he addressed
him in the following manner: 'I do not know what
hinders me, knave and coward as you are, from running
my sword through your body. You are well known
for a poltroon; and, if you had one grain of courage,
you would never have chosen your ground in the midst
of your guards, to insult a gentleman of a better house,
and of a more honourable birth, than your own; but I

shall one day have my revenge. As for the paltry company that I command in your regiment, and which I bought dearer than ever any company was bought before, it is the greatest disgrace to which I was ever subject to be for a moment under your command, and now, if you please, you may give it to your footman.'

Having thus given vent to his resentment, Simon left the apartment with his hat upon his head, and his hand upon the hilt of his sword, for fear of being assassinated. But the Lord Commissioner had not the courage to order the two centinels who were in the antichamber to arrest him; being probably apprehensive of the resentment of the guard of infantry, which Simon commanded in the court of the palace, and which was almost entirely composed of his own clan.

When the Master of Lovat got into the court, he desired his lieutenant to take care of the guard, and went himself to seek General Sir Thomas Livingston, Commander-in-Chief of the Scottish army, and who was afterwards created by King William, Lord Viscount Teviot. The General had a great regard for the Master of Lovat, and none at all for Lord Tullibardin the High Commissioner. When, therefore, Simon complained to him of the insult he had received from Tullibardin, his Colonel, in the midst of his guards, he was extremely provoked, and said to the Master: 'Your Colonel, my dear Simon, is in luck to be High Commissioner, and to represent, however unworthily, the person of the

King, for, if he were not, I would throw him this very 1696 evening into the prison with which he has so basely threatened you. But do not fear him; he dares not do you any harm. I take you under my protection, and I will remove you from his regiment into a much better situation before a week be elapsed.'

Next day General Livingston and the Master of Lovat published the infamous conduct of the Lord Commissioner to the whole army. He had never been popular in Scotland; and this action rendered him completely odious. It was the only subject of conversation at Edinburgh for several days, and the little children cried shame upon him as his carriage passed along the streets.

In this manner the public completely revenged the Master of Lovat for an affront, which he could not vindicate with his sword, as he had to do with his own Colonel, with the Viceroy of a kingdom, and with a man who was beside a poltroon by profession. It was not long after, that he refused in a very disgraceful manner the challenge of Mr. Campbel of Finac, who had distinguished himself in the enterprise of Darien, telling him that his conscience would not permit him to fight a duel; though Mr. Campbel had openly insulted him in his own apartment in the royal palace of Edinburgh, and upon the very spot where the above scene had passed with the Master of Lovat.

Simon was not willing, after this, to perform any

1696 function in the regiment, and Sir Thomas Livingston had the goodness to remove him from the regiment of Lord Tullibardin, and to give him the company of grenadiers of the regiment of Macgil. This company was superior to any other grenadiers in Scotland, being almost wholly composed of young gentlemen, uniformly tall and well shaped. The Master of Lovat enjoyed this new appointment, and Thomas Lord Lovat his father kept quiet possession of the honours and estates of his ancestors for one entire year, when they were disturbed by the insatiable cupidity and the avaricious machinations of the old Marquis of Athol.

This nobleman had rendered himself universally odious by the tyranny he exercised upon his vassals in the province of Athol, and still more by his inexcusable and infamous conduct towards the illustrious house of Argyle, a house which had been so unjustly oppressed in the preceding reigns. This rascally Marquis had been a personal enemy to the late Earl of Argyle, who was beheaded under James the Second; the bravest and the most respectable nobleman in Scotland. The Earl of Argyle had given a blow to the Marquis of Athol publicly before the whole court, which was then at Edinburgh, and the Marquis did not dare to revenge himself but by the basest and most barbarous tyranny.

Lord Athol had the command of the troops, which
1685 were sent to reduce the Earl of Argyle; a hero, most

unjustly persecuted by a cabal of courtiers, after having given the most unquestionable proofs of his loyalty to King Charles the Second, and having even followed him in his exile. This savage Marquis, seeing himself at the head of a powerful army, and master of the county of Argyle, not only pillaged the whole country and every house in it, but also caused all the beautiful plantations of the castle of Inverary, the principal seat of the Earls of Argyle, to be defaced and torn up by the roots. Nor did his malice stop here. He caused fourscore brave gentlemen of the House of Argyle to be assassinated with the most unexampled barbarity. He had at this moment in his pocket the pardon of King James for all the Campbels who were willing to submit to his clemency, and he had consented to a capitulation with these very gentlemen, by which he had obtained possession of the castle, where they had held out against the efforts of his whole army. In defiance however, both of the royal pardon and of his own capitulation, he caused them all to be hanged.

Simon, who was at that time a boy, was informed of these particulars by the late Lord Lovat, his father, who, being trustee of the Lovat estate, had been obliged by an order from the King to lead his clan against the Earl of Argyle, though he was tenderly attached to this nobleman, and was ready to have sacrificed his life for him in any other quarrel, than against his lawful Sovereign.

Mr. John Fraser, brother to Simon, and who was commonly known in France by the appellation of the Chevalier de Lovat, assured him during his residence in that country, that, in travelling to Edinburgh, he was only a mile and a half from the castle of Dunkeld, at the time of the death of the Marquis of Athol*; and that his host, who sat up in his turn, together with a guard of thirty men, in the Marquis's apartment, had informed him, that for a month before his death, Lord Athol was in the most deplorable condition, blaspheming God, and crying, that he was already in hell, and surrounded with devils, for having oppressed the Stewarts of Athol and the Frasers, and for having shed the innocent blood of the Campbels. The clergymen of the neighbourhood, all of whom came in their turn, to endeavour to compose him, were terrified from approaching his bed, he crying out, that he had nothing to do with them; and that he was already encompassed with devils. And in this infernal kind of madness the Marquis died, the very night that the Chevalier de Lovat was within three miles of his house: an exemplary judgment of God, which ought to make those tremble who oppress the just, and destroy the innocent; for sooner or later their punishment is certain, and, if they are spared in this world, it is only to aggravate their torments in the world to come.

After this digression, which relates to a fact that ought not to be concealed from posterity, I return to

*1703

the project of that greyheaded tyrant, the Marquis of Athol, and of the Earl of Tullibardin, his eldest son, the true heir to his avarice and his other amiable qualities, to possess themselves of the estates of Lovat, and to enrich their family, which was hitherto rich only in hungry lords, without property, and without appointments.

To carry this project into execution, they consulted 1697 with an infamous and unnatural rascal of the clan of the Frasers, who was at that time a barrister, without either reputation or employment, in the city of Edinburgh, and who for a little money sold himself to the family of Athol, to betray his clan, and to ruin his chieftain. Mr. Michael Fraser, his brother, and a very learned minister in the neighbourhood of Inverness, who has always continued extremely faithful and zealous for his laird, exerted himself to persuade this apostate wretch to abandon his design. But he was unsuccessful in his attempt, and concluded with cursing the day that gave birth to such a monster as his brother Robert, who for vile lucre submitted to be the instrument of Lord Athol to ruin Lord Lovat, and to exterminate the name of Fraser, which he unworthily bore.

Robert Fraser represented to the Marquis of Athol that he had no apparent right to the estates of Lovat, and had little prospect of success, if he endeavoured to possess himself of them by force; since the whole clan was unanimous to live and die with Thomas Lord Lovat, and resolved to suffer all extremities, rather than permit a stranger to enter into possession of their province. He therefore observed, that the only conduct it became him to adopt was to declare the eldest daughter of the deceased Hugh Lord Lovat, heiress to his property, and to offer her in marriage to the eldest son of Lord Salton, whose name was Fraser, and who was the representative of an inconsiderable branch of the Frasers, which had settled in the lowlands of the county of Aberdeen. He added that in that case he would undertake to insinuate to the clan of the Frasers that Lord Salton was very rich, and a Fraser as well as themselves; and that if his son united his property with that of the pretended heiress the clan of Frasers would become much more flourishing and respectable than under Thomas Lord Lovat, who was neither so rich, nor so capable of freeing the clan from the many unjust claims that were made upon them, and prosecuted in law for fictitious debts. Robert Fraser concluded, that, when the clan should by this plot, and by some bribes that might be secretly distributed, be divided among themselves, and when, of which there was no doubt, Lord Lovat and Lord Salton should have cut each others throats, the family of Athol might profit by their disorder; and the Marquis might introduce the young lords, his children, into possession of the province, either under pretext of the dowry of

LIFE OF LORD LOVAT.

their sister, or by the pretended right of the young 1697 heiress, their niece, who would then be in their power to marry as they pleased.

The Lords Athol and Tullibardin were delighted with a project which accorded so well with their own hearts. They began with bestowing rewards upon the traitor, Robert Fraser, and upon a little knave of a Fraser, the son of Dunballah, whom Robert associated with him, in order to inveigle the clan, and to lead Lord Salton into their snare.

They repaired accordingly to his seat in the county of Aberdeen, and represented to him that it would be worthy of a man of his virtue and greatness of soul to raise the name and the clan of Fraser to a flourishing condition, and to bestow his son in marriage upon the heiress of Lovat, by which means, as he was very rich, he might place the clan in a more honourable and respectable condition than ever.

Lord Salton had often heard that the estate of Lovat was the best situated and in the finest country in Scotland; and, as he was naturally the most avaricious of men, he gave willingly into their plan. At the same time he was a man of good sense and a great deal of prudence; and, as he was very remotely related to the clan of the Frasers, being incapable even of speaking their Erse language, he declared that he would never consent to the project, but upon condition of his being invited by the clan, and provided there should not be found

1697 any near relation of the late Lord Lovat, who should be proper or willing to marry the pretended heiress.

The two traitors, Robert and Thomas Fraser, who had already sold their laird and their clan, now undertook to procure for Lord Salton an address, or unanimous letter, in the name of the whole clan, to intreat him to come among them and consummate this marriage, though these knaves had no more credit in the clan than a couple of footmen. They quitted, however, Lord Salton in order to carry on their scheme.

They were sufficiently pleased that they had so far succeeded as to draw him into their snare. In the mean time they wrote to Lord Athol, that they were proceeding to Inverness, and that, even should they not dare to mention their project to the clan, they would, however, procure a fictitious letter to induce Lord Salton to set out for Lovat. They added, that Lord Athol ought by all means to send one of his children to receive him, and to buoy him up in the hope which they had inspired, of having the pretended heiress for his eldest son. Lord Athol accordingly dispatched Lord Mungo Murray, with instructions to his daughter, the dowager Lady Lovat, respecting the manner in which she should receive Lord Salton.

Robert Fraser and his coadjutors, having arrived at Inverness, near Lovat, conscious that they did not dare to open their project to the principal gentlemen of the clan, who were extremely attached to Thomas Lord

Lovat, and, who had no conception of the possibility of his title being disputed, bribed two or three beggarly relations of their own to sign such a letter as they desired. This done, they immediately dispatched it express to Lord Salton, assuring him that the three signatures annexed were those of the principal gentlemen of the clan; and that they had subscribed it in the name of all the Frasers to invite him into their country.

Lord Salton gave implicitly into their artifice: and such was the origin of all the misfortunes of Thomas Lord Lovat, and Simon Lord Lovat, his son, and of the almost total ruin of the clan of the Frasers, so celebrated for ages in the Scottish history. Robert, the prime author of these misfortunes, died under the visible judgment of God; and his fellow knave, Thomas Fraser, may yet be overtaken with the just punishment of his crimes.

These two emissaries of Lord Athol, however, divulged their design to some of their relations, who were faithfully attached to Lord Lovat; he was accordingly advertised of the particulars, and immediately dispatched an express to his son, who was then at Edinburgh, intreating him to quit the army, and come and reside with him, to defend his rights against those who were disposed to invade them. Simon, unable to resist the inclinations of his father, quitted the service with regret, and immediately set out, to place himself, together with his father, at the head of the affairs of his clan.

As soon as he arrived, and received an account of the treachery of Robert and Thomas Fraser, and three or four beggarly people of the name, who had invited Lord Salton to come and interrupt the tranquility of his father and his clan, the Master of Lovat dispatched three men to arrest Robert and his insolent coadjutors, in order to their being punished according to their deserts. It may be remarked, by the way, that the heads of the Scottish clans exercise a power nearly despotic over their vassals. The conspirators, however, escaped, and hastened to put themselves under the protection of Lord Salton.

When Lord Lovat and his son were acquainted with their escape they caused a general letter to be written to Lord Salton on the part of the whole clan, to intreat him to remain at home, and not to interfere with their repose, their chieftain, or his interests. They added, that they were unanimously determined to live and die with their laird, and that they were sorry to be obliged to tell Lord Salton, though he were a Fraser, that, if he dared to enter their country in hostility to Thomas, Lord Lovat, their chief, his head should answer the infringement, and he should never return alive into his own country. Every gentleman of the clan, the three beggars excepted, who had associated themselves with the barrister and his cousin, signed this letter.

An express was accordingly dispatched, who met 1697 Lord Salton already advanced half way on his journey. He proceeded, however, to Inverness, where he learned from undoubted authority that Thomas Lord Lovat and Simon, the Master, were in peaceful possession of the honours and estates of their ancestors, and that the clan were resolute to defend them to the last; consequently, if he advanced any farther in the prosecution of his scheme, he would not fail to run an imminent risk of his life, since the highland clans did not consider themselves as bound by the letter of the law, like the inhabitants of the low country, but to a man would regard it as their honour and their boast, to cut the throat, or to blow out the brains of any one, be he who he would, who should dare to disturb the repose of their laird.

Lord Salton, who had little knowledge of the manners of these regions, had by this time severely repented the having left his own country. He wrote upon the spot a very humble and polite letter to Lord Lovat and his son, protesting before God that he had not left his own estate in order to disturb their tranquility; but that he was come, like a good Fraser, to endeavour to terminate in an amicable manner the differences he had been told had arisen between Lord Lovat and the family of Athol; and that for this purpose he would now proceed to the residence of the Lady Dowager Lovat, which was at Beaufort, nine miles from Inverness.

Lord Lovat and his son took this letter in good part, and answered Lord Salton, that, if he were come upon so good an errand, he was welcome to Lovat, and they would hasten to do him the honours of the country; but that, if he came to intrude into their concerns against their consent, he should dearly repent it.

Still, however, Lord Lovat and his son, and the principal people of the clan, were apprehensive that the Lady Dowager Lovat and her brother, the son and daughter of Lord Athol, together with the three or four traitor Frasers who were with them, would persuade Lord Salton to persist in their project. Lord Lovat was at this time at his large estate of Stratheric, which stretches along the western banks of the Ness; the estates of Lord Lovat comprehending the almost entire circumference of this lake, which is the largest and most beautiful in Scotland. The Master of Lovat, therefore, intreated his father to cross the lake by the shortest cut, in order to meet Lord Salton at his seat of Lovat, the houses of Beaufort and Lovat being only three miles from each other. In the meantime Simon determined to proceed to the same point by the way of Inverness, in order that he might meet Lord Salton, if his lordship should be desirous of setting out on his return before their arrival.

The Master of Lovat no sooner arrived at Inverness, a town whose inhabitants are almost all of his clan, and as true to his interests as those who live at the very gates of Lovat, than he learned that Lord Salton had once more given himself up to the direction of Robert Fraser and his associates, that they had jointly concerted their affairs at the house of the dowager Lady Lovat, and that he meaned to return the next day into his own country, without waiting to see either Lord Lovat or his son, notwithstanding his having given them his word that it was for their interests that he had come into the province. Simon, who was at that time very young, and eager in his temper, was extremely irritated at this behaviour. He sent a letter with all diligence by a gentleman of his train, in which he called upon Lord Salton to adhere to his word, passed to his father and himself, and to meet him the next day, at two in the afternoon, three miles from Beaufort, either like a friend, or with sword and pistol, as he pleased.

Lord Salton received this letter at six o'clock in the evening, and immediately called together his cabal, by whom it was resolved, that it would be proper to send word to the Master of Lovat, that Lord Salton would meet him at the time and place appointed, as his good friend and servant. In the meantime they determined, that, as the rendezvous was given only for two o'clock in the afternoon, they ought to set out at break of day, and pass the bridge of Inverness before eight in the morning. It was not doubted, that thus they would escape the Master of Lovat, who would have no suspicion of so precipitate a retreat.

Lord Salton accordingly returned a polite answer, assuring the Master of Lovat that he should be happy to meet him, in order to give him the proofs of that friendship and respect he entertained for him. The gentlemen, however, who attended the Master, had a mistrust of all that was concerted at Beaufort. They recommended to him to proceed for Lovat early in the morning, before it should be possible for Lord Salton to escape.

The Master accordingly proceeded, and passed the bridge of Inverness very early, attended by six gentlemen and two servants, on horseback, and completely armed. The inhabitants, observing their alert and spirited appearance, lifted up their hands to heaven, and prayed God to prosper their enterprise.

They had not proceeded more than four or five miles beyond Inverness, when they observed a large troop of runners issuing out of the wood of Bonshrive, which is crossed by the high road. It is a custom in the north of Scotland, for almost every gentleman to have a servant in livery, who runs before his horse, and who is always at his stirrup when he wishes to mount or to alight; and, however swift any horse may be, a good runner is always able to match him.

The gentlemen who attended upon the Master of Lovat, seeing this large troop of runners, were immediately satisfied of the duplicity of Lord Salton, and assured him that it was his lordship, Lord Mungo

Murray, son of Lord Athol, and the rest of the cabal 1697 who were advancing. The Master represented to his attendants that such an affront was too atrocious for him not to exact satisfaction for it, or to perish in the attempt; and he demanded of them whether they were willing to run the same hazard which he was determined to do. The gentlemen of his party were offended at the question, and assured their chief that his own heart was not more faithful to his purpose than they were to expose their lives and fortunes for his honour and interest. He replied, that, since Lord Salton and Lord Mungo Murray were, if they might judge from the appearance of the troop of runners, four times stronger than himself, he would call out Lord Salton in duel, and Lord Mungo as his second, and he intreated his attendants not to fire till the combat should be finished between him and Lord Salton. Having thus concerted their proceedings, they marched on to the rencounter, the runners having assured them that the company that was advancing was that of the lords whom they sought.

Lord Salton and Lord Mungo Murray, with their train of attendants, issued from the wood at the moment the Master of Lovat was about to enter it. Upon sight of them he drew a pistol from his belt, and a very brave gentleman of his party, by name William of Erchette, who was behind the Master, observing this action, without uttering a word, levelled a carabine which he had upon his horse, at Lord Salton,

1697 crying out, 'Stop, traitor, you shall pay with your hide your irruption into this country in hostility to our laird.' At these words they all stopped short.

The Master of Lovat instantly spurred his horse into a slight gallop, making towards Lord Mungo, who was foremost in a narrow path leading out of the wood. As he approached him, the Master of Lovat cried, his pistol in his hand, 'Fire, traitor, or I will blow out your brains.' Lord Mungo, mounted upon a very fine horse, the property of the late Lord Lovat, his brother-in-law, instead of firing his pistol, dropped his bridle from his hand, and exclaimed aloud, 'My dear Simon, and is this the termination of our long and tender friendship! Grant me my life.' The Master replied: 'You are a base coward, and deserve no quarter, but I give you your life:' and, saying this, he disarmed him in a moment of his pistols and his sword. No sooner was this done, than, turning round, the Master of Lovat perceived one of his attendants in the very act of discharging the contents of his carabine at the distance of only three inches into the body of Lord Salton. Simon immediately threw himself before his attendant, and called to him with all his might not to fire. Thus his generosity saved in one day the lives of two noblemen, who the very night before had conspired his destruction, and who had formally broken to him their words of honour.

Since, however, the two lords had more than forty

horsemen behind them in the road, the Master of Lovat gave orders to all the gentlemen of his party, to present their carabines to the breasts of Lord Salton, Lord Mungo Murray, and the persons who were already come up, and to fire upon the first person who moved hand or foot, while he alighted from his horse, and disarmed the remainder of the troop as they arrived. In this manner the Master of Lovat took from the enemy more than forty pair of pistols, together with a number of swords, without the smallest resistance from any individual, except the valet de chambre of Lord Salton, who was a lowland Fraser, and who would not give up his arms till the Master struck him a blow upon the head with the flat side of his sword.

In the meantime the nine persons of whom the Master's troop was composed, were insufficient to guard above forty persons with their horses, to the house where the Master of Lovat resolved to hold them in durance. He therefore dispatched one of his company to muster the infantry of the province, which is constantly well armed and equipped, and animated with the most incredible zeal in the service of their chief. They assembled in crowds; and Lord Lovat himself soon arrived, together with almost every person who lived for some miles round: so that in less than six hours Lord Lovat and his son mustered between six and seven hundred brave Frasers, completely armed, under the walls of Fanellan, which was the seat to

1697 which the Master caused the two lords and all their attendants to be conducted.

Upon their arrival the Master of Lovat intreated his father to retire to one of his other estates at a considerable distance from Fanellan, as well to avoid the fatigue incident to so active a scene, Lord Lovat being then sixty-eight years of age, as because the Master was unwilling that the capture of these noblemen should be imputed to his father, or that he should be involved in any of the disagreeable consequences that might follow so spirited an action.

As two of the persons most actively concerned in the project of Lord Salton, were still with the dowager Lady Lovat at the seat of Beaufort, the Master now dispatched a gentleman of his clan with thirty followers, to bring them prisoners to Fanellan; at the same time directing him to place a guard upon all the avenues of Beaufort House, to prevent the dowager from sending to her father, in opposition to Lord Lovat and his son. Beaufort House was in reality the property of Lord Lovat, not only as a part of the Lovat estate, but as being his appanage as younger son of Hugh Lord Lovat, his father. Accordingly he had always been stiled during the life of his nephew the Laird of Beaufort, and had lived in the house till he became a widower, having afterwards bestowed it out of pure bounty upon his nephew, on account of the ruinous condition of the Castle of Lovat. Whether, however,

the persons, that the Master had sent to apprehend
the conspirators, committed any insults upon the
domestics of the house, or upon their prisoners, the
dowager Lady Lovat exclaimed warmly that she was
insulted and made a prisoner, as she said, in her own
house.

Accordingly she made her complaint to the Marquis
of Athol, her father, and to her brother, the Earl of
Tullibardin, at that time one of the Secretaries of State
for Scotland. During the whole transaction, the Master
of Lovat had remained at a distance from the dowager,
at the house where his prisoners were confined; and
those persons who were sent to Beaufort, were guilty
of no sort of disrespect to her person. In the meantime,
out of this natural and temperate procedure, unaccompanied with either attempt or design against the person
of the dowager, Lord Athol and his son created that
chimerical monster of a rape and violation, with which
they blackened the character of the Master and his
friends. It was impossible, indeed, to do other than
praise the action by which he had made himself master
of the person of the lords, who had come with a design
of expelling him from his inheritance.

Meanwhile the whole country knew that the Master
of Lovat, at the age of about twenty years, well educated, at the head of an ancient house, and of a brave
and respectable clan, might have aspired to any match
in the kingdom. Indeed he ranked among his ancestors

1697 on the female side three daughters of the royal house of Stuart, together with the daughters of the most ancient peers and the first nobility of Scotland. He had no reason, therefore, to commit the smallest violence upon a widow, who was old enough to be his mother, dwarfish in her person and deformed in her shape, and with no other fortune than a jointure of two hundred and fifty pounds a year, which itself was dependent upon his good pleasure as Master of Lovat. Add to this, that the whole north of Scotland was conscious that this pretended rape was a mere calumny, a ridiculous chimæra, invented by the Marquis of Athol for the ruin of the Master of Lovat. It is also notorious that the dowager herself, since the prosecution was commenced against the Master for a crime, that he never so much as imagined, and that it would strike him with horror to commit, even with a female of the meanest condition, has declared to more than a hundred persons, that her father and her brother were extremely to blame to accuse the Master of this crime; that he had never failed of paying her every proper respect; and that she loved and esteemed him, having been brought up with him in the same house, the late Lord Lovat, his cousin, having always regarded him as his child.

Notwithstanding, however, the evident absurdity of this imputation, Lord Tullibardin, then Secretary of State to King William, persuaded his master that Simon of Beaufort had committed a rape, accompanied with the most atrocious and aggravating circumstances, upon the person of his sister, the widow of the late Lord Lovat.

Something was still wanting: Thomas Lord Lovat could not be comprehended in the chimerical crime of his son, nor could a detachment of the royal army be obtained against the clan of the Frasers, to punish the crime of an individual. Lord Tullibardin, therefore, persuaded King William that both father and son had been the first to join the insurrection of Viscount Dundee, that they had been the last to submit to the present government, and that they had in fact always continued his Majesty's inveterate enemies. They expected, he said, to see King James in Scotland in the ensuing summer, and had already once more taken arms for his service, and collected two thousand men under their standard. He described their estate as consisting of immense forests, inaccessible islands, and impregnable castles. They had furnished these islands and castles with ammunition and provisions; they had thrown up intrenchments in their forests, in order to render a country still more inaccessible, which was already sufficiently so by nature; if, therefore, his Majesty did not issue immediate orders to the whole Scottish army to march against these rebels and villains, the flame now lighted up might soon become too great for all the exertions of the three kingdoms to extinguish.

It was natural for King William to give credit to

1697 the representations of his Secretary of State. He therefore yielded implicitly to the sentiments of Tullibardin, which were in fact the mere result of private picque against Simon, and an interested contest for the Lovat estate; and issued orders to the Scottish troops to march against the clan of the Frasers, and to the Scottish Privy Council to exert themselves on their part for their entire reduction. It was thus that King William, to satisfy the sordid and treacherous disposition of his minister, employed his authority to exterminate a house, whose ancestors in every period of the Scottish history have gained the most distinguished laurels in the defence of their king and country.

1302 In the famous battle of Rosline, ages before the illustrious house of Stewart ascended the Scottish throne [Buchanan lib. viii. page 255], Simon Fraser and John Cuming were the two commanders in chief who gained the most memorable victory ever obtained by the Scots over the English.

Simon Fraser, son of the former, and Alexander,
1333 his brother, were cut in pieces at the battle of Perth [Buchanan lib. ix. pages 284, 5], through the treason of Andrew Murray of Tullibardin against his king and country, who placed stakes of wood in the most fordable part of the river, as a direction to the English, in order to their falling by night upon the army of Scotland. The part of the camp nearest to the river

was occupied by the Frasers, and the Keiths the ancestors of the Earl Marishal of Scotland, who were all cut in pieces, and the Keiths have never recovered the slaughter of that night. The following year Andrew Murray of Tullibardin was taken and hanged by James and Simon Fraser, and Robert Keith.

The Frasers at length recovered from this misfortune, as in a more recent instance they were delivered, by a particular interposition of providence, from a still greater disaster at the battle of Loch Lochie.* In *1544 this battle Lord Lovat, his four brothers, his three sons, and all the gentlemen of his clan were cut in pieces by the different clans of the Macdonalds, who were at that time four times their number. This attack was instigated by George Gordon, Earl of Huntley, who bore the Frasers an extreme hatred on account of their attachment to the family of Argyle, with whom he was engaged in continual feuds. The attachment of the Frasers to the Campbels is as old as the very existence of their names; and accordingly the quarrel of a Campbel was always considered through the whole country as the quarrel of a Fraser. But God restored by a kind of miracle the clan of the Frasers, who were all killed upon the spot, with the exception of three persons desperately wounded. The passage is curious enough to deserve to be cited in the very words of Buchanan.

'About this time,' says he, 'by the instigation,

as it is thought, of the Earl of Huntley, a battle was fought, in which almost the whole clan of the Frasers was exterminated. There was an old quarrel between the Frasers and the Macdonalds, which had been rendered illustrious by the many bloody engagements to which it had given birth. Huntley in the meantime was deeply irritated that the Frasers alone, among so many neighbouring clans, should reject his protection. He had just collected the neighbouring islanders, and made an incursion upon the estates of the Earl of Argyle; and, while every other clan had exerted its whole force in his favour, there was scarcely an individual in the whole clan of Fraser that had not ranged himself under the enemy's standard. For this time, however, the feud was composed without an engagement, and the forces of each party having disbanded themselves, returned to their respective clans. The Macdonalds meantime, instructed by the Earl of Huntley, collected their whole force; and, having taken their enemy by surprise, engaged in a most obstinate battle: the unfortunate clan, overpowered by the greatest inequality of numbers, were killed to a man. Thus a family, the most numerous, and who had often deserved well of the Scottish weal, had wholly perished; unless, as it seems just to believe, the divine providence had not interfered in their favour. Of the heads of the clan eighty persons had left their wives at home pregnant, and each of them in her turn was delivered

of a male child, who all attained safe to man's estate.'
[Buchanan lib. xv. page 532.]

These particulars are sufficiently known, as being contained in the only authentic history of Scotland for those times. And, indeed, the life of Simon, Lord Lovat, which forms the subject of the present history, has been itself little less than a continual miracle, since he has repeatedly escaped by the favour of providence, all that the malice of men and devils could invent, to ruin him, to undermine his reputation, to rob him of his property, and to deprive him of his life.

I now return to Lord Tullibardin, who surprised King William, in the manner that has been related, into the issuing of an order, the most vindictive that ever originated with any King of Scotland, and of the nature of which King William was assuredly not sufficiently informed. Lord Tullibardin, at that time Secretary of State and High Commissioner to the Scottish Parliament, had the whole Privy Council, which was indeed almost totally composed of his own creatures, at his disposition. No one is now to be told that the Secretaries of State for Scotland, ever since her kings ascended the English throne, have had a very great, and indeed an absolute power in the Scottish Privy Council.

Nor was this ever more conspicuously displayed than upon the present occasion. Upon the groundless calumnies of the Marquis of Athol, a committee of

1697 Privy Council, chosen by Lord Tullibardin, without examining a single witness, a procedure contrary to all laws, and all precedent, and without issuing a citation to Lord Lovat or his son, an indulgence which has never been refused to the most atrocious outlaws, published a printed sentence against Thomas Lord Lovat, and Simon his son, and against all the Frasers, men, women, and children, their adherents. This sentence included an order to all the troops in the kingdom to overrun their province, to take them dead or alive, to burn, kill, ravage, and destroy the whole clan without exception; if they, or any of them, took sanctuary in churches, to burn them in the said churches, at the same time annexing a general amnesty, in case the troops employed in this execution, in burning them, should burn any person not bearing the name of Fraser. In a word, all history, sacred and profane, cannot produce an order, pregnant with such unexampled cruelty as this sentence, which is carefully preserved in the house of Lovat, to the eternal confusion and infamy of those who signed it, and to awaken the gratitude of the Frasers, to the latest generation, to that God who delivered them from this infernal execution.

While this was transacting, the Master of Lovat, little suspecting the machinations which the Lords Athol and Tullibardin were preparing against him, was employed in disposing of his noble prisoners. For some time he detained them in custody, and threatened to hang them, for having intruded into his inheritance, and sought to deprive him of his lawful and hereditary rights. At length, however, by the intercession of certain barons of the low country, who came to solicit the liberty of Lord Salton, Lord Mungo Murray, and their attendants, he dismissed them, having first obliged Lord Salton to promise that he would send him, as soon as he should be out of the province of Lovat, a formal obligation in the sum of eight thousand pounds, with four barons of the low country as his sureties, that he would never more interfere with the affairs of the Lovat estate, and that neither he nor the Marquis of Athol would ever prosecute either Lord Lovat, or his son, or their clan in general, for the disgrace they had experienced in being made prisoners, or for any of the transactions of this affair. Thus was the Master of Lovat exercising his generosity towards a part of the Athol family at the very time that they were conspiring his destruction and the extermination of his clan.

It was not long before the Master was advertised by his friends of the formidable decree of the Privy Council; that in consequence all the regular troops in Scotland were marching against him by the low countries, and that Lord Athol was assembling an army of highlanders to march round the mountains and attack him in flank. So formidable a preparation would have terrified any man who had not been a little

1697 acquainted with the manner of carrying on a war in the highlands, and who was not tolerably certain that his province was almost inaccessible, and that with five hundred men he could effectually stop the progress of five thousand in a forest, fortified by nature with rocks and an almost uninterrupted defile.

Previously, however, to the arrival of his enemies, the Master intreated his father with tears to retire into the country of his brother-in-law, the head of the brave clan of the Macleods, a family extremely rich and powerful in the islands of Scotland. Lord Lovat consented to the proposal; and the Macleods came to meet him, and received him with the same affection as they would have done their own chief, the brother-in-law of his lordship.

The Master of Lovat felt himself extremely happy in having placed his father in safety. He now assembled his whole clan, in order to learn their resolution; and all of them, with a zeal which surpasses credibility, and which ought for ever to engage the inviolable attachment of every Scottish chief to his clan, protested to the Master that they would never desert him; and that they would leave their wives, their children, their houses, their property, and all that they held most dear, to live and die with him. The Master on his side made equal protestations of tenderness and friendship. This being settled, he reconnoitred the ground which would be proper for his defence; and having

taken possession of it with a select number of his clan, 1697
he dismissed the rest to protect their houses in the best
manner they could.

The several regiments of cavalry, infantry, and
dragoons, which were stationed in the kingdom of
Scotland, now arrived at Inverness, in order to execute
the infernal sentence which had been pronounced against
the Frasers. In the meantime Lord Athol detached
the three young lords, his children, at the head of an
army of highlanders, composed of every man whom
he could collect, either by menaces or rewards, from
the Stewarts, the Robinsons, the Farquharsons, and
even the Macdonalds, though they were the neighbours
and the relations of the Master.

Upon the day appointed for wasting the whole
province of Lovat with fire and sword, the regular
troops entered into the flat country. They saw nothing
here but women and children in tears; and the officers,
animated with a more Christian spirit than the Privy
Council, declared they would sooner resign their commissions than execute so barbarous a business as the
murder of defenceless women and children, who could
be objects only of compassion, not of vengeance.

They therefore disposed themselves to advance to
the ground where the Master and his adherents were
entrenched. But here they were assured that if they
passed the river, the fords of which were extremely
narrow, not one of them would escape. Upon this,

1697 these brave and honest fellows, who had no inclination to lose their lives in order to conquer provinces for Lord Athol, returned home, after having burned and pillaged a few houses, for fear of a reprimand from the Secretary of State.

They were no sooner departed than the highland army, commanded by the Lord Murrays, appeared upon the mountains, in order to surround the Master on that side. They dared not, however, approach his place of defence; and he struck them with so complete a panic the first night they came within reach of him, that they fled with great precipitation across the fields, and retired next day, taking care, however, to burn every house, and pillage every woman and child, that came in their way. Such was the conclusion of the first and grand expedition of the family of Athol against the Master of Lovat and the clan of the Frasers.

Lord Tullibardin, the Secretary of State, who had been the author of all these cruelties, was highly enraged at so dishonourable an event. He obtained from King William an order to break several regiments which had been employed upon the expedition, and among others Lord Forbes's regiment of horse.

The Frasers, after this enterprise, had some respite from the encounter of large armies. But they were daily harrassed with flying parties from Inverness and Inverlochy, otherwise Fort William. These were in

small numbers, and the Master had always timely notice 1697
of their approach; so that he gave himself little trouble
about them. He might, if he had pleased, have cut
them in pieces wherever they appeared. But, as the
regular troops had always displayed a clemency for
his country, and a regard for his person, he treated
them with as much mildness as was consistent with
the safety of his clan.

He was, however, continually in danger of perishing
by the public attempts that were made to take him,
three or four times in a week; and his danger was still
greater from the villains that Lord Athol had shamefully bribed to assassinate him. Many of his own and
of other clans confessed that infamous crime, and particularly Captain James Maclean. In this situation the
Master of Lovat thought proper to make a journey into
the island of Sky, the province of the Laird of Macleod,
with the principal gentlemen of his clan, in order to pay
his duty to his father, and to take leave of him, provided he should be unexpectedly cut off in any of the
perils he encountered. He gave himself, however, little
anxiety about the efforts of Lord Athol; and upon his
return to Lovat, being desirous not to harrass his clan,
he dismissed his whole train, except about fifty gentlemen for the guard of his person.

Lord Athol, who had always his spies planted about 1698
the Master of Lovat, was advertised by three or four
traitors of the Frasers, that the Master was now in

great security at one of his estates, called Straheric, the part of his inheritance nearest to the province of Athol, and that a small troop of resolute men might easily take him. The Marquis accordingly selected from his vassals five hundred of his bravest men, and placed at their head the two heroes of his family, Lord James and Lord Mungo Murray.

Lord Athol directed them to march only by night, to prevent a discovery, and bid them never see his face again if they did not bring along with them the Master of Lovat, dead or alive. They accordingly proceeded in great diligence, extremely well armed, and having for their guide two Frasers, who engaged to lead them by the most private and unfrequented paths. In fact they arrived upon his estate without the Master's having received the smallest previous intimation. He was at this time gone to Inverness, to visit *incognito* some of his friends, and had with him only three or four servants, when he received an express from Straheric, that this estate was filled with the troops of Lord Athol, and his children at their head.

The Master feared, not only that his house and estate of Straheric might be ruined, but that his faithful relations in that country might be unable to escape from the hands of these barbarians. Instead, therefore, of withdrawing into his other territories, which he might easily have done by the bridge of Inverness, he dispatched his four servants full speed, to advertise his relations of their danger, and to intreat them to join him upon the top of a little mountain, which he had selected as a proper place of rendezvous. He himself proceeded thither, with only a single runner, through the woods and unfrequented paths, resolved to perish with his clan, or to save them from the hands of their remorseless enemies.

When he arrived upon the appointed mountain, he had the satisfaction to range an hundred gentlemen, and an hundred brave peasants, under his standard in the space of two hours. But the accounts he received magnified extremely the number of the enemy, representing them as a regular army of two thousand, or at least fifteen hundred men; and the most prudent were for retiring and abandoning the open country to their ravages. The Master, however, swore that he would never take so painful a step without having first a nearer view of them; and that, if he could not venture to face them in the open field, he would at least hang upon their flanks, in order to hinder as much as possible the ruin of the country, and cut in pieces the stragglers from the main body. The gentlemen of his clan, who had no fears but for his person, finding him so resolute, followed his standard with pleasure.

He arrived about sunset within a short three miles of his enemies. There he received exact information respecting their numbers by one of the guides of his own clan, whom Lord James Murray had the impu-

1698 dence to send, to command the gentlemen of the country to come, before ten o'clock the next morning, to make their submission, to deliver or abandon to him the Master of Lovat; and in case of disobedience he swore he would burn their houses, and not leave them so much as a cock to proclaim the dawn of the day.

The bearer of this message, whom the Athol army had compelled to become their guide, and who had formerly been a judge of the province, and a particular friend of the Master of Lovat, added that the young lords had with them the best troops of the province of Athol, of the Stewarts, and the Robinsons; that they were completely armed; and that they expected to be joined next day by the King's troops: therefore, if it were possible to attack them, it must be done before this junction was effected.

Four days previous to this transaction Simon had assumed the title of Lord Lovat, having learned the melancholy news that his father was dead, in consequence of a violent march, which he had made to avoid the enemy, who were reported to be setting out for the isles in order to surprise him. Simon was most sincerely afflicted by the death of a parent whom he loved with the utmost tenderness, and who had been so firm and resolute in the support of his lawful claims at so advanced an age; for he died at the age of sixty-eight years. He therefore swore that, having the authors of his father's death, and of all his personal

misfortunes before his eyes, he would now revenge 1696
himself in their blood, or perish in the attempt.

He found those who were with him ready to devote themselves to revenge the wrongs of their chief, and the devastation of their country. He therefore sent back the same person to Lord James Murray, with notice that Simon Lord Lovat, before ten o'clock the next morning, would infallibly have the honour of waiting upon him sword in hand, at the head of all the gentlemen he had appointed to meet him; and, though he had not half his complement of men, being intercepted from all communication with his estates of Air, Loirnamanac, and Straglasse, by the lake of Ness which divides them, that he had yet the utmost confidence in the favour of God and the justice of his cause. Lord James Murray was not a little surprised at the message of Simon. He immediately called together his officers, drew up his troops, and took post upon a very advantageous ground, having a steep rock behind him, and his front covered with the buildings of a village. There, thinking themselves in entire security, and satisfied of the small numbers that the enemy could draw together in that country, they lighted a number of fires, and began to prepare their supper.

Simon had at that time about two hundred and fifty men under his command, half of them ill armed, the regular troops having the year before stripped their

1698 houses, and every other place of security, of all the arms they could find. He foresaw that, if the enemy were permitted to repose for this night, they would be much better prepared for the battle which he was resolved to give them the next day. His relations, however, were averse to fighting that evening, and were desirous of waiting for a reinforcement of Lord Lovat's vassals, from the provinces of Obertarf and Glenmoriston, which are situated at the head of the Ness and in its environs.

Lord Lovat meanwhile resolved at least to beat up the quarters of his enemies. For this purpose he selected fifty active young fellows, and marched them within musket-shot of the enemy. There they gave their first fire, and immediately threw themselves upon their bellies in obedience to his orders. The Athol troops were extremely terrified at this discharge. They immediately set up their bagpipes, and formed themselves behind their fires. If Lord Lovat at this moment had had his whole force with him, the enemy might have been all cut in pieces, without the expence of ten men. He could observe their slightest movement by the light of their fires, a circumstance of danger, to which from ignorance they did not advert; and they were unable to perceive Lord Lovat or any of his men at the distance of twenty paces.

Lord Lovat sent immediately for the rest of his force, in order to make a decisive attack; but the gentlemen of his clan were peremptory for waiting the reinforcement from Obertarf and Glenmoriston. Lord Lovat perceived that nothing could be done that night; he therefore drew off his detachment, leaving only twelve men to keep up a constant fire upon the enemy. He himself slept a few hours at about a mile and a half from their camp.

At break of day he was awaked by a false alarm that the enemy were approaching. He had laid down in his clothes, and therefore rose immediately; and, drawing his sword, resolved to die upon the spot, rather than yield an inch to his antagonists. He ordered his troop to stand to their arms and prepare for battle. He marched to a neighbouring height to wait for the attack. But on his way, he was informed that it was a false alarm, occasioned by a detachment of the enemy, who had sallied from their camp to pursue the twelve men who had fired upon them in the night; and having exchanged a few shot, both parties retired to the main body.

Lord Lovat held a council with the gentlemen of his clan, to determine the manner in which it was proper to attack the enemy in so advantageous a post. He had now been joined by a part of his clan from the province of Obertarf, and his whole force amounted to about three hundred men, one half of them slenderly armed. At the same time he was perfectly informed, that the enemies force amounted to more than six hundred troops, carefully selected, and completely accoutered.

He observed to his council, that it was impossible to attack the enemy in front, on account of the walls and huts with which it was covered. It became necessary, therefore, to have recourse to stratagem. He proposed to detach sixty of his fleetest and most active young men under Mr. Alexander Macdonald.

This gentleman, the only neighbour, or person not of his own clan, that he had with him, was the famous Alexander Macdonald, otherwise called *Alister More*, on account of his gigantic stature, being the tallest man in Scotland, and not less celebrated for his brave exploits than for his prodigious height. He was of the family of Kappah, whose lands are contiguous to those of Straheric and Obertarf. He was himself related to the Frasers of Straheric; and, being extremely attached to Lord Lovat, he always offered, with much pleasure, to risk his life in his service. Lord Lovat, knowing his fidelity, valour, and skill, had recourse to him upon this important occasion.

He asked him whether he would be willing to take sixty young fellows well armed, and march to a height within sight of the enemy, where he should draw out his little detachment in so extensive a line as to lead the Athol party to believe that Lord Lovat and his whole force was on that side. In the meantime Lord Lovat proposed, with the body of his army, to make a circuit of the rock that covered the enemies rear, and take them in flank, while Alexander Macdonald attacked them in front. The proposal was unanimously approved by the council, and eagerly accepted by Mr. Macdonald.

Lord Lovat now marshalled his little troop, and selected the men most proper for Macdonald's detachment. He instructed him to gain the place appointed, and to remain there, while Lord Lovat filed through an obscure moat to the other side of the mountain in the enemies rear. Lord Lovat then proposed to make a signal of three discharges of a musket, when Macdonald was to march as near as possible to the huts in the enemy's front, and to fire upon them from the nearest station he could obtain, in order to dislodge them from their cover, or at least to throw them into disorder. Lord Lovat would in the meantime fall upon them sword in hand from the mountain; and thus he promised himself an assured victory, though his number did not amount to the half of the enemy. While this was concerting, his clan was actuated with the most incredible ardour, ready to precipitate themselves upon the enemy, without preparation and without order.

Mr. Macdonald now marched on his side to the neighbouring height, and Lord Lovat set out to make the circuit of the mountain. Being arrived within cannon shot of the enemy, without being yet in their sight, he drew up his troops, with one gentleman at the head of every six peasants, and dispatched centinels, to proceed softly, and almost creeping upon their bellies, to reconnoitre the motions of the enemy. One of them presently returned with notice that the enemy was in motion. Another gave intelligence a moment after, that he saw them marching towards Inverness in great haste. Lord Lovat immediately ascended with his troop to the summit of the mountain; and perceiving that the enemy were actually flying, he made the three discharges as a signal to Mr. Macdonald to attack and stop them.

But Macdonald, who observed them running with great precipitation, judged it better to outstrip them by the swiftness of his men, in order to stop them at a terrible defile, which was six miles onward, and which it was absolutely necessary for them to pass. He observed that Lord Lovat and his men were at too great a distance to be able to come up with the enemy, unless they were stopped at this defile. This quickness of recollection in Mr. Macdonald was a proof of masterly skill; for, if the enemy had had heart and spirit enough to rally and face Lord Lovat in the plain, they might have cut in pieces his whole force without any loss.

Lord Lovat had intreated his troop to march in order after the enemy, and by no means to break their ranks. But his brave peasants replied with one voice; 'If you chuse to attend to your regular manner of marching, you may do as you please. But for our parts we will come hand to hand with these rascals, 1698 or burst our wind in the pursuit.' Saying this, and without waiting for orders, they immediately broke away after the enemy, and he was the bravest man who could run the fastest. Lord Lovat ran for three miles along with them, on foot, and almost naked. He was now obliged to mount on horseback, without either boots or spatter-dashes, in order to stop the foremost of his troop, who rushed upon the enemy like so many madmen. A rear guard of only fifty men might at this moment have totally destroyed the Frasers.

But the enemy thought only of flight. They had been informed in general by one of their spies that they were surrounded on all sides; and they saw no other means of safety. They were, however, immeasurably astonished, when, as they approached the defile which afforded them the only means of escape, they saw it in possession of Alexander Macdonald and his sixty fusileers. They immediately stopped short. At the same time they saw the main body of the Frasers pursuing them. This body was now extremely dispersed. The very women of the country ran along with their husbands, conjuring them not to spare the murderers of their chiefs, and the villains who came to rob them of their all. The enemy, beholding this spectacle, and already impressed with the most lively apprehensions, took it for granted that Lord Lovat's troop consisted

F

of four times their number, though in reality it did not amount to one half of it.

Lord James Murray is said to have exerted himself to compel his men to engage, and to have drawn them up in line of battle. But the Stewarts of Athol, who were animated with an instinctive hatred of the Marquis, and who had no quarrel with the Frasers, declared in a peremptory manner to Lord James, that they would demand quarter of the victor, and were ready to lay down their arms. Lord James was beside himself at this declaration. Lord Mungo burst into tears, seeing himself once more in the hands of Lord Lovat, and entertaining a well-grounded apprehension that their repeated breaches of honour and humanity had cancelled all the regard he had ever entertained for them.

During this dispute among the enemy, Lord Lovat drew up his troops, as they arrived, within musket-shot of the Athol forces. As soon as they were formed, he gave positive orders to advance, but not to fire a shot, till he had discharged his piece within pistol-shot of the enemy; then to fire at once, throw down their muskets, and fall upon the enemy sword in hand in front, while Mr. Macdonald and his small detachment attacked them in flank.

The enemy believed themselves lost without redemption. They saw Lord Lovat's troop advancing in perfect order. Immediately, in the room of firing, they laid down their arms; and, covering their heads with their plaids, cried out for quarter.

At the same moment Mr. Archibald Menzies, who was their major, and who had three years before resigned his company of grenadiers in the regiment of Lord Murray in favour of Lord Lovat, then Laird of Beaufort, ran before the enemy, with a white handkerchief or neckcloth tied to a bludgeon, crying out for mercy. He advanced in order to throw himself at the feet of Lord Lovat. Two of the Frasers followed him, and demanded Lord Lovat's permission to kill him. But his lordship cried out with a loud voice to spare him. He then threw himself prostrate, and begged his life, declaring he had always been a friend to Lord Lovat, and had never done any injury to his province. His request was granted.

'I am also come, my lord,' added he, 'to demand quarter for the Stewarts, who are with your enemy, and have been forced upon this expedition as well as myself. They love you better than they do Lord Athol and all his children.' Lord Lovat replied, that he could not listen to the proposal; and was sending him back to his commanders, to tell the enemy to resume their arms and defend themselves, otherwise he would cut them in pieces; for he was determined that day to avenge the death of his father, and the tyranny of Lord Athol and all his family.

At this moment all the gentlemen of the clan of

1698 the Frasers came up to Lord Lovat, and intreated him for God's sake, to spare these miserable wretches, and give them their lives. Lord Lovat and the most resolute young people in his troop were peremptory for putting them to the sword; and many of his most valuable friends and relations have since blamed him for his lenity upon this occasion. But in fact he was not at liberty to act as he pleased. In spite of his eager desire to cut his enemy in pieces, he was obliged to follow the advice of his most venerable relatives and the heads of his clan. And these protested to him, that it would be a real murder to kill people who had laid down their arms; that their clan would infallibly be exterminated if it were perpetrated; and that not a man in the kingdom would either assist or pity them. Lord Lovat, therefore, to say the truth in spite of himself, spared their lives a second time to the children of Lord Athol, who had sought every means that hell could invent, and had put in practice both open violence and secret assassination, to put an end to his existence; though they had in reality no other cause of complaint against him than that he was born the true and legitimate heir to the estate of Lovat.

Lord Lovat contented himself upon this day of *Altnigoir* (such is the epithet that his clan bestow upon this bloodless victory), with causing the children of Lord Athol, and all their followers, to swear upon a naked sword, after the manner of the country, a horrible

oath, by which they renounced their claims in Jesus 1696
Christ, and their hopes of heaven, and devoted themselves to the devil and all the torments of hell, if they ever returned into the territories of Lord Lovat, or occasioned him directly or indirectly the smallest mischief. Beside this, Lord James and Lord Mungo Murray, and all their followers, Murrays, Stewarts, Menzies, and Robinsons, executed a paper, containing the above oath, together with an obligation under the penalty of a large sum of money, to prevail upon Lord Athol, their father, and Lord Tullibardin, their brother, secretary to King William, to do justice to Lord Lovat, and to indemnify him for the injuries they had done to his inheritance.

Having obtained these securities, Lord Lovat drew up his whole troop in two files; and, in conformity to an example he had read in the Roman history, made these miserable cowards march, like so many criminals, between the ranks of his men, and obliged them immediately to quit his territories by the same road they had entered them. Such was the event of the last expedition of the family of Athol into the province of Lovat.

The children of Lord Athol, at once irritated and ashamed of this terrible disaster, hastened to appear before the Privy Council, where they swore that Simon of Beaufort, such was the style they allotted to Lord Lovat, had surrounded them with three thousand men,

1698 and would have assassinated them, if they had not found means to escape from his cruelty by an unguarded pass. In the mean time, in spite of the tyranny of Lord Athol over his vassals, and the power of Lord Tullibardin, then Secretary of State, they were never able to induce a man of the Stewarts, the Robinsons, or any other of their vassals, to march against Lord Lovat. They swore they would never more draw their swords against a man who had given them their lives in so generous a manner. Accordingly from that day Lord Lovat possessed his inheritance in tranquility; being subject to no other inconvenience than that of being sometimes invaded by a slender detachment from the garrison of Fort William, of which the officers and almost all the soldiers were his friends.

1699 The sentence of death, however, being still in force against him, his friends and relations represented to Archibald Duke of Argyle, a great favourite of King William, that he ought not to permit the family of Lovat and the clan of the Frasers to perish; that they had been considered in all ages as a branch of his own, and that they had always been as attached and as faithful to his ancestors as the Campbels of Inverary themselves.

They added that the family of Athol, who exerted themselves for the extermination of the Frasers, were the hereditary enemies of the house of Argyle; that this very Marquis of Athol a few years before had exercised every species of tyranny and oppression over the Campbels in their own country; and that, in permitting the house of Athol to aggrandise itself by the acquisition of the Lovat estate, he was suffering so many declared enemies of his clan to erect their power upon the ruin of his friends. These motives determined the Duke of Argyle to obtain the indemnity of Lord Lovat and his clan, in spite of all the opposition the Earl of Tullibardin could employ.

The Duke of Argyle possessed ten times the sense of his rival. King William, who knew him for the best statesman in Scotland, gave him a very large share of his confidence. And the Duke employed this confidence to convince his sovereign that Lord Tullibardin served him very unfaithfully in that kingdom, that he employed the royal authority to ruin the most ancient houses in order to aggrandise his own, and that the persecution he exercised against Lord Lovat and the clan of the Frasers, was capable of exciting all the clans, and even the whole nation to revolt against the government. His grace at the same time represented the friendship subsisting between the house of Campbel and that of Fraser, and how highly his Majesty would oblige him in this affair. He added, that the King might spend a hundred times the value of the Fraser estate before he could reduce it, on account of its inaccessible situation, and its intermarriages and friendships with the neighbouring clans. King William protested that he was totally ignorant of the affair, and had no concern in issuing such orders as his grace represented; and he promised, in consideration of the services of the Duke of Argyle, to grant a full and unconditional pardon to Lord Lovat and his clan.

The Duke, having obtained this promise, wrote to Lord Lovat to lay down his arms, and come privately to London, when he might depend upon his obtaining for him an entire pardon. Lord Lovat thanked the Duke, and promised to obey; and shortly after set out for London.

When Lord Lovat arrived, he found that the King had issued orders to the Earl of Seafield, his Secretary of State for Scotland, to draw up the pardon. This minister, who was the colleague of the Earl of Tullibardin, though he was friendly and even related to Lord Lovat, yet being naturally extremely timid, stood in awe of the vengeance that he might incur from the family of Athol by expediting this pardon. He, therefore, suffered the affair to be put off from time to time, in spite of the solicitations of the Duke of Argyle and Lord Lovat, till King William set out for the United Provinces. Lord Seafield then intreated Mr. Pringle, Under Secretary of State, to present the pardon to the King at Loo, and to sign it as Secretary of State; since the papers subscribed by Mr. Pringle, when the King was in Holland, were not less valid, than if they had 1699 been signed by a principal secretary.

Lord Lovat was much afflicted at this delay. And as it was not proper for him to return to Scotland, he determined to make an excursion into France. The principal motive of his tour was as follows :—

The Marquis of Athol had been the first person who appeared for King William in the Privy Council of Scotland. Soon after he changed sides and became a declared Jacobite. And now, in order to discourage the relations and friends of Lord Lovat, he gave out, that, when King James should be restored, he would trample upon Simon of Beaufort and his clan, as completely as his son did by the authority of King William. The ancestors of Lord Lovat had uniformly signalised themselves in the royal cause, and, indeed, had nearly been ruined by their exertions for the illustrious house of Stuart; and Lord Lovat himself had rendered the most essential services to the interests of King James. He was, therefore, resolved to learn from the mouth of that prince whether the reports that Lord Athol so industriously disseminated through the north of Scotland were true or false.

Arriving at St. Germains he addressed himself to his cousin, Sir John Maclean, chief of the clan of Macleans, who introduced him to Lord Perth. This nobleman received him with open arms, and immediately led him to King James. The Queen and the young Prince, her son, were present.

After a short customary conversation Lord Lovat complained to the King of the family of Athol. King James immediately, in the presence of the Queen, the Prince, the Duke of Perth, and Sir John Maclean, all four still living, grew extremely warm, and, lifting up his hands, he said, turning to the Queen, 'This perfidious family of Athol, and that old traitor, the first man that revolted against my government in Scotland, have the folly to believe that I will protect them against a family the most loyal in the kingdom, and whose ancestors have always been loyal to mine. The father of this very lord, who is now before you, was inviolably attached to my brother and myself. No, my lord,' said the King, turning to Lord Lovat, 'I will defend you against any man in the kingdom who dares to profess himself your enemy; and that perfidious and traitorous family of Athol I will do everything in my power to exterminate.'

'Madam,' added he, turning to the Queen, 'do you ever remember, and remind the prince, your son, of what I now say. Ever make the distinction which is so justly due to the family of Lovat. I will give under my hand my sentiments upon this subject to Lord Lovat.'

Upon this King James took some paper, and wrote with his own hand the obligations that had been con-

ferred upon the crown by the family of Fraser, engaging, 1699
in behalf of himself and his successors, that he would
reinstate that family in the property they had lost by
their adherence to the crown, and that he would protect
Lord Lovat and his posterity against all their enemies
in Scotland, and particularly against the perfidious and
faithless family of Athol. The King then subscribed
this paper, and affixed to it his lesser seal. Lord Lovat
deposited it in the hands of Sir Alexander Innes of
Coxton, a gentleman distinguished by his attachment
to the interests of James.

King James having intreated Lord Lovat to make
his peace with the reigning government, in order to
save his clan, his lordship returned to London, before
the time that King William set out, as has been related,
for the Netherlands. Not having been able to obtain
his pardon in form, he followed his Majesty to Loo,
though then under sentence of death, having a letter of
recommendation from the Duke of Argyle to Mr.
William Carstares, chaplain to the King, and who had
much influence with his master.

Mr. Carstares received him in the most polite
manner, and promised to mention him to the King;
which he did the same day. The King observed to
Mr. Carstares that Lord Lovat was a very bold man to
come so far under sentence of death. Carstares replied,
that he placed an entire confidence in his royal word,
which he had given to the Duke of Argyle. 'He has

reason,' said the King, 'and I beg of you to speak to Mr. Pringle, to draw up his pardon in all the forms, and as ample as possible. I am desirous to indemnify him from everything that I can by the laws of the kingdom, and I will not forget him.'

Mr. Pringle accordingly drew up an ample and complete pardon for every imaginable crime, that it might not be possible to evade it upon the subject of the pretended rape, about which Lord Athol made such a world of noise, and which had no other foundation than that nobleman's malice, in order to ruin Lord Lovat by the imputation of a crime that he had never so much as imagined.

As soon as King William had signed this unlimited pardon Lord Lovat dispatched his cousin Simon, son of David Fraser of Brea, express, in order to cause the great seal of Scotland to be affixed to it. But whether this cousin, who is an unnatural traitor, and a rascal worthy of the gallows, had at that time sold his chief for the money of Lord Athol, as he repeatedly did afterwards, or the timidity of Lord Seafield induced him to stop this pardon in its passage through the remaining forms; thus much is certain, that the pardon executed in Holland was suppressed. Lord Seafield in the mean time caused another pardon to pass the great seal without Lord Lovat having the smallest intelligence upon the subject, comprehending only his high treasons against King William and his Government; thus affording an opportunity to Lord Athol 1699 still to prosecute his suit upon the subject of the rape.

Lord Lovat was as innocent as the child unborn of this crime: he therefore thought proper to order a citation to be served upon Lord Athol and his family, by way of recrimination, for having falsely accused him, and for the devastations they had made, without orders from the sovereign, in his provinces. He next made a progress through all the towns of the north, and the counties adjacent to his estate, where he was received in a very magnificent manner, and returned to Edinburgh with a retinue of a hundred gentlemen, who came as witnesses to support before the Court of Justiciary his action against Lord Athol.

But the very day that had been named for Lord Lovat to support his charge, the Duke of Argyle, his patron and zealous friend, was informed by Lord Arbruhel, of the Argyle family, and one of the nine Lords of Justiciary, that the families of Athol and Hamilton had entirely gained the other eight judges, and that, however clear were Lord Lovat's innocence, he would not have a single voice except his own in his favour, without an order from the King, to oblige the Lords of Justiciary to do strict justice, regardless of the interests of their relations or friends. These eight judges had been appointed to their office by Lord Tullibardin, the Secretary of State, and they considered their places as depending upon their giving sentence according to his inclination.

Upon this intelligence the Duke of Argyle sent for Lord Lovat, who was then at the house of his kinsman and friend, the Earl of Leven. Both of them accordingly repaired to the Duke's, who informed Lord Lovat of the intelligence he had received from Lord Arbruhel, and concluded that it was necessary he should suffer himself to be cast for non-appearance till the Duke should be able to speak to the King, either to obtain a new pardon, or an order to the Court of Justiciary to do justice to Lord Lovat, according to the laws of the kingdom and the dictates of equity, without suffering themselves to be biassed by personal interest.

Lord Lovat, conscious of his innocence, and having upon the spot so many witnesses to prove it, declared that he could not consent to the advice of the Duke of Argyle, but was resolved to bring the matter to an immediate issue. The Duke grew warm, and remonstrated, before Lord Leven and the other lords and gentlemen who were present, that, if Lord Lovat were as innocent as Jesus Christ, the eight judges gained by his enemies would condemn him; that for his part he would not give them that satisfaction; adding, 'My dear Lovat, I love you too well to quit you for a moment till I have absolutely seen you on horseback.' Upon this he ordered to his groom immediately to bring to the door the best horse in his stables, ready saddled and bridled. 1699

The other friends of Lord Lovat intreated the Duke of Argyle in vain to suffer him to stand the trial; his cause was so good, and his witnesses so numerous, it was impossible the decision should be unfavourable. The Duke flew into a violent passion, which was a thing very unusual, he being the man in the world that had the most self-possession. 'Gentlemen,' said he, 'do you know these rascally judges better than Lord Arbruhel and I; or are the interests of Lord Lovat dearer to you than to me? If you are prepared to consent to his ruin, let me tell you I am not. I insist upon his setting out immediately for the frontiers of England, whither I will follow him in four days.'

Lord Lovat was obliged to acquiesce in the advice of the Duke of Argyle, his patron, his friend, and his sole dependence. He mounted the horse which the Duke had given him, and set out, to his own regret, as well as to the regret of every other friend he had in the world, who were not sufficiently acquainted with the corrupt and abandoned characters of his judges. Next day the Court of Justiciary pronounced a sentence of default or non-appearance, as it is called in Scotland, against him.

Lord Lovat expected the Duke of Argyle upon the frontiers, where he was joined by his Grace the following week, and made a most pleasant journey with this amiable companion. After his arrival in London he was at the Duke's house almost every day.

The Earl of Tullibardin was to the last degree exasperated that the Duke of Argyle had, without his privity, obtained a pardon for Lord Lovat. He was convinced that King William paid more regard to the counsels of the Duke than to his. Accordingly, like an ass as he was, he carried his commission of Secretary of State for Scotland to the King, saying, that as his Majesty had more confidence in the Duke of Argyle than in him, and as he had been pleased without his privity to pardon the most incorrigible rebel and traitor in the three kingdoms, he found that he was incapable of serving his Majesty, and therefore thought fit to lay his commission at his feet. 'Consider what you are doing,' replied the King; 'the commission you are about to resign is the most desirable in the whole Scottish service.' Tullibardin replied, that he had entirely made up his mind upon the subject, or he should not have taken a step of that importance.

King William, naturally of an irritable temper, immediately flew into a passion, and said to Tullibardin, 'I always knew you for a fool and a coward; I now see that you are an absolute madman. I not only receive your commission, but I forbid you for ever to enter into my councils, or to concern yourself with any of my affairs. Retire immediately to your own house.'

When Lord Tullibardin had left the royal closet

his Majesty entered the anti-chamber where there was 1700
a great number of Scotch and English nobility, to
whom the King immediately related what this fool had
been doing. 'At the same time that he kept me in
perfect ignorance,' said the King, 'he set all Scotland
in flames, and employed himself to ruin an ancient
family of that kingdom, to revenge a pretended affront
that had been put upon his sister. But I have real
pleasure in pardoning the young nobleman, whom this
fool has been persecuting, and who has more merit than
he and all his family.' General Lord Teviot, who was
present at this declaration of King William against
Lord Tullibardin, in favour of Lord Lovat, and who
had always been much attached to the latter, wrote
to him the particulars the moment he left the antichamber.

The Earl of Tullibardin, enraged at this treatment
which he had drawn upon himself, immediately threw
himself into the party that opposed King William in
the Scottish Parliament, at the head of which was his
brother-in-law, the Duke of Hamilton. Thus the
present Lord Athol, after being the violent partisan
of King William, and the only man in Scotland to
compel the officers of the Scottish army to take the
oath of abjuration against King James and the pretended Prince of Wales, after having held in prison and
persecuted to destruction the Laird of Balleahan, and
the Stewart lairds of the county of Athol for having

1700 taken arms in favour of King James, had the impudence, finding himself disgraced by King William, to believe, not only that he should be received with open arms by the exiled family, but that he should be able to trample upon Lord Lovat and his family, which had always been loyal, by his intrigues, and by the credit of his brother-in-law, the Duke of Hamilton, at the Court of St. Germains; and this for no other reason than because he considered Lord Lovat as his personal enemy, who had it in his power to institute a suit against him, that must infallibly have terminated in his ruin.

And however absurd and presumptuous these hopes may appear, Lord Athol was not disappointed in them. The misfortunes of Lord Lovat, in first embroiling himself with the Earl of Middleton, and afterwards in manifesting a zeal in the business of Scotland more sanguine than was acceptable to the Queen Dowager, gave a most extraordinary and improbable success to the intrigues of Lord Athol, and the exertions of the Duke of Hamilton for the imprisonment of their antagonist: thus putting him out of a condition, to take possession of his estates, and to prosecute Lord Athol for tyrannical and violent oppressions which have caused him to be regarded over the whole kingdom of Scotland as a real tyrant, and Lord Lovat and his clan as the object of universal compassion, attachment, and esteem.

If Lord Perth will give himself the trouble to

peruse these memoirs, and if his near alliance with Lord Middleton will permit him to confess truths advantageous to Lord Lovat, he is qualified to bear testimony to the veracity of what I have here advanced in relation to the Court of St. Germains; and he was an ocular witness of the greater part of the events which I am about to place in their true light in the second part of this history.

<small>1700</small>

PART THE SECOND.

From the Accession of Queen Anne to Lord Lovat's Arrival in England in the Close of the Year 1714.

> 'Sed quæ præclara, et prospera tanti
> Ut rebus lætis par sit mensura malorum.
>
> Dat veniam corvis, vexat censura columbas.
> Sed spoliatis arma supersunt.'
>
> JUVENAL, Sat.

SECTION I.

1702 LORD LOVAT, after so many dangers, and such long adversity, was in the full possession of the honours and estates of his family at the death of King William. He was not ignorant of the misunderstanding which had subsisted previous to this event, between King William and the Princess of Denmark; he knew that that Princess had entertained a strong attachment to the Duke of Hamilton and the Earl of Tullibardin; believing them firm in the interests of King James, her father, to whom she had eagerly reconciled herself, exhibiting every mark of repentance and remorse for having contributed to his misfortunes. Influenced by these considerations, and having always been zealous for King James, lately deceased, Lord Lovat, upon the present intelligence, immediately pro-

claimed the pretended Prince of Wales in his province; 1702
resolved either to perform some distinguished action in
his favour, or to make advantageous terms for himself
with Queen Anne.

Averse, however, to take any considerable step
without the advice and permission of Archibald Duke
of Argyle, who was his patron, and to whom he owed
his life, he immediately waited upon that nobleman,
and told him frankly the designs he had formed. His
Grace, who, without the shadow of flattery, may be
said to have been one of the wisest men in the three
kingdoms, and who had a tender friendship for Lord
Lovat, told him that the tables were turned upon him
and all the friends of King William; that the Duke of
Hamilton, and Lord Athol whom Queen Anne created
Duke of Athol some days after her accession to the
crown,* were the greatest favourites of the new
monarch; that all the Queen's attachments were to
such as had been enemies to King William and
Jacobites by profession; that of consequence his own
head was not in safety, and, for a much stronger reason,
that of Lord Lovat was in great danger. He therefore

---

* King William died on the eighth of March, 1702. The old Marquis of Athol died in the beginning of 1703; and, about a month after his decease, John, late Earl of Tullibardin, was created Marquis of Tullibardin and Duke of Athol. Lord Lovat has everywhere given him only his father's title; partly, perhaps, because it was by this he was known at the Court of St. Germains. The partial confusion that is created by the different styles allotted to several of the English and Scottish nobility by this Court and that of London is well known.

1702 advised him to withdraw into France, and to do the best he could in that country for himself, and for the indemnification of his friends, provided his enterprise succeeded.

Lord Lovat accordingly took leave of the Duke, his faithful ally and dearest friend, with tears in his eyes, and a thousand protestations of gratitude and attachment. He had also the honour to take leave of Lord Lorn, the present Duke of Argyle, who, though very young, disapproved the advice of his father, and told Lord Lovat that he was going to ruin himself for the unfortunate and ungrateful Court of St. Germains; that for his own part he would shed the last drop of his blood sooner than take part with a family which had practised so much injustice and cruelty against the house of Argyle.

Lord Lovat, however, considered that he was in danger of his life under the reign of a princess, who had chosen for her favourites his personal enemies. He had felt from his earliest infancy an extreme bias in favour of the family of Stuart. He had obtained the consent of the Duke of Argyle, whose will was a law to him. He now, therefore, thought of nothing but giving solidity to his enterprise, by engaging the chiefs of the clans, and those noblemen of the Lowlands, whom he knew for Jacobites, and in whose intrigues he had formerly been engaged for the interests of the late King James, to enter into his design.

He immediately visited the chiefs of the clans, and 1702 a great number of the lords of the Lowlands, with William Earl Marishal, and the Earl of Errol, Lord Constable of Scotland, at their head; and expostulated with them in so spirited a manner, and urged with so much force the interests of the Court of St. Germains, that he engaged them to grant him a general commission, on their part, and on the part of all the loyal Scots whom they represented, to go into France. They assured the Court of St. Germains, and the King of France, that they were ready to take up arms and hazard their lives and fortunes for their interests; and intreated them to send over the person whom they stiled their young monarch, with an officer to command them, and the succours that might be necessary for such an enterprise.

Lord Lovat, having received the commission that he had desired with so much ardour, set out upon his expedition with extreme alacrity. He passed through England and Holland, in order to go into France by the way of Flanders, the only road which was not shut up by the war which had just broken out. After several imminent dangers in Holland and in Flanders, too long to be here recounted, he arrived at Paris with this important commission about the month of September, 1702.

His cousin-german, Sir John Maclean, chief of a very brave and considerable clan in Scotland, had

1702 resided ten years at the Court of St. Germains, and passed for a man of ability and good sense. Lord Lovat upon his arrival sent for him express, as a person proper to instruct him in the state of that Court. Sir John Maclean accordingly came to Paris; and, Lord Lovat having opened to him the subject of his journey, told him that the person to whom he should address himself was Lord Perth, who had been Chancellor of Scotland when King James came into France. Lord Drummond his son, Lord Marishal his son-in-law, and the Lord Constable his brother-in-law, were in the number of those who had sent Lord Lovat into France; and were all of them greatly able to serve the young prince. Lord Lovat, therefore, felt no pain in addressing Lord Perth, believing, upon the representation he had received, that he had more power at the Court of St. Germains than anybody else, and not having the smallest knowledge of Lord Middleton.

Sir John Maclean left Lord Lovat at Paris, and went alone to St. Germains, to speak to Lord Perth, and afterwards to the Queen; and in two days returned to conduct him to court. He led him in a private manner to the closet of Lord Perth, who received him with that goodness which is natural to him, and with unequivocal marks of friendship and satisfaction. Lord Lovat explained to him his business and the condition of affairs, and he was charmed to see so considerable a project on foot for the restoration of the King, and at 1703 the head of which were the principal nobility of Scotland, his kinsmen and relations.

Lord Perth then instructed Lord Lovat in what manner he should speak to the Queen. He said there was one thing that he must request, without which his project, and all that the persons who had sent him could do, would be ineffectual. Every 'true friend of his Majesty,' said Lord Perth, 'is persuaded that Lord Middleton is a faithless traitor, a pensionary of the English Parliament, to give intelligence of all that passes at the Court of St. Germains. The late King,' he added, 'and even the Queen herself, suspected him of having discovered their secrets to the Prince of Orange.' Sir John Maclean, who was also in the closet, confirmed what Lord Perth said. They both agreed in giving Lord Lovat a black and detestable picture of the Earl of Middleton, and intreated him to engage the Queen, upon her royal word, not to discover a syllable of his project to this nobleman.

The young nobleman was an entire stranger to Lord Middleton. He did not know that he was at that time at daggers-drawing with Lord Perth and his brother, the Earl of Melfort. He was totally ignorant that Sir John Maclean had been disobliged by him in the appointment of a gentleman of the Privy Chamber to the King, which had been promised him, and was given to another. He therefore gave implicitly into the snare, and was credulous and honest enough to attend to all the precautions that his kinsman and his patron suggested. A traitor to his King and country, he became his enemy without knowing him; and, in his first audience of the Queen, he exacted her royal promise never to communicate a syllable of his project to Lord Middleton, as he was extremely suspected by her most faithful subjects.

Such was the origin of Lord Lovat's misfortunes. The Queen readily complied with his request, telling him that the late King and herself had had reason to suspect Lord Middleton's fidelity in a discovery that the Prince of Orange had made of an affair, which regarded the King and the Electors Palatine and of Bavaria, and which had been communicated to nobody but Lord Middleton. Thus the Queen herself appeared at that time to have no confidence in him.

Lord Lovat immediately began to work with the Queen in digesting the business upon which he had been sent. At her Majesty's request the Marquis de Torcy, Minister and Secretary of State for Foreign Affairs to the King of France, and Monseigneur Gualterio, Nuncio of the Pope, entered into the project; and Lord Lovat waited, by her orders, upon each of these statesmen, to inform them of the situation and state of affairs in Scotland. M. de Torcy expressed himself to Lord Lovat, in the first audience he had of that minister at Marli, in strong terms, respecting the affection of the King, his master, for the Scottish nation, 1703 and the confidence he might place in the receiving every sort of succour.

The Marquis de Callieres, Secretary of the Cabinet to the King, his plenipotentiary at Ryswic, and who was a man of great ability in state affairs, had been thoroughly informed in the concerns of the Court of St. Germains by his friend Lord Perth. Upon this account the Marquis de Torcy and the Papal Nuncio, his intimate friends, earnestly begged of him to work with Lord Perth, Lord Lovat, and Sir John Maclean, in forwarding the Scottish project. The Papal Nuncio, soon after Cardinal Gualterio, and whom I shall here distinguish by that title, came often to the office of M. de Callieres to observe their progress, and to assist them with his advice, he being one of the most skilful men in Europe in political affairs.

All these persons were at that time witnesses to the zeal and assiduity of Lord Lovat for the interest of the Court of St. Germains. As long as the Queen kept the secret, the affair went on in the most prosperous manner; and her Majesty was so passionately desirous of its success, that she said twenty times to Lord Lovat that she had sent her jewels to Paris to be sold, in order to send the twenty thousand crowns,* which Lord Lovat represented to be necessary to arm and

---

* 2500*l*.

equip their friends, to the chiefs of the Highlands in Scotland.

But no sooner was the secret discovered, than the face of the business was entirely changed. The Earl of Middleton, having learned that Lord Lovat was incognito at the Court, and that he worked at a project which was to be executed by the relations or allies of the family of Perth, his declared enemies, for the restoration of the King, believed that he was ruined without resource if the project should succeed. He was not in the wrong; for, if the Scottish insurrection had been executed, his disgrace would have been inevitable. Preferring, therefore, his own private views to the interests of his King and master, he resolved to save himself by undermining and ruining the project.

It was impossible to succeed in this undertaking without ruining Lord Lovat, who was the first mover in the affair, and the representative of all the loyal Scots. Lord Middleton, therefore, from this moment plotted the destruction of Lovat, and never lost sight of his purpose, till he had thrust him into a dungeon. Even then he did not cease to fear that Lord Lovat might one day divulge the truth of the whole affair to the King and Queen. He therefore insinuated to them so black an idea of Lord Lovat, that they believed him the greatest traitor in the three kingdoms; though there is not a single nobleman without exception who served them more faithfully, nor a Scotsman from the death of Lord Dundee, who rendered so great services to their interests. 1702

Lord Middleton, however, in pursuit of his design, set out with decrying Lord Lovat to the Marquis de Torcy; at the same time abusing all the Highlanders of Scotland, observing, that they were no better than a kind of banditti, fit enough to pillage the Lowlands, and to carry off cattle, but incapable of forming a regular corps, or of looking in the face the enemies of the King. His lordship had forgotten, that his father had not risen to the rank of a peer of Scotland from a private soldier of the regiment of the uncle of Lord Lovat in the service of the great Gustavus Adolphus, but for having commanded, after his return into Scotland, and his desertion from the army of the Protector, who had bestowed upon him the rank of colonel, the Highland clans in the service of King Charles the Second. In reality, it was to the clans of Fraser and Macleod, that the first Lord Middleton was indebted for his subsistence for many years.

Lord Lovat was no sooner acquainted with the calumnies that had been disseminated against himself and the Highlanders, than he complained in a very lively manner to the Queen. Her Majesty had still so much goodness for him, and so much confidence in his zeal, that she usually gave him three audiences every week. She therefore paid considerable attention to his remonstrances; and replied, that if Lord Middleton

1702 said a word against either him or the Highlanders, she would immediately dismiss him from her service. The Earl, however, denied with oaths that he had ever uttered what was imputed to him; and added, that he should be the most ungrateful of men if he spoke against those to whom he was indebted for his rank; but that on the contrary he should never forget what he owed to the Highlanders, and above all to the house of Lovat.

These assurances, however, did not entirely satisfy Lord Perth; and perceiving that Cardinal Gualterio had a very particular friendship for Lord Lovat, he recommended it to that lord, to intreat his Eminence to cause the Queen to be spoken to by the Marquis de Torcy on the part of the King of France, to communicate no affair which respected Scotland, to any nobleman of her Court, except to Lord Perth, Lord Lovat, and those whom they should have admitted to a share in the business. The cardinal had much credit at the French Court, and was infinitely esteemed by the Sovereign. He therefore easily brought about what Lord Lovat desired, and the Queen anew promised compliance.

1703 Lord Middleton readily perceived that she spoke to him in a manner more cautious and reserved than usual. He foresaw her entire alienation, and his own ruin. He therefore at this moment brought his last mine to play upon the fortress; which had its complete effect, de-

feated his enemies, overturned the projected insurrection, 1703
and put a final termination to the credit of Lord Lovat.

All on a sudden he retired into the convent of the
Benedictines at Paris, from whence he wrote to the
Queen, humbly to intreat her to permit him to pass the
remainder of his days in entire seclusion from secular
affairs. He pretended that he had been miraculously
inspired to reconcile himself to the holy Catholic
Church, by hearing the blessed sacrament carried
along with the sound of a little bell before it, to the
apartment of his son, Lord Clermont, who was at the
point of death. Upon this he had immediately set out
for Paris, publicly to abjure the Protestant religion;
and his next step was, by a memorial, full of penitence
and religious sorrow, to demand permission to retire for
the rest of his life, in order to expiate the scandal of his
past impieties.

The Court of St. Germains was extremely divided
upon this new event. Lord Perth and all the most
zealous servants of the young King exclaimed loudly,
that Lord Middleton had turned Roman Catholic in
France, exactly as Lord Sunderland had done in England, for the sole purpose of betraying his Sovereign
with the greater security. On the other hand it was
vigorously maintained by his friends, that the hand of
God undoubtedly appeared in the miraculous manner
of his conversion. The Queen entered entirely into
their sentiments; and, in spite of the hypocritical re-

1703 monstrances of her minister, beseeching her to permit him to remain in the convent, her Majesty recalled, and even laid her royal injunctions upon him to return to Court. These injunctions he was unable to resist. The Queen received him with extreme joy, and from that moment he engrossed an entire ascendency over her.

Some time after Lord Lovat, perceiving how ill his business advanced, reproached the Queen with the confidence she had newly placed in Lord Middleton after all she had formerly said against that nobleman. The Queen replied, that it was true she had suspected him, and she believed not without reason, but that after a conversion evidently so miraculous she could no longer doubt his fidelity; she was even satisfied that the interference of a man so highly distinguished of Providence would bring down the divine favour and blessing on her affairs. From this period Lord Lovat perceived all his credit at the Court of St. Germains to be at an end. He found his project, and the affairs that brought him into France, overthrown. And this was so much the case that the Queen, who had often said she was resolved to sell her jewels, in order to give sixty thousand francs to the Highlanders of Scotland, exerted herself to persuade the King of France not to apply this sum of money on his part for the prosecution of the affair, after that prince had had the generosity, through her Majesty's intercession, to issue

LIFE OF LORD LOVAT. 97

an order to his Treasury to pay the money into the hands of Lord Lovat, without costing her a penny. Lord Lovat immediately determined to wash his hands of the affair, and to return without delay into Scotland. But his kinsman, Lord Perth, Cardinal Gualterio, and the Marquis de Torcy engaged him to have patience, and to stay a little while to see whether anything could be done.

The Queen, on her part, unwilling to disoblige him, obtained for him, through the interest of Madame de Maintenon, Cardinal Gualterio, Cardinal de Noailles, and the Marquis de Torcy, a private audience of the Most Christian King, who had never before granted that favour to any foreigner, let his quality be what it would.

At this audience there was no person present except the Marquis de Torcy, who stood behind the royal chair. Lord Lovat enlarged upon the antient alliances between France and Scotland, observing that the Scotch, assisted by the French, had frequently beaten the English, and that, if they were now honoured with the protection of the greatest King that had ever filled the throne of France, they would not certainly be less successful than they had been in former instances.

His Most Christian Majesty replied, with a look of much benignity, that himself and the whole French nation had their hearts unfeignedly Scottish; and that, since Lord Lovat had been chosen to represent the whole body of loyal Scots, he desired to be understood

H

1703 as from that moment renewing with him all antient alliances between the two nations. The King promised at all times to assist the Scots with troops, money, and everything that might be necessary to support them against the English. He added, that he was perfectly acquainted with the fidelity of Lord Lovat and his family, and that he might depend at all times upon his favourable remembrance.

The Most Christian King then quitted Lord Lovat with a most gracious and engaging air, extremely natural to this celebrated monarch. When Lord Lovat retired at the opposite door of the closet where the King had left him, the Marquis de Torcy and the Marquis de Callieres appeared ready to receive him, and had the politeness to say that the King had been highly satisfied with him. Two days after the Queen sent a billet to Cardinal Gualterio, informing him that she had that day received a visit from the King of France, who had the goodness to say, that he did not know whether Lord Lovat were pleased with him, but that he had been extremely pleased with that nobleman: intreating her at the same time never again to demand of him a private audience of any of her subjects, since he had at no other time exposed his person in that manner to any foreigner. The Queen concluded with intreating the Cardinal to felicitate Lord Lovat, who was then at Paris, upon the subject.

Lord Lovat, being very young and sanguine, was

charmed with the unexampled honour he had received 1703
from the Most Christian King, and sensibly touched
with the great attentions he experienced from his
Ministers. He could not restrain himself from frequently expressing his gratitude and zeal for the interests of the King of France. This was a handle
eagerly laid hold of by the Earl of Middleton, who
constantly surrounded Lord Lovat with his creatures,
to alienate from him the mind of the Queen, and to
ruin the project of a Scottish insurrection.

Lord Middleton endeavoured to persuade the Queen
that, as Lord Lovat was full of ambition and enterprise, he had been gained by the French Ministers and
by Cardinal Gualterio to excite at all adventures a
civil war in Scotland. He added, that indeed such a
war would be extremely advantageous to France, but
that it would ruin instead of advancing the affairs of
the King, her son; that the Scots could never support
hostilities against England for any length of time; and
that the most loyal houses must be expected to perish
in such an insurrection. He observed, that such a step
would also overthrow the design entertained by the
Parliament of England, of formally recalling their
rightful sovereign: a design of which he pretended to
be assured, though I believe very falsely, by the letters of
Lord Nottingham, Lord Wharton, and Lord Godolphin.*
Lord Perth, who was informed that the Queen gave

---

* A stroke is drawn through each of these names in the manuscript.

1703 into this snare of Lord Middleton to ruin the project of Scotland, communicated intelligence of it to Lord Lovat, and warmly intreated him to disabuse her Majesty.

Lord Lovat spoke to the Queen that very evening, representing to her in a strong manner that there could be none but concealed traitors who would endeavour to distinguish between her interests and the interests of France; that her Majesty had no other resource under heaven but the assistance of France to support her loyal subjects; that those who would have it believed that a civil war in Scotland would interfere with the intentions of the English Parliament in favour of their rightful sovereign ought to fix a term within which Parliament was to declare for the King as they pretended; that, if they fixed no term, it was an incontestible proof that their promises were intended only to amuse and lull asleep the Court of St. Germains, as they had successfully done for fifteen years past, and that, for these reasons, her Majesty ought to consider all persons that insisted upon such pretences as traitors.

The Queen protested before God that she had no hope in the English Parliament; that all her expectations were derived from the generosity and friendship of the King of France, from the loyalty of the faithful Scots, and above all from the Highlanders. Lord Lovat replied in these very words: 'With these views, what reason can induce you, madam, to reject the counsels of the French administration, and of 1703 Cardinal Gualterio, whose attachment is so unquestionable, for putting the loyal Scots in a condition to restore their sovereign?'

Her Majesty now promised in the most unreserved manner to conform herself to this advice for the future; and, as she saw that Lord Middleton brought every engine into play to counteract the projects and services of Lord Lovat, she resolved to reconcile them, as being the step which seemed most necessary to the success of her affairs; and to endeavour to derive advantage from their united counsels. Lord Middleton, who easily perceived that this reconciliation would place him in a more advantageous situation than ever for counteracting the expedition and ruining Lord Lovat, expressed himself ardently desirous of it. The Queen spoke upon the subject to the Cardinal, knowing the extreme friendship he had for Lord Lovat, and engaged his Eminence to persuade him to embrace it.

The Cardinal accordingly warmly intreated Lord Lovat to indulge the Queen upon this article. He observed, that he would be as much master as ever of what he chose to communicate, and what to conceal from Lord Middleton; that it was always necessary to be on our guard with a reconciled enemy; but that in the mean time it was expedient to enter into an apparent intimacy with the favourite. Lord Lovat had an unbounded deference for the Cardinal, and consented, at

1703 his intreaty, to meet Lord Middleton at his Eminence's apartments.

Lord Middleton accordingly came thither, and Lord Lovat, who went there every day like a child of the house, found the Earl and the Cardinal together. His Eminence witnessed the protestations of friendship that Lord Middleton made to Lord Lovat at this interview, expressing his gratitude for the obligations that his father had experienced from his own family, and that of his mother, who was daughter of the chief of the Macleods.

As Lord Lovat was naturally plain and sincere in his manners, he persuaded himself that the professions of Lord Middleton were honest and unfeigned. The letters, which he afterwards addressed to Lord Lovat from St. Germains, and which are still among his lordship's papers, were so full of protestations of attachment and friendship, that in spite of the precautions that had been insinuated to him by the Cardinal, this nobleman admitted them all to be as true as the gospel. He made similar protestations on his side.

The design of Lord Middleton being thus far advanced, he next employed his confident, Mrs. Fox, the great female statesman of the Court of St. Germains, to draw out of Lord Lovat all that he intended to do when he arrived in Scotland. It was this Mrs. Fox, who was constantly employed in passing and repassing between St. Germains and London, to cultivate the pretended commerce between Lord Middleton and those English noblemen who promised to cause the Queen and the Parliament of England to declare for King James the Third. These very noblemen afterwards appeared among the most zealous partisans of the house of Hanover.

I will beg pardon of this lady for a moment, while I return to mention a circumstance which I had forgotten in its place. For many months before the Queen had entirely divulged the Scottish project, Lord Lovat had worked with the ministers of Louis the Fourteenth. He obtained of the Court of France, to send an army of five thousand men to support the loyal Scots. They were also to send officers, money, ammunition, and arms, sufficient for such an enterprise. Everything had already been prepared. Lord Lovat had even received from the Marshal de Vauban, with whom he had communicated several days for that purpose, his grand secret for the construction of folding ladders, with which it was proposed to scale Fort William, formerly Inverlochy, a fortress, constructed in the midst of the mountains, and which served as a curb upon the Highlanders, particularly the clans of the Camerons and the Macdonalds.

The affair was in this state of preparation, when Lord Middleton felt himself more than ever obliged to employ the ascendancy, that his pretended miraculous conversion had given him over the mind of the Queen, for its subversion. All those subtleties, pretexts, and chicanery, in which the mind of this statesman was so remarkably fertile, were exhausted. He at length hit upon a last resource, which succeeded beyond his most sanguine expectations. He persuaded the Queen to represent to Louis the Fourteenth, that, granting all that Lord Lovat had said, respecting the resolution of the Scots to take arms, were true, when he left that country, yet, having already resided many months at the Court of France for the completion of his scheme, and in that time having received no intelligence from Scotland, the face of affairs in that country might be now entirely changed. He, therefore, most humbly intreated her Majesty to defer the execution of the Scottish project, till she should have sent Lord Lovat back into that country, in order to ascertain how far things remained there in the condition he had left them; adding, that the Most Christian King ought to depute an envoy on his part along with Lord Lovat, to learn from the mouths of the loyal Scots their real intentions in favour of their lawful sovereign and the kingdom of France.

Louis the Fourteenth perceiving that the Queen was obstinately bent upon not consenting to the Scottish insurrection till after this specious examination, consented that Lord Lovat should be sent home. He agreed at the same time to commission a gentleman on his part to learn the final resolution of the Scottish noblemen, previous to his sending them the troops, and 1703 the various other succours that were proposed.

It was at this period that Lord Lovat, seeing himself suspected, and persuaded that his project and the pains he had taken were lost, absolutely determined to give up all concern in the affair. But he was not permitted to follow his own inclinations. Cardinal Gualterio, the Marquis de Torcy, the Marquis de Calieres, and Lord Perth united to recommend it to him not to abandon an enterprise so glorious for his person and family, and so useful to his King and country.

M. de Torcy, in particular, who was highly irritated at the conduct of Lord Middleton and the weakness of the Queen, told Lord Lovat, for whom he entertained much attachment and condescension, that the counter-plot of Lord Middleton ought not to discourage him, for that he had nothing to do but to chuse what Scotsman he pleased to accompany him in the character of envoy from the King of France. He added, that, as the King wished the Highlanders to take arms immediately, in case they were in a capacity to support themselves till the arrival of the French succours, it would be proper of Lord Lovat to take with him Colonel Peter Graham and Major George Fraser, who was his distant relation, both very brave officers, to assist in the enterprise. Lord Lovat obtained at the same time a promise from the Marquis de Torcy to dispatch after him his cousin german, Sir John Maclean, with orders to join him, and to give him a thousand crowns* for the expences of his journey. The Marquis de Torcy performed this promise a few months after.

Lord Lovat, perceiving that the nomination of an envoy for the King of France was devolved upon him, chose for that purpose Captain John Murray, a most respectable and gallant gentleman, who had been many years in the French service. Mr. Murray was brother to the Laird of Abercairny, in the county of Perth, the most ancient branch, and the true head of the family of Murray, though the branch of Athol have falsely arrogated to itself a superiority, which the Laird of Abercairny, and many other branches of the Murrays, more ancient than that of Athol, have never acknowledged. Captain Murray was the fittest person in the world for that negotiation, being descended from this illustrious house, and related more or less remotely to the first nobility in Scotland. He was charmed with so honourable an employment, and he was promoted, and in some sort rewarded for his undertaking, previous to his departure.

Cardinal Gualterio, still further to sooth Lord Lovat, and in order to bestow an additional degree of security upon his person, an object to which his Eminence paid the most condescending attention, proposed to him to accept a commission of Brigadier-General in the service of the King of France. The commission was accord-

---

* 125*l*.

ingly procured for him by the Marquis de Torcy. Lord 1703
Lovat received from this Minister the written instructions of the Court of France to take arms in case a proper opportunity occurred, and six thousand francs * from the royal treasury to defray the expences of his journey. He was now upon the point of setting out with Mr. John Murray, Colonel Graham, and Major Fraser.

It was at this period that Lord Middleton, constantly apprehensive from the good understanding that subsisted between Cardinal Gualterio, the Marquis de Torcy, and the other French Ministers, and Lord Lovat, engaged the Queen to bring about the seeming reconciliation between him and that nobleman, of which I have already spoken, and in the forwarding of which I had mentioned the intervention of Mrs. Fox.

This hireling of Lord Middleton was the intimate friend of Sir John Maclean, at whose house she took an opportunity to meet Lord Lovat. Taking this nobleman aside, she told him that Lord Middleton was perfectly charmed with his behaviour, and resolved to make him his only confidential friend, of all the noblemen that had followed their exiled master. She added, that in order to take measures with Lord Lovat respecting the commissions and honours, which it was proper for his master to bestow upon him, and which he was desirous of expediting, he would take it as a favour if

---
* 250*l*.

1703 Lord Lovat would give him a private interview at his *petite maison*, hard by the convent of the Benedictines at Paris, where he often retired in pious seclusion from the world, and held his conferences with Mrs. Fox and his other spies. Lord Lovat entered without suspicion into the snare that was spread for him. He did not fail to repair at the day and hour appointed to the rendezvous, when, in the room of finding Lord Middleton, he was introduced to Mrs. Fox, who was alone, and negligently reposed upon a kind of bed. As she had a great deal of wit, she entertained Lord Lovat very agreeably for two hours with the fine qualities of Lord Middleton, and the intrigues of the administration. At the end of that time Lord Middleton arrived, and Mrs. Fox quitted the apartment.

The Secretary, after having highly extolled the generosity of Lord Lovat in the undertaking so extensive and noble a design, protested that, if the Queen had not felt herself compelled by the services of his house and his own extraordinary merit to bestow upon him uncommon favours, he would upon his knees have intreated her to accord to him such marks of distinction as had never been granted to any peer of the kingdom of Scotland. Let it be observed, by the way, that what Lord Middleton said was literally true, and that he kept his word in the most religious manner. Lord Lovat was afterwards thrust for thirty-two days into a horrible and noisome dungeon, a distinction which had never been bestowed upon any Scottish nobleman before 1703 him.

Lord Middleton had informed the Court of France that the commissions granted by the late King James were annulled by his death; and that it would be necessary for the young King either to grant new commissions or to issue full powers under his sign manual, to renew in his absence the commissions which the late King had granted to the loyal Scots. The Court of France, having reflected upon this representation, applied to the Queen to issue these full powers to Lord Lovat. Her Majesty consented, and commanded her Minister to prepare them in the most authentic form. He accordingly dictated to the young King, who wrote them all with his own hand, and signed them J. R. at top and at bottom. This instrument Lord Middleton had brought in his pocket, and, delivering it to Lord Lovat, 'See here,' said he, 'the most honourable commission, and the most ample powers that ever King granted to a subject.' This instrument, so flattering to his person and house, is still carefully preserved among the papers of Lord Lovat.

After a multitude of caresses, the Secretary asked whether Lord Lovat were determined to take arms, and in what manner he intended to begin the war. As this nobleman conceived Lord Middleton to be sincere in forwarding the expedition, and in his unbounded professions of friendship, he told him very frankly that his

1703 design was to take arms at all events, since the instructions, that the Marquis de Torcy had given him on the part of the King of France, directed him to do so, provided he could support himself till the arrival of succours. He demonstrated to Lord Middleton, that he should infallibly be able to maintain the war for many years, since, granting that the Highlanders lost several battles, the enemy could not profit of their victory in so impracticable a country. This resolution apparently renewed the apprehensions of the Secretary for the execution of a project that involved in it his ruin. He, however, dissembled his fears, and bestowed infinite commendations upon the firmness and ardour of Lord Lovat.

This interview was only two days before his lordship was to set out for Scotland with Mr. John Murray and his other companions: he had already taken leave of her Majesty and the King. After having, therefore, regulated his correspondence with Lord Middleton, and mutually promised a sincere attachment and eternal friendship, Lord Lovat took leave of that nobleman with a thousand embraces.

Next day Lord Lovat was extremely surprised, while he was employed in preparing his baggage and equipage, at receiving a note from the Queen, commanding him to wait upon her at ten o'clock in the evening at her ordinary audience, her Majesty having forgotten something of consequence that she wished to communicate

to him. Lord Lovat obeyed; and, after the Queen 1703
had had the goodness to make use of a thousand
gracious and obliging expressions, she read to him a
billet addressed to the Duke of Gordon, which contained
only three words, to intreat him to be persuaded of her
grateful remembrance, and to place an entire confidence
in the bearer. Putting this billet into his hands, she
asked him whether he intended to take up arms immediately upon his arrival.

Lord Lovat replied that he did intend it, provided
the opportunity were favourable. 'My God,' said the
Queen, 'such a proceeding would ruin everything, and
prevent the Court of France from sending you any
assistance.' Lord Lovat replied, that so far from
having that effect, it was the only method by which
the Court of France could be obliged to become an
auxiliary; that the Marquis de Torcy considered it in
that light; and had commanded him on the part of
the Most Christian King to take arms if he were able
to support himself till the arrival of succours. 'And
I,' rejoined the Queen, 'positively enjoin you not to
take arms till you have particular orders from myself.'
Lord Lovat remained silent, and the Queen immediately with the most affectionate expressions wished
him all possible success. He accordingly kissed her
Majesty's hand, and took leave for the second time.

The following day he took leave of his friend,
Cardinal Gualterio, who recommended it to him, to

1703 regulate himself by the written instructions he had received from the Court of France, and not by the verbal orders of the Queen, who was governed by a man notoriously the inveterate enemy of the Scottish project. Lord Lovat set out with the design of taking arms, in order to oblige France to send the succours, which the Most Christian King had so positively promised with his own mouth.

Mean time Lord Middleton, who never lost sight of a single opportunity of ruining the Scottish insurrection, secretly dispatched James Murray,* his sworn creature, his spy, and a man who had no other means of subsistence, post for Scotland. This James Murray went by the way of Holland; and, as Lord Middleton had a regular commerce with the English nobility in the administration of Queen Anne, he had no difficulty in obtaining passports for his creatures, who went backward and forward to manage his intrigues in both the British kingdoms. On this account James Murray arrived in Scotland six weeks before Lord Lovat had been able to quit the coast of France.

Lord Lovat indeed was obliged to seek through all the towns upon the coast, from Brussels to Calais, in order to pass in safety: having no other provision for that purpose, than the orders of the Marquis de Torcy to the commandants of these places to assist him with their power. Accordingly he was constrained to wait

---
* Brother to Sir David Murray of Stanhope.

an entire month the arrival of an English packet for the exchange of prisoners, the captain of which was gained by dint of money, by the Count de la Tour, governor of Calais, to take Lord Lovat and his friends on board as English prisoners of war, and to put them on shore during the night in his boat, at some place in the neighbourhood of Dover, or at Dover.

The captain performed his engagement very faithfully; and from Dover Lord Lovat and Mr. John Murray set out for Scotland. During this journey they were exposed to various dangers; and particularly at the town of Northallerton were upon the point of being taken into custody, through the imprudence of a French valet de chambre.

A justice of the peace, who happened to be drinking in the kitchen of the post house where Lord Lovat and Mr. Murray had taken up their lodgings in that town, understood by the conversation of this valet, who was drunk, that his master was just come from France, and that he was a partisan of King James the Third. The justice was the very same man who had arrested Mr. Law upon his arrival from France some years before, and was liberally rewarded for it by King William. Upon this intelligence he assembled with much speed all the constables in the town, and surrounded the apartment where Lord Lovat and Mr. Murray were sitting.

Lord Lovat was informed of these proceedings by a

1703 gentleman of his clan, who was his servant. He proposed to Mr. Murray, to put themselves upon their defence, and to fight their way through everybody that opposed them, or to die in the attempt rather than suffer themselves to be taken alive. Mr. Murray replied that he was not ready to die; that he was a naturalised Frenchman, and an envoy of the King of France; and that Queen Anne dared not put him to death for fear of reprisals. Upon this Lord Lovat desired him to retire into the next room, as if he did not belong to his company: for himself, he was resolved to die upon the spot, or to force his way through the enemy, since he expected no better, if he were taken, than to be hanged and quartered.

He gave orders to his attendant, to lay hold of two pistols that were upon the table, and a blunderbuss that carried eight bullets. He took similar arms himself. Understanding that the justice of peace was foremost on the stairs, he ordered his gentleman to post himself upon the landing place, and to permit the magistrate to enter the apartment, where Lord Lovat stood with his pistol cocked, ready to fire. He bid his gentleman, the moment he heard the report, to discharge his blunderbuss upon the constables upon the stairs, telling him, that, as soon as this was done, they would both force their way through all their opponents, who for the most part had no other arms, than the long staves that are usually carried by people of their profession; that the night was very dark, and that, could they once gain the street, nothing would be easier than their escape.

But providence inspired Lord Lovat with a presence of mind, which saved his own life and that of his company much more easily and infallibly, than their courage could have done. He told his gentleman, that he would inform the justice of the peace that he was brother to the Duke of Argyle, who was colonel of the regiment of guards of Queen Anne, and well known and much beloved in that country. And as Lord Lovat had the honour to be really kinsman to the Duke of Argyle, and his intimate friend; and had been many times with him at the races that were held in the neighbourhood of Northallerton, it did not seem very difficult to pass himself for his brother.

While Lord Lovat was giving these orders, the justice of the peace drew up his constables in the yard, and at the foot of the stairs. He then came up to Lord Lovat's apartment. The nobleman advanced a few steps to meet him, and without giving him time to speak a word, said to him, 'My dear sir, how happy I am to see you. It is almost two years since I had that pleasure with the Duke of Argyle, at the races near this town.' The justice was struck with these words, and replied with a faltering voice, 'My lord, I ask your lordship a thousand pardons for having broke thus abruptly into your apartment. But my business was to beg your lordship's permission to treat you with a bottle of wine in this town, where I am a man of some consequence.' Lord Lovat replied that he should accept and return his compliment with extreme pleasure, and begged him to be seated.

The peace-officer answered that he would return in a moment, but that he would beg his lordship's permission to go and give orders in person to the hostess, for the best Spanish wine she had in the house. As soon, however, as he got to the bottom of the stairs, he told his army of constables with an authoritative tone, that the gentleman above stairs was brother to the Duke of Argyle; that he was going to drink a bottle with him; and that for their parts, they had nothing to do but to get home as fast as they could. Having disbanded his forces, he returned again immediately, and Lord Lovat made him so drunk, that he was obliged to be carried off without sense or motion to his own house.

When he was gone, Lord Lovat told Mr. Murray that it would be advisable to mount on horseback immediately, and to quit the town, though it was then only one o'clock in the morning. They accordingly set out: and Lord Lovat had more trouble, to hinder Mr. Murray from stabbing the French valet, who had occasioned this adventure, than to outwit the penetration, and escape from the hands of the justice of peace.

Having left this place, he arrived in Scotland with

Mr. John Murray, who did not leave him for a moment day or night; without stopping in any other town in England, and exactly two months after the arrival of James Murray, the emissary of Lord Middleton.

Lord Lovat had been obliged, when at London, to send Colonel Graham and Major Fraser before him into Scotland, with orders to wait for him upon the borders of that kingdom, nearest to England. Here therefore he met them; and, as soon as they saw Lord Lovat and Mr. John Murray, they informed them of the arrival of Mr. James Murray; adding, that he was acquainted with the particulars of the project, and had declared to the Duke of Hamilton, to Lord Athol, and the rest of the Lords of the Privy Council of Queen Anne, that Lord Lovat was gained by the Court of France and the Nuncio of the Pope, to excite a civil war in Scotland, contrary to the positive orders of the King and Queen; though the latter was so violent a Roman Catholic, that no Protestant could live in peace at St. Germains, and even Lord Middleton had been obliged to dissemble for a time, and pretend to reconcile himself to the Holy See, though still in his heart a true Protestant, and having only taken this step the more effectually to protect the cause of the Reformation.

Mr. Livingston, a French officer of distinction, then in Scotland for an affair of honour which had happened to him in France, having obtained his pardon, and returned to that court, declared to Marshal Villeroi, his patron, to the Marquis de Torcy, and to the Queen herself, that he had heard all this with his own ears, and a thousand other injurious aspersions, that were thrown out by Mr. James Murray against his Queen.

In the mean time, the Scottish Privy Council issued their proclamation a month before Lord Lovat arrived, to take him dead or alive, fixing a price upon his head, and prohibiting, under pain of death, all the subjects of Queen Anne to hold any commerce with him, either by word or writing. This astonished beyond measure Mr. John Murray, who gave himself up for lost. But Lord Lovat intreated him not to be disheartened; adding, that he had nothing to fear, and that for himself he had been inured to such menaces.

Immediately upon his arrival in Scotland, Lord Lovat sent intelligence to his brother, and a few of the gentlemen of his clan, who hastened to join him. He then waited with Mr. John Murray upon the heads of the clans, and the principal loyal noblemen in Scotland. When Lord Lovat produced his commissions, and his comprehensive full powers signed by his King, and Mr. Murray had assured them, on the part of his Most Christian Majesty, that he would send them every kind of succour, they were perfectly ravished; and made a thousand protestations of fidelity to their King and the interests of France, and of their resolution to hazard their lives in the cause.

But if they received this news with the extremest

pleasure, they were not less indignant at the base 1703
proceedings of Lord Middleton, the effects of which
Lord Lovat had now too dearly experienced, to be able
to doubt of them any longer. Nor were they less
exasperated with the unlicensed insolence of James
Murray; so that the Laird of the Stewarts of Appin, a
gentleman well born and extremely loyal, together
with some other lairds, was ready to set out for
Edinburgh in order to cut off his nose and ears. But
Mr. John Murray, who feared that this action might
prove disadvantageous to him, intreated Lord Lovat
to divert the Laird of Appin, who was married to his
cousin german, the daughter of the chief of the
Macleods, from his purpose.

Lord Lovat complied with the request, and at the
same time employed himself daily to all her faithful
subjects in making the eulogium of a queen, who has
since become his inveterate enemy; telling them that
this princess instilled the best sentiments into her son,
and taught him to regard the Scottish nation as his
most faithful subjects; for which reason they ought to
treat with the fullest contempt the impostures and
calumnies with which that villain, James Murray, was
continually blackening the character of his benefactress.

Lord Lovat and Mr. Murray having now held
particular conference with all the Scottish leaders
most attached to their sovereign, his lordship resolved to invite them to a general council of war in

the Castle of Drummond. In this council he proposed to them to take up arms immediately, with an entire confidence of being speedily succoured from the kingdom of France. Mr. Murray at the same time confirmed to them the expectations with which Lord Lovat sought to inspire them on the part of the Most Christian King. The chiefs of the Highland clans were unanimously of Lord Lovat's opinion.

But Lord Drummond, whose loyalty to his sovereign never incurred the shadow of an imputation, observed to them that there was one consideration which was absolutely decisive against their taking arms at that time. It was that the King had appointed no general; and that the Scottish nobles, equally persuaded of their capacity and loyalty, would never brook submission to one of their own body unless he was expressly nominated by a particular commission.

Lord Lovat replied, that, though he had as good a title as any man to pretend to the command in the execution of a project of which he had been the first author, he would, however, cheerfully accept Lord Drummond for his commander; that, if Lord Drummond declined, and any of the principal nobility, whose loyalty was unquestionable—the Earl of Breadalbane, the Earl of Errol, Earl Marishal, or the Duke of Gordon —were willing to take the command of the army, he would readily obey them, and he was persuaded that the other heads of clans would follow his example.

Lord Drummond returned his grateful thanks to Lord Lovat and the chiefs that declared themselves of his opinion, but added that he would never accept the command, and he was persuaded the other Lowland lords would be of the same mind, since such a step would infallibly excite the jealousy of his Majesty's subjects, and prevent the Lowland lords not invited to the command from joining the army. They must therefore expect a reinforcement, or at any rate a general from France, to whose command the Scottish nobility might feel it no indignity to submit.

In this manner, in spite of all the efforts of Lord Lovat, Mr. Murray, and the heads of the clans, to effect an immediate insurrection in expectation of a reinforcement from France, and of several officers, whose mission into that country would then be infallible, it was unfortunately concluded in this fatal council to defer for some months the decisive step. Meanwhile they resolved that it was expedient to send back Mr. John Murray, or Lord Lovat, without delay into France to demand succours in general, and to counteract the pernicious effects that might be produced in the mind of the Queen by the falsehoods of James Murray, supported by the influence of Lord Middleton.

The Countess of Errol, sister to Lord Perth, the soul of the King's affairs in the Lowlands, and a woman of a masculine and superior genius, was the only person in all that part of Scotland to support the opinion of

Lord Lovat for immediate extremities. Indeed, this lady observed fairly to Mr. John Murray that she did not find in anybody but that nobleman the firm and resolute spirit which was indispensibly necessary in the desperate condition of the royal affairs.

Mr. Murray immediately and absolutely refused to return into France upon the errand proposed in the general council, and that for two reasons. The first, that there still remained a great number of lairds affectionate to the royal cause whom he had not yet seen, and that the business of the commission which had brought him into Britain was therefore, not yet fulfilled. His second reason was, that he assured the council that Lord Lovat had much more credit at the Court of France than he had, as well as with the Queen by the intervention of his friend, Cardinal Gualterio, who had great influence over that princess.

Lord Lovat, therefore, finding all the nobility of the Lowlands averse to the taking arms, and desirous to gain these noblemen to rise in concert with the Highlanders, suffered himself to be carried away by their intreaties. In an evil hour he consented to return immediately into France, in spite of the tears of the gentlemen of his clan, who, in despair, tore their hair when they saw him ready to abandon them a second time.

Greatly were it to have been wished that he had followed his own inclination and judgement in taking

up arms with the rest of the Highland lairds, his near
relations and friends, regardless of the timid counsels of
the nobility of the flat country. He could have repelled
his enemies without difficulty till the arrival of a reinforcement from France. And in that case he would
have become one of the first men in that part of
Scotland; or, at worst, have made a brilliant and
enviable fortune in France in consequence of so important a service, and so distinguished a zeal for the
cause of his sovereign, and the interests of the Most
Christian King. But providence had otherwise decided,
and reserved for him in that country dungeons and
prisons rather than riches and honours.

Mr. Murray was obliged to return to Edinburgh to
concert matters with the Earl of Errol, Earl Marishal,
the Duke of Gordon, and other noblemen attached to
the royal cause. It has already been seen that this
gentleman, though extremely sincere and possessed of
much ability, was naturally mild and timid in his
disposition. He was therefore greatly apprehensive
that he should be put in prison through the treachery
of James Murray. He knew that the Dukes of Argyle
and Queensberry and the Earl of Leven, who may at
this time be styled the triumvirate of Scotland, had
formerly supported Lord Lovat against the tyranny of
Lord Athol at a time when the latter was Secretary of
State to King William, and seemed to have the whole
power of the administration in his hands. He there-

1703 fore applied to Lord Drummond in an earnest manner to engage Lord Lovat to wait upon these noblemen, his antient friends, to amuse them with a fictitious account of their journey, and to intreat them to give no trouble to Mr. Murray, who was come into Scotland purely to visit his relations and friends.

Lord Lovat would have been happy at another time to have waited upon the Duke of Argyle and Lord Leven, his relations, his intimate acquaintances, and persons to whom he was placed under the most essential obligations. But, now that he was unalterably fixed to engage in a war for the service of his King and the interests of France, for which these noblemen had no partiality, it was difficult for him to persuade himself to have an interview with them. But above all, the last man he would wish to have seen was the Duke of Queensberry, the inveterate and irreconcileable enemy of King James the Third.

Mr. Murray and Lord Drummond were, however, urgent in their arguments with him to comply with the proposal. They even suggested to him the idea of making his peace with Queen Anne, remaining at home in his clan, and sending Major Fraser, who had come with him from France, to demand the proposed reinforcements. Overcome by their arguments, he at length consented to see these lords; but at the same time observed to Lord Drummond and Mr. Murray, that the half of Scotland should not buy him to make his peace with Queen Anne, and that no consideration 1703 should prevent him from passing immediately into France, to learn the present purposes and final resolution of the two courts.

Lord Lovat accordingly waited upon the three noblemen, and he was particularly upon his guard with the Duke of Queensberry, in order to amuse, and throw him upon a wrong scent. The Duke himself gave Lord Lovat an immediate opportunity of doing so without much exercise of his invention.

He told Lord Lovat, that he was already acquainted with the whole of the business that had brought him into Britain; that the brother, or brother-in-law of James Murray, who was a member of the Scottish Parliament, to which Queensberry was High Commissioner, introduced to him that emissary, and that he had discovered to him the whole plan of the Scottish insurrection concerted between the Courts of France and St. Germains. He further told Lord Lovat, that he knew that he had seen, or was about to see all the Highland chiefs, and the other friends of the King in the north; that he did not, however, ask him any questions upon that subject; but that he had one favour to demand of him, which Lord Lovat must not refuse: he ought to remember, that Lord Athol and the Duke of Hamilton were two persons who had for a long time endeavoured to deprive him of estate, reputation and life; he ought not to forget, that he

1703 himself had united with the Duke of Argyle to defend him against their malice; he had therefore no reason to spare them. The Duke accordingly hoped that Lord Lovat would frankly inform him, whether the report were true, that Lord Athol and the Duke of Hamilton corresponded with the Court of St. Germains, at the very time that they displayed an ostentatious zeal in the service of the present Government.

The Duke of Queensberry at this time breathed the most inveterate enmity against Hamilton and Athol, because they opposed the projects of that nobleman in his Parliament. He would therefore have given everything he had in the world, to be put into a method of depriving these two lords of the power of counteracting and opposing his administration. Lord Lovat on his part was not less delighted, that the Duke had chosen his field of battle so opportunely.

He accordingly replied, he would give his Excellency every kind of satisfaction upon that head, on condition that he would grant him in return a small favour for one of his friends. The Duke returned, that he had nothing to do but to ask, and that he might be confident of obtaining everything that depended upon him. Lord Lovat then intreated him not to disturb Mr. John Murray, who was not come into Scotland, as James Murray had falsely given out, to excite an insurrection, but purely to see his brothers and kinsmen, and from whom his Excellency might be assured he had nothing to fear. The Duke without hesitation gave his word 1703 that Mr. John Murray should meet with no trouble.

Lord Lovat, having thus obtained the favour he desired, was now to pay the Duke of Queensberry for it in the manner he demanded. He had been informed by all the faithful partisans of King James the Third, and among others by Mr. John Murray, that the Duke of Hamilton intended no good to the royal party, but that on the contrary he was devoured with the absurd idea of becoming himself King of Scotland. Mr. Murray had received this particular intelligence from his brother-in-law, Mr. Graham of Fintry, one of the bravest and most honest men in Scotland, and who could not be surpassed in attachment to his sovereign.

The Laird of Fintry reported that the Duke of Hamilton, with whom he was very intimate, had weakly discovered his secret to him, as to his best friend, in a private conversation they had held in the Duke's closet. The Duke had observed, that he had pretensions of great antiquity by one of his ancestors on the female side to the Crown of Scotland, and that he was assured that the Scottish nation, and particularly the Presbyterians, who were both the strongest and the most numerous party, would never receive a Popish sovereign; adding, that he had put himself at the head of the Jacobite party with no other design, than to embroil the two kingdoms, and to profit of their disorder, by exalting himself to the Crown. Mr. Graham s of Fintry, who was a zealous partisan of King James, was so incensed at this discovery, that he did not hesitate to say, 'My Lord Duke, your design is as unjustifiable as your hopes are groundless. You have five hundred brave gentlemen, who are now your good friends, that would be the first to poignard you, if they saw you mad enough to declare yourself King of Scotland.'

Nor was this the only consideration that influenced Lord Lovat in his present conduct. He himself knew, by ocular demonstration, that the Duke of Hamilton had accepted the commission of General of the Scottish Army from the late King James; that he had promised an hundred several times to join himself to the Highland forces with a body of cavalry; that he had regularly broken his word, and that he had never expended so much as a sixpence, for a prince, who had laid him under accumulated obligations. Combining therefore what he had himself observed with the discovery of Mr. Murray, Lord Lovat thought that he had no reason in the world to spare such a man as the Duke of Hamilton.

With respect to Lord Athol, he was notoriously the incorrigible enemy of King James. His accumulated treasons rendered his person odious to all his Majesty's faithful servants. Much less therefore was Lord Lovat bound to spare this incomparable villain, than the Duke his brother-in-law. In a word, he was persuaded that he could not do a better service to his King, than to put the Duke of Hamilton and Lord Athol, the two greatest hypocrites in Scotland, and of whose duplicity and selfish policy no man was ignorant, out of a condition to injure his project, or to prejudice the interests of their sovereign.

Lord Lovat therefore made to the Duke of Queensberry this pretended discovery, which had no foundation in anything he knew upon the subject, except in the groundless assertions of a few Jacobites, attached to the party of the Duke of Hamilton and Lord Athol. He assured his Excellency that these two noblemen were the most faithful friends and servants of King James; that Mr. James Murray had brought them over commissions from the Court of St. Germains; and that they had promised to take up arms at a very early period, and to put themselves at the head of the whole Jacobite party, in order to restore the King; that his Excellency might assure Queen Anne that this was the real state of the case.

The Duke of Queensberry was overjoyed at this chimerical discovery. He made a thousand professions of service to Lord Lovat. He offered to make his peace with Queen Anne, to obtain for him a regiment and a considerable pension, and to make him chief justiciary and commandant of the county, which was the seat of the Lovat estates. Lord Lovat returned him his grateful thanks for these great offers. But he replied, that he could not at present accept of them; that he was obliged in honour and conscience, to return into France for the service of his King, and to carry on a project in which he was engaged.

He however promised his Excellency, that, if he had then nothing to do for King James, he would in the following spring demand permission to make his peace with Queen Anne, adding that he should then be happy to accept the offers that his Excellency had the kindness to make. In the meantime, he promised, that, if the Duke would favour him with a passport for his immediate return into France, he would communicate to him with the earliest opportunity a more particular account of the engagements of the Duke of Hamilton and Athol with the Court of St. Germains, in order that his Excellency might have proofs, sufficient to ruin these noblemen at the Court of London.

The Duke of Queensbury gave into the snare in the most unsuspecting manner. He granted upon the spot a passport to Lord Lovat, written and signed with his own hand, as Viceroy of Scotland, to enable him to proceed in safety from Edinburgh to London. Lord Lovat has still in his possession this document, sealed with the arms of the Duke of Queensberry, as well as the great offers that his Excellency made him in writing.

When the Duke had given him the passport, he mentioned that he should take post in two days for Court, adding that Lord Lovat had only to come *incognito* to his house in London, and that he would procure for him, from an English Secretary of State, a passport under borrowed names for his journey to Holland, that of the Duke not being sufficient for that purpose. Lord Lovat thanked his Excellency, promised to pay his duty to him at London with the earliest opportunity, and took leave, wishing him a good journey.

Next day Lord Drummond and Mr. Murray arrived at Edinburgh. Lord Lovat related to them *verbatim* all that passed between him and the Duke of Queensberry. They agreed in approving what he had done, and even applauded the dexterity with which he had delivered himself from an imminent and unforeseen danger by his romances of the Duke of Hamilton and Lord Athol, whom all the true friends of the King regarded as impostors, that, for their private interests, were desirous of playing off both parties, without having a sincere friendship for either.

Such were the very words of Lord Drummond and Mr. Murray, and such the first and sole guilt of Lord Lovat. Far from being a real crime, it ought to be regarded as a good and essential service to his King, and the sincere, political, and ingenious fruit of his zeal for his project and the interests of his sovereign.

With respect to his interviews with the Duke of Argyle and Lord Leven, to my knowledge he often took God to witness that he had endeavoured, as if his life had depended on it, to gain over these lords, his relations, and intimate friends, to the party of the King and the interests of France, representing to them that it was the only method they could take to save their families, France being at that time completely in a condition to restore King James in spite of his enemies.

The Duke of Argyle was much affected by what he said respecting the power of France, and her firm resolution to restore King James, as well as of the dispositions of a strong party in Scotland and in England to receive him.

His Grace, however, replied: 'My dear friend, though I perish in the party of the revolution, I will never desert it. I cannot trust the pretended son of a king who cut off the head of my father in so unjust and cruel a manner after the services he had rendered to that very king, and his brother, Charles the Second. In the meantime, my dear Lovat, if by the fortune of war the party for which you have declared yourself prevail, do what you can for me and my family; and I promise on my part, if our government continue, as I hope it will, effectually and at all times to protect you and your house in spite of all your enemies.'

After mutual protestations of friendship, the Duke of Argyle, without asking a single question concerning an individual in the royal party, bid adieu to Lord Lovat, embracing him tenderly, while, on his part, he was so much affected that he could not speak. This 1703 was a kind of presage of the melancholy news Lord Lovat received a short time after of the death of the Duke of Argyle. He was touched to the bottom of his soul with this intelligence. The Duke had always loved him as a father, and respected him as his faithful defender against the powerful and arbitrary houses of Hamilton and Athol. He was, however, well pleased with the unbounded expectations that the whole kingdom entertained from the valour and genius of the young Duke of Argyle, who has since surpassed the most sanguine ideas that his early youth inspired, and is acknowledged throughout all Europe, as well as in these three kingdoms, as the greatest hero and ornament of the Scottish nation.

With regard to the commerce of Lord Lovat with the Earl of Leven, who is still living, the Earl will not pretend to deny that Lord Lovat, from a leader in the revolution interest, made him a compleat convert to the royal party, and that he gave him an ample commission to make his peace with the Court of St. Germains, promising, if the King would grant him the same appointments he possessed under Queen Anne, to declare for the royal party, and constantly adhere to it.

It is certain, indeed, that, if the insurrection in Scotland had been executed, and Lord Leven had been assured of the terms he had demanded of the

Court of St. Germains, he would infallibly have delivered up to the royal party the Castle of Edinburgh, of which he was then governor. His commerce with the Court of St. Germains for several years past is sufficiently notorious, and abundantly proves the disposition which Lord Lovat had created, and left him in for the interests of that Court.

It proves, however, at the same time, this Earl of Leven to be the most ungrateful and unnatural of mankind, the greatest liar and impostor on the face of the earth, when, knowing the disgrace into which Lord Lovat had fallen at the Court of St. Germains, and that he could not better make his court to the Queen and her ministers than by blackening the reputation of his kinsman, he sent thither pretended letters, in which he was represented as betraying to him from time to time all the measures of that Court.

The reader has here before him all the high treasons and criminal and perfidious informations so loudly expatiated on and painted in such lively colours by Lord Middleton of which Lord Lovat was guilty in this expedition. In the meantime Lord Drummond and Mr. John Murray regarded these very transactions as the best services he could have rendered his King in discovering a method of saving Mr. Murray and himself without the smallest prejudice to the interests of his party, and at the same time of shaking the fidelity, and almost persuading the enemies of the King to desert their party. God knows what reward these services have procured him!

But if Lord Lovat had indeed been such a character as Lord Middleton represented him, he needed only to have accepted the offers of the Duke of Queensberry. In that case, without having been guilty of treason to his party, he would have been put into complete possession of his province and estates. And, if he had wished to incur the treachery and villainy which his enemies had falsely imputed to him, had he not the heads of all the King's friends in his pocket, and were not the documents in his possession sufficient to have brought to the scaffold every loyal nobleman in the kingdom? But God gave him religion and honour and courage enough rather to have suffered himself to have been torn in pieces by four horses than ever to have betrayed or taken away the life of the poorest lacquey or artisan whom he knew to be faithful to that prince for whom he so generously sacrificed his dearest and most unquestionable interests.

The Duke of Queensberry meanwhile set out for London, and Lord Lovat, not chusing to take any step but in concert with Lord Drummond and Mr. John Murray, envoy for the King of France, consulted them respecting the method of his return. They both intreated him for his greater safety to proceed to London and accept the passport the Commissioner had offered. Lord Lovat consented; and, having nobody at London

1708 in whom he could confide, he begged Lord Drummond and Mr. Murray to address him to some faithful subject, who might be his counsel and the witness of his actions, in order to his exculpation in case any unforeseen accident should abridge him of his liberty or ruin his project.

Mr. John Murray addressed him to his nephew, Mr. William Keith, the son of Sir William Keith, as a proper person to assist and attend him during his residence in the metropolis. He was a gentleman full of honour and good sense, a zealous partisan of the King, and for that reason the declared enemy of the Duke of Queensberry. Mr. Murray, who was brother to Lady Keith, his mother, wrote to Mr. Keith to render every service to Lord Lovat, to communicate to him without reserve whatever he knew respecting the King's affairs, and, if it were necessary, to expose his life to insure him a safe passage out of England.

Lord Lovat set out for London with this recommendation, and he took with him Mr. Campbel, the son of the Laird of Glendaruel, of the family of Breadalbane, his cousin german, and half brother to Sir John Maclean. Mr. Campbel appeared extremely zealous for the royal cause, and was the person that conducted Lord Lovat to the house of Lord Breadalbane. This nobleman was the soundest head, as well as the most loyal subject in the kingdom. He had more experience than all the Scottish noblemen of the royal party, and more courage, though upwards of sixty years of age, to 1703 expose himself, sword in hand, at the head of his vassals, for the service of his King, than any young fellow in Scotland. Add to this that his power was very extensive in the mountains of Perthshire.

Campbel of Glendaruel being of this family, and at the same time cousin german to Lord Lovat on the mother's side, had been the confident between these two noblemen in the business that had brought the latter into Scotland. For these reasons Lord Lovat trusted him as his own brother. And neither he nor Mr. Keith, who received Lord Lovat with open arms and in the most affectionate manner, quitted him day or night during the short period he continued in London.

Mr. Keith approved extremely of what Lord Lovat had done to amuse the Duke of Queensberry, and the trick he had played the Duke of Hamilton and Lord Athol. 'Though,' said he, observing upon this point, 'I am in appearance the friend of the Duke of Hamilton and Lord Athol, there is not in reality a person in the kingdom that hates them more than I do. In the first place nobody is better acquainted with the absurd and ambitious views of the Duke of Hamilton upon the crown. And for Lord Athol, all the friends of the King know but too well that he only appears of our party from an avaricious and immeasurable thirst of the places and pensions which he expects from the present government to induce him to betray, as he has repeatedly done, the interests of the King, and enable him to support his numerous and necessitous family, who have no other property than the empty title of my lord.'

Mr. Keith, in order the better to inform Lord Lovat of the situation of the King's affairs in England, introduced him to old Ferguson, so well known for the author or accomplice of so many conspiracies, plots, and criminal intrigues. He had been in many plots against King Charles. He had conspired against the life of the late King James; but he afterwards became his zealous servant and public partisan. And as he had a very sharp and satirical pen, the royal party employed him in writing libels upon King William and invectives against his government and friends.

Mr. Ferguson received Lord Lovat with open arms, and, having been previously informed by Mr. Keith of the credit this nobleman possessed at the Courts of France and St. Germains, he made to him a magnificent detail of all he had done for the King, and how much he had advanced his interest in the English Parliament. Two days after he gave to Lord Lovat commissions on his own part, and on the part of several illustrious personages in the English Parliament, addressed to the Queen and Lord Middleton.

He also gave him a letter of recommendation to his brother, Major-General Ferguson, who had entered into

the service of King William, and at that time com- 1703
manded the Scottish regiment in garrison at Boisleduc,
intreating him to render the same services to Lord
Lovat as he would to himself in his situation. This
letter was the means of saving Lord Lovat's life about
a fortnight after. He now took leave of Mr. Ferguson
with mutual protestations of friendship and esteem, the
latter most humbly intreating him to represent to the
Court of St. Germains what he had done and what he
was resolved to do for her service.

Lord Lovat waited with impatience for the passport
which the Duke of Queensberry had promised him.
His friend, Mr. Keith, conjured him to press the Duke
to forward that business with all speed, since his life
would probably be the forfeit of his being taken into
custody. Mr. Keith even went with Lord Lovat to
the Duke of Queensberry's gate, and remained in the
carriage, not daring to be seen, while Lord Lovat and
his cousin were with the Duke. As soon as he had
obtained his passport, he thought of nothing but his
journey, and the faithful Keith did not leave him till he
saw him fall down the Thames.

This young gentleman remarked to Lord Lovat,
with tears in his eyes, at the moment of their separa-
tion, that it was necessary to employ a degree of policy
in the affairs of Scotland; that it would be a melancholy
consideration for the interests and the friends of the
King to see so noble a project miscarry; but that for his

1703 part, he was greatly apprehensive of the subtle and dangerous character of Lord Middleton; he was persuaded he would do his utmost to ruin a project which had the family of Perth, its relations and allies at its head. He added that Lord Lovat had need alike of discretion and perseverance to counterwork all that Lord Middleton might advance against the insurrection; and that if at any time the vivacity of his temper led him to embroil himself with the minister, he and his project must be ruined together. The event was literally as Mr. Keith had predicted.

As Lord Lovat was in continual apprehension of being taken in England and in Holland, he did not wish to carry about him the portrait of his sovereign, which his Majesty had recently bestowed upon with extraordinary marks of his bounty. He therefore caused a very neat box to be made, with an inscription, that it contained the portrait of his King, which his Majesty had given him in return for the services he had performed for his Majesty and for the King his father during his exile. He included in the same box the commission which his Majesty had bestowed upon him as colonel of a regiment of infantry. This box he placed as a sacred deposit in the hands of his cousin german Campbel of Glendaruel, conjuring him to carry it, together with its contents, as a thing dearer to him than his life, to his clan.

Lord Lovat had, by extreme good fortune, left in

Scotland, with one of the bravest gentlemen of his clan, the box in which he had adroitly concealed THE GRAND APPOINTMENT, OR UNLIMITED FULL POWERS, which the King had given him to represent his sacred person, and to renew in his name, in case the occasion should make it proper to take up arms, all the commissions which the late King James had granted in Scotland. This appointment, not less honourable than rare, is still faithfully preserved by the gentleman to whom it was originally confided.

During the whole time of Lord Lovat's residence in London he had lodged at the house of a very zealous partisan of King James the Third. He had not the smallest intercourse with any individual in England that was not noted for attachment to the royal cause except the single quarter of an hour that he spent at the Duke of Queensberry's by the advice of his most respectable friends in order to obtain his passport.

In his passage to Holland he was in much danger of his life, there being on board the Dutch vessel in which he was embarked two creatures of his enemies, Major Duncan Mackenzie and Scatual Mackenzie, his eldest son. Lord Lovat had no other means of safety in this situation till they got out to sea but that of concealing himself in the hammoc of a common sailor.

A few days after his arrival in Holland, he received a letter from Campbel of Glendaruel informing him that Sir John Maclean, half brother to Glendaruel and cousin german to Lord Lovat, was arrived in England with his lady, and had surrendered himself prisoner; that Lord Lovat had not left London six hours before a posse of constables came to apprehend him; that they had treated his landlord very roughly, and thrown him into a dungeon in Newgate; and that, if he had stayed a day longer in England, his destruction would have been infallible.

Upon the receipt of this letter Lord Lovat wrote to Glendaruel, to Mr. William Keith, and to Mr. Ferguson, the famous partisan of King James, and enemy to the Duke of Queensberry. He felicitated himself upon having escaped from the hands of the English Government, and so ingeniously amused the Duke of Queensberry. At the same time he observed, how much he was afflicted at the adversity to which his landlord was exposed for his fidelity to his King and to himself.

He inclosed a letter to his brother, Sir John Maclean, in which Lord Lovat exhorted him, in the name of God, to suffer death itself, rather than to act hostile to the interests of his sovereign. He observed that a single false step in his situation would destroy the merit of all he had hitherto done, and obliterate the service of ancestors, the most celebrated for their loyalty; adding, that he had rather hear that he was torn to pieces by horses, than that he had bartered away his loyalty and his honour. Lord Lovat wrote in this urgent manner

to Sir John Maclean, because he feared that Lady
Maclean, his wife, who was a woman of much policy
and finesse, might prevail upon him to make shipwreck
of his honour for the sake of his estate. At the same
time he expressed his sentiments of this lady in a very
open manner to Glendaruel, her brother-in-law.

What Lord Lovat predicted respecting her and her
husband, happened in a very short time. Sir John
Maclean, to his shame and eternal confusion, as the
most contemptible of cowards, after a few days' imprisonment, and having first conditioned for a pension
from Queen Anne, made an ample discovery of everything he knew respecting his cousin Lord Lovat, the
Scottish insurrection, and all the projects of the Court
of St. Germains. He was accordingly, as all the world
knows, immediately set at liberty and pensioned, and
has ever since been universally regarded as the most
worthless of the human race.

Lord Lovat's dispatches from Holland were either
intercepted or treacherously delivered into the hands of
the government, and printed by the express order of
the English Parliament. They ought alone to convince
the whole world of his zeal, his faithful and unalterable
attachment to the interests of his King, and those of
France, from which the former were inseparable. It
was not however till after Lord Lovat's arrival in
France, that he knew himself to have been betrayed
by his cousin german, Campbel of Glendaruel. This

unnatural monster, this perfidious traitor, this execrable villain conceived and carried into action the barbarous design, in spite of their relationship and intimate friendship, in spite of the unbounded confidence Lord Lovat had placed in him, of accomplishing the entire ruin of that nobleman in the Courts both of England and France.

The infamous idea of Glendaruel found harbour in his avaricious soul, first, in order that he might turn to his own use eight fine horses that Lord Lovat had left in his care, together with four military trunks filled with various articles of dress, gold and silver plate, and with a variety of jewels, to the value of 800*l.*, which this villain took possession of upon his return to London.

The other part of the monster's idea was as black as the former. Glendaruel was lieutenant of the company of volunteers of Mr. Campbel of Finac, his relation and a gentleman who had shown himself his sincere friend.

It may be proper in this place to mention, that Mr. Campbel of Finac is one of the most gallant and worthy men in Scotland. His integrity and honour are known and revered by all his acquaintance. His courage, intrepidity and military skill, were greatly conspicuous in the affair of Darien, where with an handful of brave Scots he beat an army of Spaniards, disarmed with his own hand the enemy's general, and brought away his sabre, as a token of his victory, upon his return into Scotland. His victory, however, was rendered useless, by the combination of the English with their inveterate enemies for the ruin of the Scottish colony established at Darien.

Mr. Campbel of Finac was upon bad terms with Lord Athol. I have already had occasion to relate, that, upon some despotic proceedings of Lord Athol, while Earl of Tullibardin, this gentleman sent his lordship a challenge. Lord Athol however saw no merit in exposing his life against a valour so well known as that of Finac. He therefore shamefully declined the invitation, and was forced with infamy to ask pardon and forgiveness of his antagonist, who threatened to bestow upon him the appropriated reward of cowards and poltroons, by publicly caning him at the high cross of Edinburgh, where this affair made a great deal of noise.

I quit this hero in order to return to the treacherous Glendaruel. The villain was sufficiently informed, that Lord Athol and Lord Viscount Tarbat were the intimate friends and favourites of Queen Anne, and for their private interests the declared enemies of Lord Lovat. He did not doubt, that, in betraying and delivering into their hands this nobleman, his cousin german, he should obtain for the price of his villainy the company of volunteers of the brave Campbel of Finac, who was also his cousin and his captain, which was worth at least 170*l.* a year. He was satisfied, that

1703 Lord Athol would be charmed to meet with a decent opportunity of disgracing Finac, who had affronted him in so public and unqualified a manner.

Thus was Glendaruel blinded by an infamous spirit of avarice and ambition. He forgot, that a few weeks before, he had been the zealous partisan of King James, had conducted Lord Lovat to the houses of Lord Breadalbane and many other loyal chiefs, and that his discovery would put their lives in imminent danger, as well as subject his own to the mercy of the English government. He forgot everything that ought to be dear to a man of reason, honour and probity, and rushed headlong into the presence of Lords Athol and Tarbat, the very day that he took leave of Lord Lovat upon the departure of that nobleman for Holland.

He discovered to these noblemen everything that he knew respecting the affairs of the King, and of his cousin Lord Lovat, who at that time conducted them. He delivered up to them the box that Lord Lovat had confided to him, containing the portrait of the King, and his commission of colonel of infantry. Finally, he disclosed to them the commerce which Lord Lovat had carried on with the Duke of Queensberry, and the passport that his Excellency had procured him for his journey to Holland.

Lord Athol and Lord Tarbat were particularly gratified with the last part of his discovery, by means of which they hoped immediately to accomplish the ruin of the Duke of Queensberry. They went without a moment's pause to Queen Anne, and accused the Duke to her Majesty, as guilty of high treason, having maintained a commerce with the most dangerous emissary that had ever been employed by the Courts of France and St. Germains. To substantiate their accusations they produced the villain Glendaruel, who declared, that he had himself been witness to a conference of Lord Lovat with the Duke of Queensberry, once at Edinburgh, and once in London, and that he was ready to make oath, that the Duke had given him a passport for his journey into Holland. At the same time, by concert with these noblemen, he delivered to Queen Anne with his own hand the portrait of the King, and the commission of Lord Lovat, which had been confided to him as the most sacred deposit: a circumstance, which ought to render the name of this modern Judas odious to the latest posterity.

Lords Athol and Tarbat warmly pressed the Queen, to permit the Duke of Queensberry to be tried for his life upon these accusations. And indeed he must probably have lost his head in the affair, if he had not previously advertised the Queen, that the slight intercourse between him and Lord Lovat, had been solely intended to discover and establish the intrigues of the Duke of Hamilton and Lord Athol at the Court of St. Germains. And in this he averred the precise and literal truth.

But the Duke of Queensberry had nothing to support his assertion but the presumptions with which Lord Lovat had furnished him against the Duke of Hamilton and Lord Athol; while, on the other hand, Lords Athol and Tarbat had legal evidence of the commerce of the Duke of Queensberry with Lord Lovat, the emissary of the Courts of France and St. Germains. The Duke was therefore obliged to defend himself against this accusation by suing for a pardon from the Queen. And he was so much irritated against Lord Lovat, whom he conceived to have duped and betrayed him to Messieurs Keith and Ferguson, his declared enemies, that he became from that moment his inveterate foe. At the same time he treated in an inhuman manner Mr. William Keith, because he was informed that he had been every day with that nobleman during his residence in London.

The Duke however was extremely in the wrong with respect to Lord Lovat. Lord Lovat had discovered nothing to him of the affairs of the King and of France, nor did his Grace ask him a single question but in relation to the Duke of Hamilton and Lord Athol, whom his informant and all the King's true friends hated as much as he did. Far at the same time from wishing to betray the Duke of Queensberry, and to repay with ingratitude the good offices he had received from him, he was constantly ready to do his Excellency every service which consisted with his honour, his loyalty, and his conscience. Willingly would he have furnished the Duke, had it been in his power, with the means of ruining the Duke of Hamilton and Lord Athol at the Court of Queen Anne, persuaded that he could not render a more essential service to his King than by destroying the credit and influence of these noblemen, who equally betrayed both parties, and were the objects of public detestation to the zealous partisans of either.

Such is the simple and sincere detail, exclusive of the secrets of the King and of France, which it would at all times be improper to publish; such, I say, is the exact detail of all Lord Lovat's transactions in Scotland. And this ought for ever to confound the author of a book, entitled, *Memoirs Concerning the Affairs of Scotland from Queen Anne's Accession to the Throne to the Commencement of the Union,*[*] printed at London in the year 1714.

I know not what epithet to bestow upon this miserable author, who is so full of contradictions, even in the characters he draws with so much bitterness and impudence of the most able and illustrious gentlemen and the first nobility of Scotland. The mildest censure that can be passed upon him is that he has been insolent, ignorant and witless.

Indeed, he confesses as much himself; he asked pardon beforehand. It were therefore pity to treat his

---
[*] By George Lockhart of Carnwath,

book with too much severity, since he has suppressed his name for fear of being cudgelled to death by the footmen of the many noblemen he has maltreated, and who are unwilling themselves to soil their hands with shooting him through the head, as a gentleman did the father of this author, if he be the person whom all the world believes him to be. Indeed, the father was worth a million of such sons as this, who have the folly to set up for an author before they have acquired the means of subsistence, and without possessing the smallest particle of knowledge respecting either the transactions of the world in general or their own country in particular.

But it is not my business to refute his whole book. Abler men than I are equally involved in his calumnies. Since, too, the author appears to be animated with an inextinguishable zeal for the honour and prosperity of Scotland, his country and mine, he would have deserved some indulgence if his blind spirit of party had not led him to the dissemination of so many absurdities and falshoods respecting persons of the highest quality, and to the groundless flattery and preposterous applause of those, whom he imagined to be of his own opinion. My only design is to establish the honour and integrity of Lord Lovat, whom this writer has the insolence to attack. I will therefore confine myself to the clear and unanswerable refutation of those articles of his book which in so pitiless a manner tear to pieces the character of this nobleman, under the name of Simon Fraser of Beaufort. The following is the passage to which I allude.

'About this time a flying report was spread about, as if a plot had been discovered, wherein a certain number of the chiefs and heads of the Cavaliers had engaged to rise in arms against Queen Anne in favour of the pretended Prince of Wales, (as they termed the King) and this story was propagated to blacken those people's endeavours to liberate their country from the slavery and dominion which England usurped over it.

'But because this sham plot was the foundation of a mighty superstructure, made a great noise, and was the handle the courtiers laid hold on to ruin the Cavalier and country parties, I must go back a little, and trace it from its original, that the design and conclusion of it may be the better understood, and the whole looked upon with that detestation and horror by future ages which all good men had of it at the time.

'You must know then, that after the Duke of Queensberry had broken his vows to the Cavaliers, and seen them, when joined to the country, so strong and zealous a party, there was no hopes of being able to stand it out against so violent and united a torrent; he bethought himself to undermine their reputations, and so diminish their interest with the Court, and find a pretence to vent his wrath and execute his malice against those that thwarted his arbitrary designs. And knowing, to his certain experience, that the poet was very much in the right when he asserted that

> "Plots, true or false, are necessary things
> To set up commonwealths, and ruin kings,"

he, with the special advice and consent of his dear friends, the Duke of Argyle, the Earls of Stair and Leven, and Mr. Carstares (a rebellious Presbyterian preacher, and one of her Majesty's chaplains), resolved, one way or other, to frame such a plot, as, when lodged upon those they designed it against, should, in all human probability, be their utter ruin and destruction.

'They pitched upon one Simon Fraser, of Beaufort, as the tool to carry on this wicked design, and be an evidence to charge such persons as they directed. This gentleman, some three or four years before, had been guilty of a most scandalous rape upon the person of the Lady Dowager Lovat, sister to the Duke of Athol, for which crime the lords of justiciary condemned him to die; and letters of fire and sword were raised, and a detachment of King William's troops sent against him and his adherents, who were pretty numerous, betwixt whom several skirmishes happened. But finding the Duke of Argyle, who was his great patron, (for no other reason that I know of but because he had been guilty of a vile, lewd, and detestable crime, and likewise upon the person of one of the family of Athol, which two houses bore each other a constant grudge:) I say, Fraser,

LIFE OF LORD LOVAT.

finding Argyle was no longer able to protect him against the force of law and justice, quitted the kingdom, and retired into France. But King James having got an account of the crimes he was found guilty of, for which he had left his native country, would not during his life allow him to come to the Court of St. Germains.

'This person being made choice of, as well qualified for such a design, was sent for from France to England, and afterwards brought from thence to Scotland. But before he left France, by the advice of his friends at home, he turned Papist, and, finding a way to be introduced to the French King by the Pope's Nuncio, he represented himself as a person of great interest in Scotland, and oppressed for his zeal to the royal family, and that, with encouragement and a small assistance, he could contribute to make a great diversion to the English arms, and much promote the royal interest, and for that end proposed that his Most Christian Majesty should furnish him with two or three hundred men and a good sum of money to take along with him to Scotland, where he would perform wonders. But the French King, unwilling to hazard his men and money without a farther security and more probability than his assertions, gave him a fair answer, desiring him to go first to Scotland, and bring him some credentials from those persons over whom he pretended so much power, which he agreed to, and got for that purpose a little money, and, by the French interest, such credit at St. Germains as to obtain a commission from King James to be a Major-General, with a power to raise and command forces in his behalf, which was the main thing he aimed at. But at the same time, Captain John Murray, brother to Mr. Murray of Abercairny, and Captain James Murray, brother to Sir David Murray of Stanhope, were likewise, under the protection of Queen Anne's act of indemnity, sent over to Scotland to be a check upon him, and bring intelligence how they found the tempers of the people and their inclination towards King James.

'Thus provided, Fraser arrived in England; and on the borders of Scotland was met by the Duke of Argyle, and by him conducted to Edinburgh, where he was kept private; and being fully instructed what he was to do, the Duke of Queensberry gave him a pass to secure him from being apprehended, in obedience to the letters of fire and sword emitted against him. And now he goes to the Highlands, introduces himself into the company of all that he knew were well affected to King James and his interest, there produces his major-general's commission, as a testificate of the trust reposed in him, and proposing their rising in arms, and signifying the same under their hands, *That the King might know assuredly, who they were, and what numbers he had to trust to, and regulate his affairs accordingly;* some were so far seduced, as to assure him, they were ready to serve the King (though I believe there was none that did it in the terms he demanded;) but generally there were few, that did not regret the King's reposing any trust in a person of so bad a character, and, fearing he would betray them, refused to treat or come to particulars with him.

'After he had trafficked here and there through the Highlands with small success, when the Parliament was adjourned, he went to London, to consider of what further use he might be to his constituents, resolving (though the *primum mobile*, and his patron, the Duke of Argyle, was now dead) to continue in their service. And they, finding he had made but a small progress, and could not as yet fix anything at the doors of those persons against whom they levelled, resolved to send him again to France, to demand letters, and further encouragement, to the Dukes of Hamilton and Athol, the Earls of Seafield and Cromarty, and the Cavaliers: and for that end, the Duke of Queensberry procured him, and two others with him, a pass from the Earl of Nottingham, Secretary of England, under borrowed names. If he went upon a good design, as the Duke of Queensberry afterwards alledged, why needed he have made their persons and business such a secret to the Queen's Secretary, as that he must know neither?

'But before Fraser reached Paris, and had executed his black design, it came to light in great measure, for the famous Mr. Ferguson soon discovered, and consequently defeated the project, when it was as yet but in embrio; for Fraser, whilst he was in London, having addressed himself to him, and one Mr. William Keith, (a great depender on the Duke of Athol) he acquainted them with his pretended design and project for King James, and mightily pressed Keith, that he would use his endeavours to persuade the Duke of Athol to forgive him, and allow him access to his Grace, since he was heartily sorry for the crime he had committed, and was promoting so good a design; but Keith (though he played the fool, and dipt deep enough with him in all other points) told him, that was what he could not presume to propose, and what he knew the Duke of Athol would never grant.

'But Ferguson, an old experienced plotter, understanding his character, suspected his integrity; and, it coming to his knowledge, that he was often privately with the Scottish courtiers, was by them supported, and had obtained a pass, as above related, he soon concluded, that there was some base design in hand, and thereupon gave the Duke of Athol notice of it; and he again, having enquired at the Earl of Nottingham's, and finding Ferguson's information to hold good, and his suspicions to be well grounded, acquaints Queen Anne of the whole procedure, accusing the Duke of Queensberry in particular, and his other friends and partisans, of corresponding with, and protecting a person, outlawed in the kingdom of Scotland, guilty of the most horrid crime, and a trafficker with France.

'Whereupon the Duke of Queensberry, to vindicate himself, declared, that Fraser, when he came to Scotland, wrote to him that he could make great discoveries for the Queen's service; and that upon that account he had sent for him, given him a protection in Scotland, and again procured him a pass in England, with a design he should go to France, and make a clearer discovery, which he did not doubt he would have performed, had not the matter come too soon to light; and, as a convincing proof thereof, he produces a letter from the Queen-mother, directed to L. M. which he interpreted, the Lord Murray (formerly the title of the Duke of Athol, before his father died). But his Grace made use of such solid arguments, and convincing proofs to show the fallacy of that letter [that is, that L. M. might as well stand for fifty other noblemen as himself], that Queen Anne herself could not deny, but that she thought it not genuine.

'Now let any impartial judge consider, if it is probable that Fraser, with whom no honest man in Scotland would converse, who was under sentence of death, and not such a tool as to imagine, that he had an interest to do anything of moment for King James's service, could have had the impudence to address the French King in such terms as he did, and come over to Scotland, unless he had been put upon it, and protected by such as could support him at home? If he proposed to cheat the French King of a little money, why came he to Scotland with it; since he knew he could not fail, in time, to be discovered, and then could neither hope to be protected there, or to dare to return to France? These, I say, and many other such shrewd presumptions, make it clear, what was the design of this pretended plot, and, if successful, how dismal the consequences of it would have proved (*viz.* the destruction of those who opposed the designs of the Scottish courtiers and English ministry against Scotland); how happy it was in being rendered abortive, before the designed conception had come to full maturity, and how odious the thoughts of such a hellish conspiracy, and the abettors thereof, ought to be in the eyes of all good men!'*

It is somewhat extraordinary, that, contrary to all honour, justice and common sense, this author has had the impudence to let loose his spleen upon Lord Lovat, whom he did not know, and who is by his birth so extremely his superior, being the twenty-second Lord Lovat from father to son, allied to the royal family and to the first houses in Scotland; not to mention his personal merit, which had shone forth in France, as well as at home, in spite of the malice of his enemies. It is still more extraordinary, that this author, who

---

* *Memoirs of Scotland*, p. 74-84.

pretends to advance nothing but unquestionable facts, and to write entirely from his own knowledge, should invent and give to the world such a farrago respecting Lord Lovat, composed entirely of incredible lies and palpable contradictions, without the shadow of probability, reality or common sense.

The design of the author is sufficiently evident. His book is entirely calculated to undermine the reputation, the interest, and the lives of the Dukes of Queensberry and Argyle, and the Earl of Leven, the most formidable enemies of his party, and to give to the world as undoubted realities, the dark inventions of the Duke of Hamilton and the Lords Athol and Tarbat, produced by the fear of punishment for their correspondence with the Court of St. Germains, at the same time that they pretended to be the zealous partisans of the Court of London.

In prosecuting this design he endeavours to throw upon the shoulders of the first mentioned noblemen the contrivance of a project, of which they knew as much as the Khan of Crim Tartary. He represents them as sending for Lord Lovat, their intimate friend, whom (probably by a miracle) this visionary writer represents as acquainted with the nature and particulars of their plot, at the distance of two hundred leagues, and at a time, when the commerce of letters was totally rendered impracticable by the war. In the next place, by a miracle not less wonderful, he converts Lord Lovat to the Popish religion, by the advice and command of his patrons, Queensberry, Argyle, Leven and Carstares, the pillars of the Presbyterian religion in Scotland: a most admirable means which this author has discovered, for advancing the interests of the Protestant succession!

And upon this foundation, equally chimerical, false, scandalous and diabolical, the author commences his narrative with calumniating Lord Lovat. He makes him, in the first place, guilty of a rape; a crime of which he was as innocent as the child unborn, and which the whole north of Scotland, where Lord Lovat has always been, and is at this day much loved and respected, knows to have had no foundation, but in the malicious invention of Lord Athol; in order to accumulate the crime of high treason against King William, with which he charged him, and to make himself master of his estate; for which tyranny the name of Athol is regarded with odium and horror through the whole north of Scotland.

The author proceeds with his ridiculous suppositions, and sends Lord Lovat into France three years before he quitted his own country; not knowing probably, that Lord Lovat obtained a pardon from King William; and that, at the time of that prince's death, he was in quiet possession of his estates, and about to commence a prosecution against Lord Athol, which would have reduced him to the same beggary, as the young Lord Murrays his brothers; not knowing, that it was at the accession of Queen Anne, and her declared favouritism to Lord Athol and his other enemies, that Lord Lovat proclaimed his sovereign in his own province, and afterwards entered into an engagement with the most considerable of the loyal nobility and heads of clans, previous to his passing into France.

The author of the memoirs represents Lord Lovat as obtaining a commission of major-general from King James, and a power to raise and command forces in his behalf, which, telling the truth for once in his life, he adds, was 'the main thing Lord Lovat aimed at.' But, as impostors are generally deficient in memory, the author forgets that he had, in the preceding page, represented Lord Lovat as repulsed in the most disgraceful manner by the late King.*

But I know not whether I ought to have paid any attention to the calumnies of this insolent writer, or to have given myself the trouble to refute an idiot, who contradicts himself in every page respecting this chimerical plot. It is evident, that he is not only ignorant of the whole north of Scotland, but that he knows neither the character nor history of Lord Lovat, except from the misrepresentations of Lord Athol and

---

* Mr. Lockhart is not perhaps in this instance guilty of the contradiction imputed to him. In the passage last alluded to, he speaks of King James the Second; and in the former he probably alludes to the prince, whom he styles King James the Third.

his creatures. It is not less evident, that he is equally ignorant of the politics of France and St. Germains, except from the confused and nonsensical ideas, that he has imbibed from the drunken Jacobites who frequented Peter Steele's tavern at Edinburgh.

He ought not surely upon the report of people of that class to have calumniated Lord Lovat, who was from his earliest infancy engaged in military and political affairs, in which assuredly the genius and courage of this author would have been not unfrequently embarrassed. This will be sufficiently evident from a few instances, which I think it necessary to cite, and in which I shall be obliged to repeat certain particulars which have already been related.

The author of these memoirs was probably ignorant, that Lord Lovat was imprisoned for his exertions in the royal cause at the age of thirteen years, and at the very time that his elder brother was the first to join in the expedition of Lord Viscount Dundee.*

*1689

He was ignorant, that at the age of sixteen years,† and after the death of his elder brother and of Lord Dundee, Lord Lovat joined the insurrection in favour of King James of General Thomas Buchan. ‡

†1692

The author was ignorant, that at the age of twenty years ‖ Lord Lovat exposed his life with Lord Marishal, Lord Drummond, Lord Kilseith, and other noble

‖1696

---

‡ There in some mistake is this place. General Buchan's insurrection belongs to the year 1690.

prisoners, by concerning in a design to surprise the castle of Edinburgh in favour of King James, who was then expected in Scotland.

The author was ignorant, that at the age of twenty-three years,* being persecuted by the present Lord Athol, and knowing that it had been menaced by the old Marquis of Athol, that, in case King James should be restored, he would trample upon Lord Lovat and his clan, as completely as his son did by the authority of King William, this nobleman went into France in order to expostulate with the late King James, who received him, in the presence of the Queen, the young Prince, Lord Perth, and Sir John Maclean, all four still living, with as much friendship and condescension as he ever extended to a subject; at the same time giving Lord Lovat under his hand the most honourable testimony, and the most magnificent promises, which are still in the possession of a man of rank, and Lord Lovat's intimate friend. *1699

Such was the dishonourable manner in which King James drove Lord Lovat from the Court of St. Germains; and such the only voyage that Lord Lovat made into France during the life of King William, and which lasted only for fifteen days: circumstances, which ought to confound the author of these memoirs, when he sees the whole fabric of his plot overturned by so simple a tale.

That author ought to be extremely confounded,

when he knows, that, after the death of King William, not only the loyal Highland lairds, but also the Earl of Errol, the Earl Marishal, Lord Drummond, and all the other noblemen of the low country sincerely attached to their sovereign, entered into an engagement with Lord Lovat, to risk their lives and fortunes for the restoration of their exiled prince; and that, upon his arrival at the Courts of St. Germains and France, he was received with more distinction than any Scotsman had hitherto been.

Add to this, that, even after the discovery of his project both in Scotland and England, Lord Lovat, upon his return into France with new assurances from the King's faithful subjects, was equally well received as at first; that he negociated for six months with the ministers of state and the marshals of France for the completion of the expedition; and that the naval and land armaments were ready, when the Queen, governed by Lord Middleton, with an unexampled weakness refused to issue commissions to her subjects to join the troops of France: a conduct, which was the visible cause of preventing the restoration of her son, and of infinite mischief to the affairs of France.

And what ought for ever to confound the author of the Scottish memoirs, is, that, after the insurrection had thus completely failed, and Lord Lovat for the loudness of his resentment was persecuted with great rancour by the Queen and Lord Middleton, the Court of France, so celebrated for its wisdom and sagacity, knowing the advantageous commission this nobleman had brought into France, and the strength of the party in Scotland with which he was engaged, and convinced of his zeal and fidelity, far from uniting with the Court of St. Germains in his persecution, protected him against all their machinations and malice. The King of France had the goodness to bestow upon him various gratifications, beside a pension of four thousand francs,* which is the ordinary half-pay of a major-general. His Majesty had the kindness, in spite of the reiterated and incessant calumnies of the Court of St. Germains, to continue this pension to Lord Lovat, for more than ten years, till his departure into England: and in the course of the last war, when France was obliged to pay all the world in paper, Lord Lovat may say, that he was perhaps the only man in the kingdom, who received his pension in money. Indeed he was protected to the last by the Marquis de Torcy and other French noblemen, his friends, against all the fury of his enemies in Scotland and at St. Germains.

From what has been advanced, it is as clear as the day, that the project of Lord Lovat was real, solid, well founded, and well conducted, and the most promising that ever was formed for the restoration of King James; and that the 'sham plot' of the author of the memoirs had no foundation but in the malicious invention of

---

166*l*. 13*s*. 4*d*.

Lord Athol and Lord Tarbat, in order to ruin the Dukes of Queensberry and Argyle in England and Lord Lovat in France; a circumstance, that ought to render their memory odious to the latest posterity.

In supporting the impeached honour of Lord Lovat, I have found myself obliged to do justice to the Dukes of Queensberry and Argyle, who were noblemen incapable of the baseness imputed to them by the author of the memoirs, and who knew no more of the project than the Great Mogul till it was betrayed by Mr. James Murray and Sir John Maclean. After this treachery, which was yet incapable of ruining the scheme, the Dukes of Argyle and Queensberry never desired Lord Lovat to disclose to them the smallest circumstance respecting it if we except the question of the Duke of Queensberry in regard to the Duke of Hamilton and Lord Athol. I leave, therefore, this miserable author to the pungency of his remorse, for having invented a plot not less malicious than chimerical, and which he has not been able to patch together without the most palpable contradictions. I return to Lord Lovat's journey, and the narrative of his real project for the restoration of his King, the relation of which, in all its parts, is calculated to overturn the absurd and imaginary plot of the author of the Memoirs of Scotland.

SECTION II.

LORD LOVAT, arrived at Rotterdam, was extremely embarrassed concerning the manner in which he should pass, from the frontiers of Holland to the French army in Flanders. The Dutch had strictly prohibited to all their subjects, either to go into Flanders, or to let out horses or equipages to hire for that purpose, without their orders, under pain of death. Every person was searched and strictly examined as he entered or went out of the frontier towns of the United Provinces.

Unable otherwise to extricate himself from this dilemma, Lord Lovat repaired to the Hague, and applied to an Irish Roman Catholic merchant, to whom he had recommendations, to procure him a passport at a stipulated price. This merchant introduced Lord Lovat to the secretary, by whose means he was accustomed to obtain passports, but he found it impossible to succeed in the present conjuncture. He observed however to this nobleman, that it was necessary for him to quit the Hague immediately, since he would infallibly be a dead man if he were known.

Lord Lovat accordingly took his passage that very hour in the trechschuyt of Delft, having remained at the

1703 Hague only seven or eight hours. He left behind him his brother and Major Fraser, who had accompanied him from Scotland, and who staid that night at the Hague in order to see the Archduke, then upon his passage from Spain, having assumed the title of Charles the Third, King of Spain and the Indies.

It may be observed by the way, that Major George Fraser had actual rank in France, where he had served fourteen years, and that Lord Lovat had obtained of the Marquis de Torcy, as an extraordinary favour, to have his company to Scotland on account of his high and deserved reputation as a very brave man and an excellent officer. The brother of Lord Lovat had been almost compelled by that nobleman, he having obtained for him a provisional pension of ten thousand livres* from the Courts of France and St. Germains, to quit Scotland in order to be educated with his young sovereign at Paris. And a circumstance, which further overthrows the ideas of the author of the Memoirs of Scotland is that the brother of Lord Lovat, during the term of his residence upon the Continent, constantly received a pension from the King of France, under the name of the Chevalier Fraser, distinct from that which was bestowed upon Lord Lovat.

Lord Lovat had left the Hague scarcely two hours, when the officers of justice searched all the taverns and coffee-houses in the town for him, at the same time

---

* 400*l.*

describing his person: whether it were, that he was
betrayed by the Irish merchant, or was known by any
Scotsman residing at that place. He received intelligence of the danger he had escaped from Major Fraser
and his brother; and, apprehensive that it was not yet
over, he resolved to set out without delay for the
frontiers.

In this situation he recollected the letter he had
received from old Mr. Ferguson at London to Major-
General Ferguson, his brother, who commanded the
troops at Boisleduc. With this recommendation he
determined to set out for the fortress; himself, his
brother, and Major Fraser having disguised themselves
in the uniform of Dutch officers.

Upon their arrival Lord Lovat was immediately
known by an officer of General Murray's regiment
who was upon guard at the gates, and by two soldiers
of the Fraser clan. These last informed a great number
of Frasers who were in the Scottish regiments that
garrisoned that place. They accordingly flocked to the
tavern where Lord Lovat had taken up his quarters,
and with a thoughtless and unreflecting zeal threw
themselves at his feet, saying, that having now the
happiness to meet with their chief, they would never
more lose sight of him, but would follow him wherever
he went, into France, or to the end of the world. Lord
Lovat, perceiving the imminent danger in which these
poor fellows had involved him, commanded them, each

man to return to his station, and not to visit him again till night, adding, that his life would be the forfeit of their disobedience.

In the evening he waited upon General Ferguson, who, having read his brother's letter, intreating him to communicate to Lord Lovat every thing that he knew respecting the interests of the King, and to bestow upon him all the attentions in his power, desired that nobleman to sup with him alone, observing that he could inform him of several things of the last importance to the two courts. When Lord Lovat waited upon him in pursuance of his invitation, the General assured him, that, though he had been obliged for subsistence to enter into the service of King William and the Dutch republic, he had always been in his heart faithfully attached to King James. He said, that he should be charmed to meet with a favourable occasion of shedding his blood for the restoration of his Prince.

The more unquestionably to prove his zeal for this interest, he gave Lord Lovat a copy of the secret intelligence that M. Ivoye, at that time Governor of Boisleduc and a general officer of the Dutch artillery, had received from the secretaries of M. Chamillard, the French minister for the war department. In these letters all the designs of France respecting Spain, Flanders, and the other countries that were the seat of war, were detailed; designs, which the King of France conceived to be unknown to any person beside his minister and favourite, M. Chamillard. This statesman, 1703 under the influence of a weakness fatal to his country, discovered them to his secretaries, who sold them again to the enemies of their King; and M. Ivoye had a round sum of money every year from the States of Holland for this business. It is indeed notorious that this infamous traffic was carried on with more success under the administration of M. Chamillard than it had ever been before; it being extremely rare for Frenchmen to betray the interests of their monarch. Lord Lovat staid with General Ferguson till after midnight; and the General told him, that he would send his valet de chambre to introduce him again the next day by a private door.

In the morning however the commander found his garrison alarmed and mutinous. Some officers of the regiments of Orkney and Murray, relations and friends of Lord Athol, understood that Lord Lovat was in the town, and had been addressed by several soldiers of the Fraser clan who were enlisted in their regiments. These gentlemen immediately spread a report that he was come thither to debauch the Scottish garrison and induce them to desert. The officers in general had heard this report, and represented it to their commander, desiring him to arrest Lord Lovat as an enemy to the State and a partisan and emissary of France.

Upon this event General Ferguson dispatched im-

1703 mediately a message to bring Lord Lovat incognito to his quarters. He told him with concern, the great danger in which he was; that it was necessary he should disguise himself and set out upon the spot, since, if the Dutch had the least rumour of the intelligence which had been spread by the Scottish officers, it would be impossible to save his life, or hinder him from being cut into a thousand pieces. Lord Lovat thanked General Ferguson with great warmth, and told him, that he was ready to set out instantly, provided he had the means of arriving safely at Antwerp.

The affair was difficult, but Mr. Ferguson accomplished it by means of a sum of money, and by the assistance of a rich Dutch Roman Catholic merchant, whom he knew to be extremely attached to the French interest. This merchant brought to Mr. Ferguson and Lord Lovat a Catholic postilion, whom he used when he went to Antwerp and Brussels in time of peace. The postilion had three saddle and one draught-horse. He agreed to conduct Lord Lovat and his brother to Antwerp upon two of the saddle horses, himself being mounted upon the third, offering his little country cart to convey Major Fraser and Lord Lovat's page. At the same time he demanded a hundred louis d'or* upon the spot in ready money, fifty for the risk of his horses and fifty for the risk of his life, both of them being forfeited in case of a discovery.

---
* 100*l.*

Lord Lovat counted down the sum required, and, 1703 by the advice of Mr. Ferguson, disguised himself like a carter, in order to drive the cart out of the town. In this disguise he passed all the gates and redoubts of Boisleduc on the side of Antwerp, the centinels being extremely numerous in that direction. Major Fraser and Lord Lovat's brother escaped in the habit of poor citizens of Boisleduc. The rendezvous was fixed with the postilion at a league from the town, and he arrived about half an hour after sunset with his three horses. Lord Lovat immediately mounted, and, having recommended themselves to the care of providence, they travelled all night, in order to reach the neighbourhood of Antwerp before break of day. This was the road in all Europe the most dangerous, upon account of the partisans and detachments that roamed up and down the country day and night.

Near to the large town which lies half way between Antwerp and Boisleduc, the night being very dark, Lord Lovat, his brother, and the postilion found themselves in a manner surrounded by a party of fifty or sixty men. The postilion proving faint-hearted, Lord Lovat was obliged to threaten him, and to desire his brother to blow out his brains, if he did not follow them without hesitation. In the mean time, with his pistol cocked in his hand, he spurred his horse across the high road in which the party were, in order to gain the heaths on the side of Breda.

Having galloped half a league across this wide plain, Lord Lovat said to his guide, 'You see we are now out of reach of the detachment; are you able in the dark to find once more the Antwerp road?' 'No,' said the postilion, 'I do not know how to find the high road; but I know that there is a bridge, somewhere about three leagues from hence, which we must cross if we would not make an elbow of six. But at this bridge,' added he, 'there is almost always stationed a small party of the garrison of Breda, and we must not go near it without learning whether or not it is guarded.' Lord Lovat had travelled over this very country the preceding year; and, having accurately marked the situation of Antwerp, he replied to the guide, 'Fear nothing, I know perfectly well which way Antwerp lies, and I will find my way by the stars without going a league out of the right direction one way or the other.'

Saying this, they proceeded; and the postilion observing in a short time that they were not above a quarter of a league from the bridge he had mentioned, they agreed to advance to a neighbouring cottage. The postilion having called to the peasant in the jargon of the country, he rose, and Lord Lovat gave him a crown* to go before and reconnoitre whether the bridge were guarded. The peasant found nobody, and returning, Lord Lovat gave him a trifle more. Approaching meanwhile with a cautious pace towards the bridge,

---

* Two shillings and sixpence.

and hearing no noise, he spurred his horse vigorously, 1703 and passed over at a hand gallop. From this place they continued to travel the same rate till they arrived, at break of day, within a league and a half of Antwerp, Lord Lovat being extremely glad to find himself out of danger.

Having entered the city, he ordered himself to be conducted to the quarters of Marshal Villeroi, who received him in a most obliging manner, and insisted upon his dining with him. Lord Lovat was alone with Marshal Villeroi and the Duke de Villeroi, his son. Upon this occasion he acquainted them with the particulars he had learned respecting the Archduke, as well as with the treachery of the secretaries of M. Chamillard. Villeroi immediately dispatched a courier with this intelligence to Versailles, at the same time desiring Lord Lovat to do him the honour to repose himself for a few days at Antwerp, and entreating him to accept of his equipage when he chose to set out for Paris. Lord Lovat thanked the Marshal very much, but added that he was resolved to take post as soon as Major Fraser, his relation, whom he had left upon the road, and respecting whose safety he was in some pain, should arrive.

It was not without reason that Lord Lovat was anxious upon this head. The Major and Lord Lovat's page, in passing from Boisleduc to Antwerp, went seven or eight leagues out of the way, and, being obliged to

1704 conceal themselves in the day time, they were four nights in the most imminent risk of their lives before they joined Lord Lovat. This nobleman, thinking that they had been assassinated or made prisoners, was delighted to see them arrive at Antwerp. He dismissed the postilion with an additional gratuity, so that the seventeen leagues from Boisleduc to Antwerp, besides the danger of his life, cost Lord Lovat more than an hundred and ten louis d'or; and he thought himself too happy, at that price, to be sheltered in the midst of the French army.

Lord Lovat, having made his court, during the few days he spent at Antwerp and Brussels, to Marshal Villeroi and the Duke, his son, took post with the gentlemen who were with him for Paris, where he arrived in twenty-four hours after he had left Brussels.

He went immediately to pay his duty to Cardinal Gualterio and the Marquis de Torcy, and to give them an account of his expedition. They received him with their usual kindness, and were charmed to see him escaped from so many dangers, and still in a condition to execute his project. The next day he repaired to St. Germains, where the Queen received him with extraordinary marks of condescension and amity, thanking God that he had escaped the numerous perils which he had encountered for her service.

Lord Middleton and the Duke of Berwick, who was just setting out for Spain to support King Philip against the Archduke, came together into the antichamber of 1704 the Queen to embrace Lord Lovat. They received him with open arms, and conducted him to the apartments of the Duke, where they both expressed themselves towards him in the most polite and obliging terms. Lord Lovat recounted in a brief manner the adventures of his journey. Lord Middleton was overjoyed to see him arrived in safety after so many dangers, adding that he must now think no more of returning into Scotland till his King should accompany him in person; that he saw innumerable difficulties in his scheme; and that it was necessary at length to give it up, as attended with too many perils.

Lord Lovat told him that his Queen and the Court of France must dispose of his project as they pleased; for himself, he should always be ready to obey their instructions. Lord Middleton, in order to convince Lord Lovat of the sincerity of his attachment, added, that he would speak to the King to bestow upon him the blue ribbon of his country, assuring him, that he would add new lustre to that honourable order.

Lord Lovat returned from St. Germains to Paris perfectly satisfied with his reception. In arriving however at his own apartments, he fell sick of an illness, contracted by the incredible fatigues he had suffered for eight months past. This was the fatal accident, which ruined at once his own affairs and those of his prince. Lord Middleton eagerly embraced the opportunity, to

1704 eradicate from the breast of his mistress every impression she yet retained in his favour.

The Queen in the mean time being informed of the illness of Lord Lovat, and yet continuing to regard him with her accustomed complacency, sent him the following letter entirely written with her own hand, and which Lord Lovat still preserves as a testimony, to confound the calumnies of those who afterwards persecuted him.

'My Lord,

'I am extremely afflicted at the news of your illness, and I sincerely pray God to restore your health, that I may oblige the King, my son, to bestow upon your person and family such distinguished marks of his esteem, as may suffice to convince posterity, that the King is indebted to you for every future degree of prosperity he may enjoy as much as to any subject.

(Signed)

'M. R.'

After receiving this letter, Lord Lovat conceived himself to be so firmly established in the mind of the Queen that nothing could shake him; but he was extremely mistaken. By the intrigues and insinuations of Lord Middleton, her Majesty soon after became his declared enemy, and continued so for eleven years in spite of all the efforts of himself and his friends to excite her Majesty's clemency or convince her of her injustice.

Lord Lovat's illness lasted three weeks, and when he left his chamber, he received from Cardinal Gualterio and the Marquis de Torcy the agreeable intelligence that the Most Christian King was as determined as ever to execute the project, and to send, in order to support the loyal Scots, an army of five or six thousand men, with every other necessary assistance of arms, money, ammunition, and provisions. They added, that he must immediately, in conjunction with the Marshal de Coeuvre, Vice-Admiral of France, and, since the death of his father, Marshal d'Etrées, employ himself in digesting the business. At the same time the Cardinal observed to Lord Lovat, that he should join with him, in his employment the Marquis de Callieres, Secretary of the Cabinet to the Most Christian King, and the intimate friend of the Cardinal and the Marquis de Torcy.

The Marshal de Coeuvre was endowed with an understanding active, penetrating, and heroic. He was of a distinguished valour, and possessed much of the confidence of the King. He had entered into very close connections with Cardinal Gualterio and the Marquis de Torcy.

The Marquis de Callieres was a man of a clear and solid understanding, of a superior genius for the affairs and intrigues of State, and consummate in every thing

1704 that constitutes the character of an able minister. He was better acquainted with the affairs of foreign countries, than the natives themselves. But what was most admirable in his character was his rare integrity and inviolable probity, and that he was the best friend that ever existed. He was so invincibly attached to his word and his friendship, that no power and no misfortune upon earth could ever lead him to depart from them, or prevent him from supporting oppressed innocence, and asserting the truth with which he was acquainted

Lord Lovat entered into the affair with these two great men; and the Cardinal and M. de Torcy frequently visited them at their labour to observe their progress, and assist them with their advice. Lord Middleton, being informed by his spies that Lord Lovat was shut up for hours together with these distinguished personages, no longer doubted of the determination of the Court of France respecting the Scottish insurrection. Always impressed with the infallible ruin that awaited him if the project succeeded, he now applied himself wholly to engage the Queen to oppose it effectually and in earnest.

For this purpose he exerted his utmost endeavours to make Lord Lovat appear in the blackest colours to the Queen, and even to the French administration; and this at the very time that he wrote to him letters, filled with the most liberal expressions of amity and attachment. Lord Lovat having shown these letters to the 1704 Cardinal de Noailles, Cardinal Gualterio, the Marshal de Coeuvre, and the Marquises de Torcy and de Callieres, Lord Middleton has always been regarded by these noblemen, as false, insincere, double, and hypocritical. It was their undoubted persuasion of this fact, that in the event was the means of saving Lord Lovat.

At this period the impudent traitor, James Murray, arrived from Scotland, bringing with him supposititious papers, fabricated by Lord Middleton, and other calumnies sent by Lord Athol. From this moment Lord Middleton threw off the mask. He openly assured the Court of France, that Lord Lovat had betrayed his own project to the Dukes of Queensberry and Argyle and the Earl of Leven, though all Scotland knew, that the project had been betrayed by this very James Murray two months before the arrival of Lord Lovat, and that the traitor had published the most bitter invectives against his Queen, which Lord Lovat every where counteracted by the warmest eulogiums. In the mean time this wretch, being the creature of Lord Middleton, was graciously received, implicitly credited, and obtained the highest rewards from the Queen. Her Majesty entered with equal readiness into all the sentiments of Lord Middleton for the destruction of Lord Lovat.

They were so urgent in their infamous charges against him that the Marquis de Torcy thought proper

1704 to send for this nobleman to his closet, and minutely to examine for four hours into all his proceedings in the execution of his commission, of which he had already given an account to this minister in writing. This great statesman then did him the honour to express his sentiments upon the subject in these words; 'I am persuaded of your fidelity and innocence. You are, however, extremely to be lamented, since the Court of St. Germains spares nothing to paint you as black as hell. But fear nothing; you have the King my master on your side.' It will not be improper to say a word here, *en passant*, of the character of the Marquis de Torcy, though I am extremely incapable of placing it in the light it deserves.

M. de Torcy was the most bland and condescending minister in Europe. The equanimity of his character was so great that he was never known to lose his temper. His understanding was so penetrating that nothing could escape it. His genius was so solid and persevering that all his projects succeeded, or at least never failed through his fault. His great talents made him one of the ablest statesmen in the world; and his amiable qualities gained him the hearts of every man, native or foreigner, who had any intercourse with him.

He had other perfections, by so much the more admirable, as they are not always found in conjunction with agreable talents and first-rate abilities. It may be said without flattery of the Marquis de Torcy, that there was not an honester man in the world. His probity was so invincible, that the mines of Peru would have been incapable of making him say or do anything inconsistent with duty, justice, and truth. To this rare quality it may be added that there never existed a friend more sincere or more unchangeable. It was impossible to have an opportunity of nearly examining this great minister without loving and respecting him.

Lord Lovat was penetrated with grief and indignation when the Marquis de Torcy related the disgraceful character given of him by the Court of St. Germains, and when he of consequence saw all the dangers he had encountered, and the services he had performed, repaid only with the most unexampled calumny and the blackest ingratitude. He took leave of the Marquis, and retired to his *auberge*, in the lesser place at Versailles, determined never more to interfere with the affairs of that ungrateful Court. He seated himself in a disconsolate posture, and, leaning upon a table, ruminated upon the means of quitting France with honour.

While he was in this humour, his landlady entered the room, to tell him that there was below stairs a gentleman in a gold-laced coat, who wished to speak to him in private, but would not come into Lord Lovat's apartment. Lord Lovat took his sword in his hand, and went towards the stairs. Mean while the visitor ascended, and bid the landlady withdraw the candle.

He came up to Lord Lovat, complimented him

upon having done the greatest services to the Court of France and to his King; but added, that he had very powerful enemies; that they had at last obtained an order from the Most Christian King to throw him into the Bastile; that the warrant was already in the hands of the officers of the *grand prevôt;* that they were upon the hunt for him; and that one of his friends, being acquainted with the affair, had desired this messenger to inform him, that he must fly immediately if he would escape irretrievable ruin.

Lord Lovat answered his intelligencer with great firmness, that he did not at all understand what he meaned; but that he had nothing to do but to return to the person who sent him, with assurances, that he was as sincerely attached as any man to the Most Christian King; that he had faithfully served his prince and the interests of France; and that he was therefore under no apprehensions, but should wait in perfect tranquility for every thing that might befal him.

At this reply the stranger appeared to be much confused. Lord Lovat immediately comprehended, that, as he was upon good terms with the Court of France, this must be a contrivance of his enemies at the Court of St. Germains in order to ruin him, if he had been fool or coward enough to give into their snare. He afterwards learned that this treacherous intelligencer was no other than James Murray, whom Lord Middleton had sent, either to assassinate or entrap him.

Lord Lovat having passed a very bad night, between 1704 mortification and resentment, arrived at seven o'clock in the morning at the house of the Marquis de Callieres, who always protected him, being better acquainted than any other person with his loyalty and zeal. Having acquainted this minister with the malicious turn that had been played him, M. de Callieres was extremely irritated, and said, that it was one of Lord Middleton's infamous tricks, but that he would immediately wait upon the Marquis de Torcy to consult with him upon what had happened. In the mean time he desired Lord Lovat to wait in his apartment till he returned.

When he came back, he had the goodness to console Lord Lovat by informing him, that M. de Torcy was perfectly satisfied of his zeal and fidelity, that he need therefore fear nothing from the Court of St. Germains, and that he ought not to lose courage, or even relax of his zeal for the Scottish expedition, since he had the Court of France on his side, which was alone able to carry it into execution. Being thus supported by the Marquis de Torcy and consoled by M. de Callieres, Lord Lovat returned to Paris to work in his usual manner with the Marshal de Coeuvre.

Soon after this interview, the more to confound the enemies of Lord Lovat, his Grace the Duke of Perth, a man of high and punctilious honour, and who may without flattery be said to have been, of all the ministers at St. Germains, the King's most zealous

1704 and faithful servant, received a letter from Scotland from his eldest son Lord Drummond, who, of his own mere motion, and totally ignorant of the persecution which was at this time begun against Lord Lovat in France, wrote in a manner, which not only most amply justified, but implied the highest applause of the conduct of his lordship.

He asserted that Lord Lovat had rendered the most essential services to the royal interest in Scotland, and that it was not possible sufficiently to praise his zeal, his fidelity, and the intrepidity he had displayed in so warmly urging the resolution to take arms at all events. He added, that above all, his dexterity ought to be greatly admired and munificently rewarded in having with so much readiness and policy amused the Duke of Queensberry, and by that means saved the lives of Mr. John Murray and himself, without incurring the smallest injury to the royal cause. At the same time he referred to Mr. John Murray for an explicit detail of all that had been done in the affair.* This,

---

* In Macpherson's Original Papers, in which the evidence against Lord Lovat is carefully collected, a letter upon this subject from Lord Drummond to the Duke of Perth is mentioned in a billet of Lord Middleton, but the letter itself does not appear. Whether it were suppressed by Mr. Macpherson, from the apprehension that contradictory evidence would only serve to bewilder his reader, or were destroyed by Lord Middleton and his friends, this circumstance may seem calculated to confirm Lord Lovat's narrative. It may be observed, that, so far as appears, Lord Drummond and Mr. John Murray were uniform in the assertion of his lordship's innocence.

by the way, serves further to overthrow the assertions of the author of the Memoirs of Scotland.

1704

Lord Perth triumphed extremely at the receipt of this letter, as he had been deeply embarked in the Scottish project, and Lord Drummond his eldest son, Earl Marishal his son-in-law, and the Earl of Errol his brother-in-law, were at the head of it. Lord Perth upon this occasion vindicated with so much zeal and fervency the honour and incorruptibility of Lord Lovat to the Courts both of France and St. Germains, that he embroiled himself irretrievably with the Queen. He repaired with equal haste to show this letter to the Marquises de Torcy and de Callieres, Cardinal Gualterio, and the Marshal de Coeuvre, who were all of them extremely delighted with its contents. Mean while the friends of Lord Lovat exclaimed loudly against Lord Middleton, his calumnies, and his unjust proceedings.

The Marquis de Torcy and the Cardinal now spoke afresh to the King of the benefit he would derive to his affairs from favouring the Scottish insurrection, and his Majesty was accordingly induced to undertake it without delay. The next day he spoke to the Marshal de Coeuvre to form suitable arrangements with M. de Pointis, who was to command the squadron. Mean time the Marshal worked without intermission with Lord Lovat and the other persons destined to assist in the expedition.

1704 Lord Middleton now understood, that the Court of France had taken its determination, and that Lord Lovat exclaimed loudly against him and the intrigues he had formed to ruin the Scottish affairs. He saw, that the French administration paid no attention to his malicious memorials, and that the letter of Lord Drummond was constantly objected to him, as fully justifying Lord Lovat. Thus circumstanced, he had the impudence, having been at daggers-drawing with Lord Perth ever since their arrival in France, to accuse this respectable nobleman of having invented, forged, and suborned this letter, to serve the interests of his faction.

Lord Perth, whose rectitude and probity were never before called in question by his greatest enemies, was constrained upon this occasion to prove the hand writing of his son, by a comparison with several letters that Lord Drummond had written to the Queen. He further proved, that this letter had been conveyed to him, by a secret address, through the hands of Mr. Drummond, banker at Amsterdam. In fine, Lord Middleton universally passed for a base calumniator. The Queen herself, who was the only person that had ever given into his unworthy suspicions, was at length convinced of their falshood and injustice.

The minister was not yet deterred by the shame and confusion he had incurred in thus aspersing Lord Perth. He saw himself upon the eve of being ruined for ever

LIFE OF LORD LOVAT.

by the project of the Scottish insurrection. He tortured his invention to find out calumnies against Lord Lovat, that might finally remove his apprehensions, and enable the Queen to demand from his Most Christian Majesty that he should be committed to prison. The scheme he at length selected was the most extravagant and absurd that could be conceived. He persuaded the Queen that Lord Lovat had engaged Sir Alexander Maclean, captain in the regiment of Dorrington, to join with him in attacking the Duke of Berwick and Lord Middleton, in the middle of the night, in the galleries of St. Germains.

As Sir Alexander Maclean was poor, and had just married an English woman, one of the sempstresses to the Queen, Lord Middleton entertained no doubt, that, by an offer of ten thousand francs* in ready money, and a pension of two thousand livres,† he should easily induce him to advance any thing he pleased to effect the ruin of Lord Lovat. It appeared however in the event that he was extremely mistaken.

In the mean time the Queen received this romance for an undoubted truth, and made her complaints respecting it to the Court of France. Cardinal Gualterio was so highly irritated and ashamed at this conduct of her Majesty, that he went purposely to St. Germains to tell her, that she ought never to mention

---
* 400*l.* † 80*l.*

to the Court of France, a thing so extravagant, and so entirely destitute of probability, that such a procedure must necessarily give the Most Christian King and his ministers the most unfavourable impression of her Majesty.

At the same moment Sir Alexander Maclean declared publicly, in what manner he had been tampered with, and the extraordinary reward that had been offered, to induce him to maintain what was necessary for the destruction of Lord Lovat. He had rejected the proposal with disdain, and was extremely incensed that such an idea had been entertained of him. He said, that he would not accept the bribe of a kingdom for the ruin of his countryman and friend, in opposition to honour and conscience; that he had never heard Lord Lovat speak but with extreme respect and affection of the Duke of Berwick, who had always treated him with the greatest condescension; and that neither Lord Lovat nor himself were fools or mad enough, to think of attacking the principal persons of the Royal Court, in the palace of their sovereign, and in the midst of the French guards.

I do not believe that the Queen had any other share in this flagitious calumny, than by the weakness, with which she gave implicitly into the representations of Lord Middleton. Be that as it will, it is certain that she and even the minister and his emissaries were so extremely ashamed of this diabolical romance, that they suffered Lord Lovat to remain unmolested for some 1704 time afterwards.

The Scottish expedition, being now perfectly digested, was presented to the Most Christian King by the Marshal de Coeuvre. His Majesty approved of it, and told the Marshal that, as he was determined immediately to carry it into execution, it was proper that he should give it to the Marquis de Torcy, to propose and get it passed in the Privy Council.

Upon this reply, M. de Coeuvre, Cardinal Gualterio and the other friends of Lord Lovat felicitated him upon the success of his undertaking. They told him, that he must be infallibly in a short time one of the first of the Scottish nobility; since he would be called upon to head the insurrection, not only as a general officer to King James, but as a general officer in the army of France; and since every thing necessary for the success of the expedition, land forces, a squadron of ships, money, arms and ammunition, was already prepared, and nothing remained but the form, which was fixed for a very early day, of carrying it through the Privy Council.

Lord Lovat was extremely delighted to see his project, after so great dangers and so many cross accidents, upon the point of being executed. He thanked these noblemen in the warmest terms, for their zeal and generous attention to the interests of his King. He told them, that he had no longer any apprehensions, but from the intrigues of Lord Middleton; that nothing could hinder the project from having the completest success, but the sinister transactions of that nobleman, with the King, in England, and in Scotland.

It was not without reason that Lord Lovat apprehended the black designs of this perfidious minister. Having learned how nearly the business was ripe for execution, the secretary, as his last resource, acquired such an ascendant over the mind of the Queen, as to induce her to refuse to the King of France to issue the necessary commissions to her subjects. A few days after the Most Christian King waited upon her Majesty, to acquaint her with his resolution, and to desire her to hold her commissions in readiness, to call upon her subjects to join his troops, as soon they should disembark upon the island.

The Queen, governed by Lord Middleton, without having said a word to Cardinal Gualterio and the Marquis de Torcy, who had laboured with so much zeal and attachment for the interests of her son, replied, that she was persuaded this project was calculated to ruin the loyal inhabitants of Scotland, and that she could not therefore in conscience comply with what his Majesty proposed. Louis was astonished, and, if I may dare to say it, exasperated at this answer. But, as he is the prince in the world the most polished in his manners, he dissembled his real sentiments, and only told the Queen, that she might then be assured that she was at liberty to retain her commissions, till 1704 she and her ministers were as fully convinced of the excellence of the Scottish project, as he and his servants already were.

The day following, the Marquis de Torcy proposed the Scottish project in the Privy Council. M. Philipeaux the Chancellor, the Duke de Beauvilliers, the Count de Pontchartrain, and almost all the ministers, made separate speeches, in order to demonstrate the utility of the measure.

The King replied, 'Messieurs, I am satisfied that the Scottish project would be of more utility to me than all my alliances; I am convinced, that a civil war in England and Scotland would at once dissolve the league, that has been formed against me, and which subsists only by the money and exertions of that country. But I am not at liberty to carry the project into execution. The Queen of England to my great surprise, has refused to issue orders to her subjects to join my troops. I have given my protection to this princess, and granted her an asylum in my dominions, and it would ill become me to compel her to a measure, which she believes inimical to her interests. It is necessary therefore to defer this salutary project, till the Queen of England has opened her eyes to the advantages with which it is attended. I never designed to make a conquest of Scotland; but on the contrary to succour and support the loyal

Scots, in their exertions for the restoration of their sovereign.'

The whole Council was equally confounded and offended with this astonishing refusal on the part of the Queen of England. The Marquis de Torcy, who had hitherto employed much attention and ability upon the subject, was now so violently disgusted, as to protest, that, unless by the orders of the King his master, he would never more concern himself with the affairs of this stupid and perfidious Court, or with those of the unfortunate Queen, who seemed to employ all her power in ruining the prospects of her son. M. de Torcy saw with perfect clearness, all the consequences that could have resulted from this project, and the irreparable misfortune that the Queen of England, by placing implicit confidence in her perfidious secretary, caused, not only to the affairs of her son, but also to the interests of France. From that time therefore he seemed to have conceived an aversion even to the hearing of the Queen of England, or any of her concerns.

It is indeed certain, and no person of good sense can deny it, that by this fatal refusal, the effect of a headlong and unexampled weakness, the Queen gave so decisive a blow to the interests of the Court of St. Germains, that neither she nor all her friends will probably ever be able to recover so favourable an opportunity. King James, morally speaking, must by this project have been infallibly restored. The Scottish 1704 nation were resolved to hazard their lives in his favour. England was torn by the highest rage of contending factions. Queen Anne was in her heart a well-wisher to the cause. France, at that time every where victorious and triumphant, was in a condition to have afforded him every kind of assistance. There was nothing, but the immediate interposition of heaven, the strange imbecility of his mother, and the ignominious perfidy of the Earl of Middleton, that could at this time have prevented the restoration of King James to the throne of the three kingdoms; and of consequence the advancement of the Most Christian King to the situation of undisputed arbiter of Europe.

Lord Lovat was impressed with the deepest despair at this termination of all his hopes, and all his labours. He instantly resolved to return into Scotland without taking leave of the Queen, or ever hereafter having the smallest concern in her affairs. With this determination he hastened to wait upon Cardinal Gualterio. His Eminence had from the first treated Lord Lovat with so much condescension, and had continued to entertain for him so untainted a friendship, that he had long been in the habit of taking no step that regarded the two courts, without first communicating it to the Cardinal. And here I must attempt a sketch, though it will necessarily be very imperfect, of the various perfections of this great man.

1704 Cardinal Gualterio was handsome and well made. He was the most affable and engaging of the human race. His friends were always received by him with open arms, and a visage full of complacency. A French nobleman justly observed to me, that his Eminence had no kind of resemblance to the rest of his countrymen. The Italians commonly appear to carry their heart upon their lips, while in reality they are full of dissimulation. Cardinal Gualterio had their frank and honest air, but at the same time was in reality one of the sincerest and most indefatigable friends in the universe.

Lord Lovat experienced in his own person the reality of this amiable quality. The Cardinal lived with this nobleman for two years in all the habits of the most unrestrained intercourse; he served him like a brother; he made all his best friends in the court of France common to Lord Lovat. And though he was the nuncio of the Pope, and well knew that Lord Lovat was a Protestant, he never spoke a word to him upon the subject of religion; though the author of the Memoirs of Scotland has the impudence to assert, that Lord Lovat was reconciled to the Church of Rome, in order to ingratiate himself with the Cardinal. Little did this author know of the true character of Cardinal Gualterio. This great man left to the preacher and the confessor the business of converting souls. The theatre, in which he employed all his talents and all his industry, was that of the affairs of 1704 state.

In the science of politics he was consummately skilful; and it may be said of him without exaggeration, that he was one of the first and ablest ministers in the world. He had secret correspondencies in all the considerable courts of Europe, and very frequently received from them letters entirely written in cypher. He had himself so great a facility of language, and such a command of his attention, that I have seen him at the same time dictate to his three secretaries, and write with his own hand more than fifty letters in six hours.

His incomparable ability in all kinds of affairs, his mild and unassuming disposition, and the openness and affability of his character drew upon him the special friendship and regard, not only of the Most Christian King, but of all his ministers, and all the nobility of France to whom he was known. Indeed he seemed to be regarded by Louis the Fourteenth and his servants, less as a foreign ambassador, than as a leading member of the French administration.

Lord Lovat having waited upon the Cardinal, acquainted him with his intention to abandon the affairs of St. Germains, since the Queen, contrary to her promise and her oath, had ruined all by this last fatal stroke, to please Lord Middleton.

The Cardinal replied, 'My poor Lord Lovat, you

are young and ardent; you carry your heart too much upon your lips; but nothing is more necessary, than to dissemble your feelings and your resentment, if you would succeed in affairs of state. Do you not see,' continued he, 'my poor Lord, that I am obliged to dissemble with certain people three hundred and sixty-five days in the year? And you cannot dissemble for a single hour with the Queen and Lord Middleton. Let me entreat you, my dear friend, to follow a little my example. Cultivate perseverance and firmness in the pursuit of difficult objects: you see I am never disheartened. In the mean time you have several times recalled the Queen to her original purposes by your spirited remonstrances on the part of the loyal Scots. I would have you once more write to her Majesty, remonstrate on the extreme injury she is doing to the affairs of her son, by following the counsel of those, who are desirous of defeating the Scottish project for their private interest. As soon as the Queen has received this letter,' added the Cardinal, 'I will wait upon her, that I may inforce your representations as far as is in my power.'

Lord Lovat, agreably to the advice of the Cardinal, wrote a letter to the Queen, possibly somewhat more spirited than the Cardinal desired. It was in reality this fatal letter, that so incensed the Queen against him, that she has not yet forgiven it, notwithstanding the penitence the author has performed of thirty-two

days in a dark and unwholesome dungeon; of three 1704
years imprisonment in the Castle of Angoulême; and
of seven years imprisonment in the city of Saumur.
This unfortunate letter therefore being the immediate
cause of all the calamities that afterwards overtook
Lord Lovat, it is proper that the substance of it should
be related in this place.

Lord Lovat declared in this letter, that he was
greatly mortified that he had so often exposed his life,
and sacrificed his property, in bringing to perfection a
project, which her Majesty, in contradiction to the most
formal and positive promises, had overturned at one
blow; and which would, in all human appearance, have
seated King James upon the throne of his ancestors.
He observed, that every loyal subject in the Scottish
nation would be as much afflicted at the unfortunate
event as he was; and affirmed, that, while her Majesty
implicitly followed the advice of the people who were
at the head of the English Parliament, Jesus Christ
would come in the clouds before the King her son
would be restored. He concluded, that for his own
part he would never more draw his sword in the royal
cause, so long as the regency was in her Majesty's
hands; but that, when his King should be major,
or of an age to be at the head of his affairs,
he would expose himself with his whole clan, to the
last drop of their blood, for his service. In the
mean time, he should always maintain the respect

1704 for her Majesty which was due to the mother of his sovereign.

The Queen put this letter immediately into the hands of Lord Middleton, who declared, that it was full of high treason, and the most formal disobedience; and that, if Lord Lovat had written such a letter to a queen, reigning in Scotland, his head must have paid the forfeit of his insolence. Incited by these representations, the Queen took the letter in high resentment, and immediately waited upon the King of France, intreating him, for his rebellion to commit Lord Lovat to the Bastile, and adding that she must otherwise be obliged entirely to withdraw herself from the world, that she might no longer be exposed to such insults on the part of her subjects.

Cardinal Gualterio in the mean time, in pursuance of his promise, having repaired to St. Germains, found the Queen in all the exacerbations of the most furious rage against Lord Lovat. He immediately engaged the Cardinal de Noailles; the late Duke de Noailles, his brother, a great favourite of the King; and the Marshal de Coeuvre, to speak to his Most Christian Majesty in favour of Lord Lovat. These noblemen undertook the cause, and expressed themselves to the King with all possible ardour. The Marshal de Coeuvre, who had worked so long with Lord Lovat, had the goodness to say upon this occasion to the King his master, that the Queen of England bestowed an ill reward upon the zeal and fidelity that Lord Lovat had displayed in the cause of her son; that he knew him for a most honourable man; and that, if his Majesty would consent to accept his surety, he would answer, body for body, for his perseverance in the interests of France, and his loyalty to the King of England. The King replied that he was precisely of the Marshal's opinion, and that M. de Coeuvre did him a great pleasure, in confirming the thoughts he had always entertained of Lord Lovat.

Scarcely had this conversation passed, when the Queen of England arrived, in order to request the commitment of Lord Lovat to the Bastile. The King made no other reply, than by telling her he was firmly persuaded of the zeal and fidelity of that nobleman, and that in consideration of this, her Majesty ought to pardon a failure of respect, which originated only in the thoughtlessness of youth, and the fervency of his zeal for the King her son. The Queen returned repeatedly to the charge, without being able to obtain for Lord Lovat the punishment she desired.

Some months after, Cardinal Gualterio did Lord Lovat the honour of observing to him, that his story had the air of being a perfect romance; that he ought to be eternally grateful to the King of France; and that his Majesty had to his Eminency's certain knowledge done more for him, than he had probably ever done for any peer of France, in resisting for so long a

1704 time, not only the intreaties, but even the tears of the Queen of England, who demanded with the extremest earnestness, his commitment to the Bastile. This circumstance gave Lord Lovat so high an idea of the natural equity and justice of the King's disposition, and excited in his bosom so lively a gratitude for his persevering goodness, that he resolved from that moment, let the consequences be what they might, not to quit France without a complete and perfect justification of his conduct, or without the consent of the Most Christian King.

Lord Middleton, perceiving that all his efforts were not sufficient to ruin Lord Lovat at the Court of France, invented at this time a new calumny, which in the end overwhelmed him with the utmost confusion. He saw that Mr. John Murray, the envoy of the Court of France to the loyal Scots, was not yet returned; and he knew by his correspondents that he had set out from Scotland four months before. Since in all this time he had not been so much as heard of, he concluded, according to all human appearance, that he was either lost at sea, or had perished amidst the various dangers of his journey. This was the basis he chose for his imposture. Supported by the evidence of his creature and that reprobate villain, James Murray, he informed the Court of France, that, however they might think proper to entertain a good opinion of Lord Lovat, he could assure them, he had caused their envoy, Mr. John Murray, to be assassinated in Scotland, 1704 in order to prevent his report of the treasonable proceedings of Lord Lovat in that country.

This accusation was of so terrible a nature, that none of the friends of Lord Lovat could persuade themselves to mention it to that nobleman. In the mean time Mr. John Murray did not return. Lord Lovat perceived a degree of coldness and reserve in the countenance of his friends, which he particularly remarked in Cardinal Gualterio, and was extremely afflicted by it; this illustrious character having always lived with him upon the footing of a brother.

The aspersion of Lord Middleton continued to gain credit. In the mean time the Queen was incessant in her importunities with the King of France; and Lord Lovat on his part delivered to the French administration memorials, conceived in terms of considerable asperity, against the Court of St. Germains. Tired out with the complaints that poured in upon him from every side, Louis lamented with some earnestness to Cardinal Gualterio and the Marquis de Torcy, the two patrons of Lord Lovat, the unpleasant situation in which he was placed. Thus circumstanced, these noblemen resolved to send Lord Lovat to Bourges, to reside with two of their particular friends, the Archbishop, who was son to the Duke of Gêvre, a man of ability and merit, and much esteemed at the Courts of France and Rome; and M. de Roujeault, at that time intendant of Bourges.

1704 The Cardinal at last intimated to Lord Lovat, that the King and the Marquis de Torcy wished him to reside at Bourges, till Mr. John Murray should arrive in France, in order to quiet the mind of the Queen of England. He added, that he might depend as much as ever upon the resolution of the Most Christian King to execute the project, and upon his being called upon to conduct it. Lord Lovat replied, that he was ready to go wherever the King pleased, provided he had wherewith to subsist, and to pay his little debts at Paris; adding, that he was unwilling to leave that metropolis in a dishonourable manner, after having spent in it such considerable sums of his own money for the interests of his King, without having in his life touched a single penny from the Court of St. Germains. The Cardinal answered, that what he desired was reasonable, and he would mention it to the Marquis de Torcy.

In a short time after, his Eminence acquainted Lord Lovat, that the King had granted him for his subsistence at Bourges a hundred crowns[*] per month, which was the ordinary pension of a major-general, and was equal to four times as much at Bourges as at Paris; that the Marquis d'Argenson, lieutenant-general of the police, had orders to take an account of his debts, which his Majesty was determined to pay

---

[*] 12*l*. 10*s*. or three thousand six hundred livres per annum. This does not exactly coincide with p. 189.

as also to give him such a sum of money as was 1704
requisite for his journey. Accordingly, the Marquis
de Torcy some days after paid into Lord Lovat's hands
a thousand crowns * for his journey from Paris to
Bourges, which was but fifty leagues, and which might
be made at the expence of fifteen pistoles.†

Lord Lovat, having received this money, and
bought everything necessary for him, prepared to set
out. He went to receive the commands of Cardinal
Gualterio, and to know of him the day, in which it
was proper he should leave Paris.

In this interval Mr. John Murray arrived from
Scotland, having been near five months in his journey.
As he carried with him the written engagements of the
loyal Scots to take arms for their King and for France,
he was afraid of being taken in his journey, and was
obliged to pass from Scotland into Norway, from
thence to Dantzic and Hamburgh, and so across the
whole German empire, with much fatigue, and great
hazard of his life. The arrival of this gentleman
agreably surprised the Court of France, who began
to believe that he had actually perished.

In giving an account of his journey and his negociations to the King and the Marquis de Torcy, Mr.
Murray fully justified Lord Lovat, and related a
thousand circumstances much to his advantage. He
made the same narrative to Cardinal Gualterio, who,

---

* 125*l.* † 13*l.* 2*s.* 6*d.*

1704 on account of his great friendship for Lord Lovat, and zeal for the affairs of the King of England, was extremely delighted with it. His Eminence had scarcely received this narration, when Lord Lovat entered his apartment.

As soon as he saw him, he leaped upon his neck, and embraced him with extraordinary marks of friendship, crying out, ' My dear Lord, you had no need of being justified in my opinion, in the opinion of the Marquis de Torcy, or even in that of the Most Christian King. But Mr. John Murray is arrived most opportunely to confound and astonish your enemies, who were base enough to suggest that you had caused him to be assassinated in Scotland. He has already given an account of himself to the King and the Marquis de Torcy, and has said things a hundred times more favourable of you and your services, than all the malice of your enemies could induce you to advance of yourself.' The Cardinal added, that he would himself conduct Mr. Murray to St. Germains, before it was possible for Lord Lovat to see him, in order that he might repeat to the Queen, in his presence, all he had said to the Court of France of the fidelity and services of Lord Lovat, and then his Eminence would intreat the Queen to do justice to Lord Lovat with the King of France.

Mr. John Murray went the next day with the Cardinal to St. Germains, and made the same favourable report, that he had done the day before to the 1704 Court of France, affirming, that, by his clan, the intermarriages of his family, and his personal credit, Lord Lovat was the great support of his Majesty's affairs in the North of Scotland. The Queen was so much affected with Mr. Murray's representations, that she admitted, she could no longer doubt of Lord Lovat's loyalty; but added, she could never forget his personal disrespect and insolence: and these words she repeated the next day to the King of France.

Cardinal Gualterio was highly pleased with what Mr. John Murray had reported to the two Courts. He told Lord Lovat that he must no longer think of going to Bourges; that on the contrary it behoved him to stay at Court, and triumph over his enemies; and he would speak for that purpose to the Marquis de Torcy. Lord Lovat replied, he was ready to do every thing the Court of France and his Eminence should think proper.

In two days after this conversation the Cardinal told Lord Lovat, that, upon his representations to M. de Torcy, the Marquis observed, that it was true, Mr. John Murray having fully justified Lord Lovat, it was no longer just that he should go to Bourges; but that if he did not go, not only the Queen of England, but possibly the King his master would reflect upon him: that the Queen had renewed her charges of the ill treatment of Lord Lovat at Marli, and had complained that he was still at Paris, venting calumnies against her, and menacing to return into Scotland to ruin her affairs; to which the King had replied in a very cold manner, 'Madam, it is a month ago since Lord Lovat was at Bourges, M. de Torcy has told me so;' that the contrary would appear if Lord Lovat remained at Paris, and might cause M. de Torcy considerable uneasiness.

Lord Lovat replied, that he would go not only to Bourges, but into Spain, rather than cause a moment's pain to the Marquis de Torcy, who had always treated him with so much attention. He now took leave of Cardinal Gualterio with the most pungent grief, at seeing himself upon the point of being separated from a man, who had distinguished him by so generous a friendship, and for whom he entertained so profound and tender a respect.

The Cardinal embraced Lord Lovat, intimating that he should not stay at Bourges above a month at the utmost, and protesting that at all times, and in all places, he should find in him a brother, rather than a friend. Lord Lovat penetrated with gratitude, could only answer the Cardinal with his tears. And his emotion was not without reason; for from that time he has never seen, and according to all appearances never shall see again, this excellent nobleman, his patron, his support, and his best and most intimate friend.

Lord Lovat set out next morning for Bourges, in

opposition to the opinion of his brother, and of Major 1704 Fraser his cousin, who exerted their utmost efforts, to engage him to return into Scotland, or to repair to the Court of Hanover. They enlarged upon the unsuitable reward and unworthy treatment he had received from the Court of St. Germains. They observed, that his honour was more than vindicated in France, by the return of Mr. John Murray, and the justice that was done him by that gentleman. Lord Lovat however could not come to the resolution of quitting France, without the consent of the Most Christian King, and in contradiction to the sentiments of Cardinal Gualterio and the Marquis de Torcy, after having experienced so much condescension from the King, and so much friendship from these noblemen.

Major Fraser seemed overcome at this parting with his chief, and wept like a child. It seemed as if this brave lad foresaw, that he should never again behold the head of his family, and his relation, whom he so tenderly loved. In fact the poor Major was afterwards killed at the siege of Lerida,* by the last musket-shot *1707 that was fired at that place, after having given the most extraordinary proofs of his valour. He was universally regretted by the French and Irish officers who knew him, being esteemed, not only for his gallant behaviour, but also as one of the best officers of foot in the army in which he served. He bequeathed all of which he died possessed, and his arrears from the regiment, to

Lord Lovat, who however never received a farthing of it.

Major Fraser contributed extremely to the preservation of the city of Cremona to the French, in that surprising and almost miraculous action which covered the whole nation with immortal glory.* It was he who gave orders for breaking down the bridge of Cremona, over which Prince Thomas of Vaudemont must necessarily pass with a large body of cavalry, which, together with the forces that had already made themselves masters of the town, would infallibly have cut in pieces every Frenchman and Irishman in the place: such was the acount I received from the Major, and assuredly he was not a man to varnish his conduct with a deceitful lustre. After having thus stopped the progress of the Prince of Vaudemont, he assembled a body of Irish in a large bastion on the side of the bridge, and caused the cannon of the bastion to be pointed upon the cuirassiers of the Emperor, who were drawn up at a small distance. The shot had their entire effect. The enemy were thrown into disorder, and the Major, immediately causing his Irish to sally from the bastion, attacked the imperialists sword in hand with so much spirit, that he cleared that quarter of the town of them in a moment. Such was his share in the glorious day of Cremona.

He also very much distinguished himself at the head of his regiment, in the various sieges and battles gained by the French, under the command of the celebrated Marshal Catinat, and the gallant Duke de Vendôme, in Savoy, in Piedmont and in Italy, during the two wars of 1688 and 1701. The justice I have done to his memory is richly due to a man, who, at that time a captain in the regiment of General Vahope, followed the fortunes of his King into France and into Ireland, and who continued to serve his native sovereign, and to advance the interests of France with courage, distinction and fidelity, for twenty years, down to the moment that he was killed by a musket-shot in the head, at the siege of Lerida, at the time the Duke of Orleans made this celebrated conquest.

I return to Lord Lovat, whom we left travelling post to Bourges. Before his arrival M. de Roujeault, intendant of Bourges, received a letter from the Marquis de Torcy, requesting him to render to Lord Lovat, who was about to spend some time in that city, every service in his power; adding, that this nobleman was the head of an ancient and considerable family in Scotland, celebrated for loyalty to their prince, and attachment to the French nation. In a word, this great minister spoke in the most flattering manner of the family, the person and the merits of Lord Lovat. 1704.

M. de Roujeault, being prepared by this letter, received Lord Lovat in the most obliging manner, and procured for him every gratification he could wish in his present situation. From that time there commenced a most strict and affectionate friendship between Lord Lovat and this famous intendant, so that M. de Roujeault is to be considered as one of the best friends Lord Lovat has in the world. This circumstance induces me to say a word of the character of that gentleman, who is at the present moment intendant of the generality of Rouen.

He was descended from a good family of the profession of the law at Paris, and nearly related to Marshal Catinat. When very young he was promoted to the appointments of counsellor to the Parliament of Paris and master of requests. Being known for a man of understanding and excellent sense, he was raised to the office of intendant of the generality of Bourges. In this capacity, instead of oppressing and trampling upon the people, as other intendants do, he commenced his administration by relieving the poor peasants, and thus putting his province in a better condition for serving their prince. From that time he acquired, and with justice preserved in all his intendancies, the appellation of father of the nobility, of the people, and the poor. From Bourges he was called to the intendancy of Maubeuge and of the army on that side. The province of Berry lamented his departure with tears, and are not yet consoled for his loss. At Maubeuge, he attracted in a particular degree the esteem of the Elector of Bavaria, the Duke de Vendôme, and all the officers of the army. He was at this time the intimate friend of that great minister M. de Bergheic,* and he engaged in all the intrigues of war and state on that side. He also entered, from the commencement of his friendship with Lord Lovat, deeply into the affairs of England.

After the disasters of Flanders he quitted Maubeuge, to the great regret of the nobility, and the officers of the army. He was now appointed intendant of the extensive generality of Poitou. It was there that I saw him in 1709 not only save the province from a general revolt, but render corn in every part of it almost abundant, at a time in which the rest of France suffered extremely, and the people died in the high roads and in the towns by a most terrible famine.

The city of Rouen was to a proverb the rock, which gave occasion to the ruin of the intendants of France. Two of these gentlemen had just been treated in a very uncivil manner within a short time of each other. M. Desmarêts† observed to his Majesty, that he did not know what intendant to send to these hot-headed and untractable Normans. The King replied, that he knew what would exactly fit them; all that was necessary was to send them M. de Roujeault, who would attach the Normans as warmly to his person, as he had

---

* Superintendant of the Spanish revenues in Flanders, and the Catholic King's chief minister in that country.

† Appointed Comptroller-General of the Finances in 1708 in the room of M. Chamillard, who had for some years united that and the war department in his own person.

done the other provincials among whom he had presided.

When it was known that M. de Roujeault had orders to set out for Rouen, the Poitevins were struck with the deepest consternation. They offered to increase the taxes of the government, if his Majesty would permit M. de Roujeault to remain among them. It was necessary however to conform himself to orders that did him the highest honour. I was at Poitiers when he set out from that place. Every thing wore the face of a murmur, almost of a general revolt through the whole province. Men and women, the old and the young, drowned in tears, exclaimed aloud, that they lost their father, their protector. For some days before his departure, whenever he left his house, he was in a manner overwhelmed with a crowd of the lower people and the poor, weeping, and crying, that they would follow him wherever he went: they could not live without their father.

As he went through Paris in order to receive the orders of the King, his Majesty said to him in the most gracious manner, ' You have been loved and regretted at Bourges, at Maubeuge, at Poitiers: the same thing will happen to you at Rouen; I am persuaded of it. Be not offended that I think proper to draw you a little nearer to Versailles.' From Paris M. de Roujeault went strait to Rouen; and what is entirely without example, he is as much beloved in his present government as the most rascally intendant was ever hated.

After this short sketch of his history, it is scarcely necessary to add, that he was a man of uncommon merit. His abilities were solid; he was much given to reflection; he was penetrating, collected, fertile in expedients, and capable of affairs, the greatest and the most arduous. But what is peculiar to him beyond every man of his rank I ever knew, is, that while other intendants and people in places of trust, not only in France, but over the whole face of the earth, have no other object than that of enriching their families, and elevating themselves to the highest dignities, the purpose and policy of all the actions of M. de Roujeault, his single study from morning to night, was to do good and contribute to the gratification of others. He could never say, like the celebrated Roman emperor, 'I have lost a day;' the day never passed over the head of M. de Roujeault in which he did not contribute to the happiness, or confer important benefit upon some of his fellow-creatures: a circumstance, which ought for ever to render his name immortal.

I have made this digression upon the subject of M. de Roujeault, because he was the support, and the principal consolation of Lord Lovat, during the whole term of his imprisonment and exile. It was to him that he owed the extraordinary advantage of being always paid his pension in money, while all France was paid in paper at a very great loss; an indulgence for which Lord Lovat and his friends can never be sufficiently grateful to this gentleman, and all those who are connected with him.

1704 That nobleman spent his time in a very agreable manner at his present residence. He received every week letters from Cardinal Gualterio, and frequently from the Marquis de Torcy, the Marquis de Callieres, and his other friends. He had not been a month at Bourges when he was informed, by Cardinal Gualterio and from other hands, of the great condescension which the Most Christian King had displayed in his favour. M. de Torcy being with the King at Marli, his Majesty said, 'You know, *monsieur le marquis*, that your friend Lord Lovat has but a slender provision in his residence at Bourges. Send him four hundred crowns* by way of addition to his pension; and tell him, that I granted him this without being solicited to it by any body.' The friends of Lord Lovat felicitated him upon this generous and most gracious action; and observed to him in the most agreable manner, that this gratification, under the circumstances in which it was given, ought to be more pleasing to him, than if his friends had obtained for him twenty times as much.

Lord Lovat was indeed so highly delighted with this act of condescension, that, Cardinal Gualterio having done him the honour to send him immediate intelli-

---

* 50*l*.

gence of the birth of the first Duke de Bretagne, he 1704 resolved to spend four or five hundred pistoles* of ready money, to celebrate this illustrious birth and to display his attachment to France in the most magnificent manner. As wine was very cheap in the province of Berry, Lord Lovat bought several tons, which he caused to be formed into fountains, that ran during the whole evening for all the populace of Bourges. The *fête* was considered as throughout so beautiful and superb by the inhabitants of Bourges, that the people of the town caused an account of it to be published.

Lord Lovat is ignorant whether the Queen of England were irritated with his having assumed the air of giving magnificent entertainments at a time, when her Majesty regarded him as disgraced and in exile. It is certain that Lord Middleton had constantly his spies upon him. He marked the favour of the Court of France towards him, and he trembled with apprehension, that Lord Lovat would remain at Bourges no longer than till the period destined for the execution of the Scottish project. Once more therefore he called all his engines into play in order to bring this project to a final termination.

He represented to the Queen, that Lord Lovat was yet as formidable as ever; that he regarded all her displeasure with contempt, and intended shortly to pass over into Scotland, where he expected to revenge his

---
* About 400*l.*

1704 disgrace by the ruin of the royal affairs in that kingdom. What had yet been done against him, he therefore observed, must go for nothing; it was absolutely necessary to proceed till he was reduced to a state of impotence. By such arguments the Queen was prevailed upon to give the last fatal blow, which completed the ruin of Lord Lovat, and the entire and irretrievable destruction of the affairs of her son, of which that nobleman was in the present case the principal and essential spring. After having experienced multiplied refusals, she at last obtained of the Most Christian King an order for Lord Lovat to be arrested and sent prisoner to one of the royal castles. The following was the account that Lord Lovat received some months after from an intimate friend, who had undoubted knowledge of the transactions of the Court of France at that time.

The Queen, tutored by Lord Middleton, waited upon the King of France, carrying with her the last will of King James the Second, and expressed herself nearly in the following terms. 'Monsieur, I am well assured, that Lord Lovat is resolved to return immediately home, and that he threatens to ruin the affairs of my son in Scotland. It must be confessed, that he is very capable of carrying this threat into execution, by the power he possesses in that country, and the perfect acquaintance he has with my son's affairs. I am therefore at length obliged to acquaint your Majesty, that I have here brought the last will of 1704 my royal husband, by which I am appointed to the regency during my son's minority. If you finally refuse to give orders for Lord Lovat's imprisonment, I must beg leave to lay my commission at the foot of your Most Christian Majesty, and to retire into the convent of Chaillot for the rest of my days. Your Majesty must answer before God for the tremendous calamities which I foresee will ensue.'

The King, though surprised at a language which he did not at all expect, replied with his usual magnanimity; 'Madam, I am as perfectly persuaded at this day, as I was at first, of the zeal and fidelity of Lord Lovat to your Majesty's interests. Since however you are pleased to think that your son's affairs will infallibly be ruined, if he be not thrown into prison, I consent. I will send him to one of my castles, from which it will not be possible for him to escape.' Next day his Majesty gave orders with regret to the Marquis de Torcy to send Lord Lovat to the castle of Angoulême; but to assure him of his royal protection, and that his Majesty would not forget him when the project of Scotland was ready for execution. Such was the manner in which the fatal measure of the imprisonment of Lord Lovat was attained and adjusted.

For himself, ignorant of what was transacting, he expected every day to be recalled. He was at dinner, on the fourth day of August, 1704, at the house of M.

1704 le Roy, *procureur de police*, at which M. de Roujeault had fixed him, as being the best house in Bourges. A grand prevôt, accompanied by his lieutenant and twenty-four archers, stole into the drawing room, and seized Lord Lovat as if he had been an assassin, demanding from him his sword in the King's name. Lord Lovat delivered it with great tranquility, saying, that he had never designed to draw it, but in the cause of his King or for the interests of France, as he had always hitherto done. They paid no attention to what he said. They took him by the arms and the legs, and dragged him like a dog, from the saloon in which he had dined, to his apartment above stairs. Here the prevôt pillaged him in the most inhuman manner of his papers, of his purse, his watches, his jewels, and in a word, of every thing he had. It was only by the greatest menaces on the part of M. le Roy, a man of ability and merit, and the most incorruptible integrity, that this brute of a prevôt was induced to return to Lord Lovat,—just what the rascal pleased.

This ruffian, not contented with having maltreated Lord Lovat in his own apartment, conducted him on foot at high noon through the middle of the town on a market day, hemmed in with the files of his archers, and a whole crowd of the populace, as if he had been conducting to the gallows. In this manner he was obliged to submit to all the raillery of an insolent and uncivilised mob, while every respectable inhabitant of the city, in which he was honoured and esteemed, wept over his misfortune, and the ignominy of his disgrace. [1704]

The villain of a prevôt was so obliging as to attend Lord Lovat with his archers all the way to Angoulême. He had the luck to procure a cursed little chaise, where Lord Lovat was in a manner buried alive under the unwieldy bulk of this enormous porpoise. Such a situation, united with the extreme heat of the season, had so dreadful an effect, that his lordship was apprehensive of dying upon his route. The illness however of this unfortunate nobleman, and the various unpleasant circumstances with which he was overwhelmed, were not able in the smallest degree to mollify the barbarous manners of this rude officer, who probably imagined, that a British lord was a kind of monster in the shape of a man.

Lord Lovat is not able precisely to determine, whether it were through the generous recommendation of the humane prevôt, or rather through the malice of Lord Middleton and his enemies at the Court of St. Germains, that upon his arrival at the castle of Angoulême he was thrust into a horrible dungeon, which had been from time immemorial the unviolated habitation of coiners and murderers. It was a gentleman of this last class, whom the consideration of Lord Lovat's friends obliged to give way to him in the present instance. His page, who was a young gentleman of the Fraser clan, and the only person permitted to witness his sufferings, conceived so extreme a horror at this dungeon, as to fall ill the first night, and to be for six months given over by the physicians.

Lord Lovat remained in this apartment, shut up for thirty-five days in perfect darkness, where he every moment expected death, and prepared to meet it with becoming fortitude. As an express prohibition had been given, to communicate any thing to him in writing, or even to utter a word in his presence; and as he was unable to conceive the reason of this barbarous treatment, conscious of his entire innocence of all that his adversaries had laid to his charge; all that the enemies of France have imputed of most horrible to the French government was continually passing through his mind. He listened with eagerness and anxiety to every noise, and, when his door creaked upon its hinges, he believed that it was the executioner come to put an end to his unfortunate days.

SECT. III.

SINCE however Lord Lovat perceived, that the last 1704 punishment continued to be delayed, he thought proper to address himself to a grim jailoress, who came every day to throw him something to eat, in the same silent and cautious manner in which you would feed a mad dog. He intreated her to have the goodness to give him paper, pen and ink, in order to write a letter to the minister. She replied, it was more than her life was worth to comply with his request. Lord Lovat answered that he would give her the letter open, that she might see he wrote nothing that could have any sinister consequence to her, or could give offence to the Court. He added, that to reward her civility, he would put his purse in her hands that she might take whatever she thought proper. The clink of the louis d'or subdued the inexorable virtue of the fair jailoress. She furnished Lord Lovat with the materials he wanted, and he immediately wrote to Cardinal Gualterio, the Marquis de Torcy, and the Marchioness de la Frezeliere.

About twelve days after this transaction M. de Borés, lieutenant of the town and castle of Angoulême, and who has ever since treated Lord Lovat as his

1704 son, came himself to liberate him from his dungeon. He conjured him to believe that he was in the utmost degree afflicted that a man of his rank had been thrust into that horrible place; it was the fault of a stupid wretch of a captain, who commanded at that time in the castle, while he was at his country house, where he usually spent a good part of his time. He added, that he had orders from the Marquis de Torcy to grant him the entire liberty of the castle, at the same time taking his parole of honour in writing, that he would not leave France without the consent of the King, which engagement he was to send to the Marquis de Torcy. It was this interview, that first convinced Lord Lovat, that the Court of France had no share in producing the inhuman treatment he had received.

His friends now began to correspond with him, and he received two days after a letter from the Marchioness de la Frezeliere, inclosing a copy of the Marquis de Torcy's to M. de Borés. The Marchioness informed Lord Lovat, that, when she went to solicit his release from the Marquis de Torcy, this amiable minister appeared extremely surprised at the treatment Lord Lovat had received, and declared that it was very much beside both the King's intention and his own; he had sent Lord Lovat to the castle of Angoulême as a friend. This castle was in a manner an open prison, having an extensive park included within its walls, in which were the pleasantest walks of the city, where the better sort of inhabitants resorted every day to take the 1704 air, and whose company M. de Torcy conceived might be some alleviation to Lord Lovat under his unfortunate restraint.

Indeed the Marquis's letter to the King's lieutenant affords an unanswerable proof of what that nobleman had at first suspected, that his barbarous treatment had originated solely in the enmity of the Court of St. Germains. The minister wrote to the lieutenant of Angoulême, that he deserved to be cashiered for having in so inhuman a manner maltreated a man of Lord Lovat's quality; that he did not deserve to have a prisoner of rank committed to his charge; that Lord Lovat should no longer be the prisoner of any King's lieutenant in France; but that he should be solely the King's prisoner and his own, upon his parole of honour, not to go out of the country without the royal consent. The Marquis commanded M. de Borés to take this parole of Lord Lovat in writing and send it to him, and in the mean time to give him the liberty of the castle.

The King's lieutenant immediately executed these orders; and Lord Lovat lived, from that time, more agreably in the castle of Angoulême, than he would have done had he had the range of a province. He was much respected and beloved by the most considerable persons in the city and neighbourhood, who united their endeavours to soften to him his adversities. Indeed I

1704 have often heard him say, that, if there were a beautiful and enchanting prison in the world, it was the castle of Angoulême.

1705 A short time after, Lord Lovat's correspondents informed him, that the King was resolved to execute the Scottish project; and for that purpose had sent Mr. Hooke and Mr. John Murray into Scotland, in order to renew the engagements that had been entered into by the nobility of that country for the restoration of their prince.

This Mr. Hooke was an English gentleman, who had originally been deeply engaged in the intrigues of the Duke of Monmouth, and, having been pardoned by the late King James, in order the more fully to demonstrate his fidelity and gratitude, followed his Majesty in his retreat into France. He was there struck out of the list of those persons who received pensions from the Court of St. Germains. Upon this event he determined to enter into the service of the King of Sweden; but, in his journey for that purpose, he met at Hamburgh the Count de Guiscard, who was returning from an Embassy to the Court of Stockholm. The Count had here several interviews with Mr. Hooke, and finding him a man of ability, he prevailed upon him to abandon his design, and brought him back to France.

The Count de Guiscard here recommended him to his intimate friends, the Marquis de Torcy, and the

LIFE OF LORD LOVAT. 227

Marquis de Callieres, as a man formed by nature for ripening negociations and managing intrigues of state. Soon after, M. de Torcy employed him in a secret negociation in Holland, in which he perfectly succeeded, and exactly carried into execution the designs of his employer. Upon his return the minister obtained for him a pension of five hundred francs* per month, and a brevet of second colonel in the Swedish regiment of Count Sparre.

When Lord Lovat, in conjunction with the Marquis de Callieres, digested the project of the Scottish insurrection, the Marquis mentioned to him Mr. Hooke, as his intimate friend, and begged Lord Lovat to permit him to introduce that gentleman into the Scottish secrets, as a man very capable of rendering essential service to the project. Lord Lovat, who had an infinite attachment and respect for the Marquis de Callieres, his generous friend, told him, that he had not the honour to know Mr. Hooke, and that he was by no means partial to the idea of admitting an Englishman into a Scottish project; notwithstanding which he would receive with pleasure a man who had the happiness to be his friend, and whom the Marquis knew to be faithful to the cause of the King of England, and the interests of France. Mr. Hooke immediately began to take his share in digesting the Scottish affairs; and from this period commenced a most intimate friend-

---
* 20*l.*

ship, and cordial union between him and Lord Lovat. Mr. Hooke presently discovered, and from his natural penetration and long experience saw further than any body, into the impostures and imbecility of the Court of St. Germains.

This gentleman was afterwards promoted to the rank of a brigadier in the French service. He had the reputation of some distinguished actions performed by him in Flanders; and to do him justice it must be confessed, that Mr. Hooke was a man of unquestionable courage, a penetrating genius, a clear understanding, sagacious, judicious, and capable of moulding to his purpose the most inauspicious events, whether in affairs of state, or the transactions of war. He was extremely short-sighted; but his uncommon gallantry excellently supplied this defect upon all necessary occasions.

I have spoken thus at large of this gentleman, because he was the principal mover in conducting, in the kingdom of Scotland, the affairs of the unfortunate project, which so completely miscarried in the year 1708. He passed backward and forward several times in order to prepare the minds of the Scottish nation for the execution of the business. He had a considerable intercourse with the Earl of Errol, Earl Marishal, Lord Athol, Lord Stormont and all the nobility of the Lowlands who were loyal to King James. In the last place, a few months before the French fleet, destined for this enterprise, sailed from Dunkirk, Mr. Hooke made a tour of all Scotland, not excepting the most inaccessible mountains and remotest islands. He concerted measures with the lairds of the Highland clans for an universal rising, as soon as the French army should arrive in the vicinity of Edinburgh. I am indeed persuaded, that this unfortunate project did not miscarry in the execution by any error or neglect of Mr. Hooke. Had his counsels been uniformly followed, I am fully satisfied, that the King of England would have been long ago restored to his throne.

I resume the letters of Lord Lovat's correspondents, acquainting him with the progress of the affairs of the Scottish project. They informed him, that Lord Middleton had infused the largest hopes into the Court of France, from the favourable dispositions of the Duke of Hamilton, Lord Athol, and many other noblemen of the Lowlands of Scotland. He affirmed, that they would rise in arms as soon as a French fleet should appear upon the coast; and that they had concerted signals, which they would make in such places as were proper for the debarkation of King James and his troops.

Lord Lovat however knew by experience the unbounded avarice of the Duke of Hamilton, which would infallibly prevent him, as it had hitherto done, from running the smallest risk for the royal cause. He was perfectly acquainted with the watry soul, the ingrained imposture, and the steady falshood of Lord

Athol. Upon these grounds he wrote his sentiments in a very explicit manner to the Marquis de Torcy, and did not fail to predict to this minister, with the most literal exactness, everything that happened in the execution of this unfortunate project.

Such was the only crime that Lord Lovat committed against the state during his residence at Angoulême. Unless we should be disposed to qualify with that title the continual offers he made for the service of his native sovereign, in spite of the frowns and prejudice of the Queen. Or unless we should quarrel with the arrest that was made by his orders, at the castle of Angoulême, of an Irish priest of the name of O'Daly, whom the enemies of Lord Lovat had sent to surprise and betray him, disguised in the uniform of a captain of the regiment of the Duke of Berwick, with a gold-laced coat and a feather in his hat.

This emissary, having first desired a private interview with Lord Lovat, and opening himself in a very cautious manner, informed that nobleman, that he was gentleman of the bedchamber to the Duke of Modena, a prince, very deeply engaged in the interests of the Emperor; that his master had sent him into France to execute some secret projects of the Emperor and Queen Anne; and that he expected in a short time to receive a hundred thousand crowns* at Bourdeaux, in order to be distributed in the Cevennes, and among

---
* 12,500*l*.

the other French religionaries. He added, that, if Lord 1706 Lovat would consent to escape out of prison and accompany him in his return, he would engage his master the Duke of Modena to interfere with the Emperor, to obtain his pardon from Queen Anne, and his reinstatement in all the property and estates, which he had so idly lost in endeavouring to serve the most ungrateful and stupid Court in the universe. Captain Macartney (this was his style) promised, that he would in that case transmit to him from Bourdeaux all the money he should want till his complete reinstatement.

The wretch however presently perceived, that Lord Lovat would hear nothing against the Queen at St. Germains, and gave little attention to the scheme he proposed for his escape, and his passage into England. Upon this he began to speak in the most disrespectful and insolent terms of the Most Christian King. Lord Lovat, unaccustomed to bear any injurious expressions against a prince, to whom he was indebted both for life and subsistence, and immediately suspecting, that the villain was either a spy employed by the enemies of France, or an emissary on the part of his enemies at the Court of St. Germains, caused him to be arrested by the commandant of the castle, who happened to be the very person, to whom Lord Lovat had been indebted for his very rough treatment on his arrival at the castle of Angoulême.

While the captain disarmed him, this impostor

endeavoured to swallow a paper, which the commandant wrenched out of his mouth, torn through the middle. This paper contained a false route, which the villain had employed under the name of Captain Macartney, and which was enough to have hanged him, forgeries of this kind being made capital in France. They now proceeded to examine the impostor's portmanteau; the contents of which were chiefly such things as a priest usually carries about with him, and being shown to the prisoner, he confessed himself to be a priest.

His brother, a cordelier who resided at Limoges, came to see him some days after, and lamented that our adventurer, imagining himself to be rendering the most important services to his King, her Majesty, and the interests of religion, had suffered himself to be enticed by the enemies of Lord Lovat into so dangerous and unjustifiable a proceeding. He was persuaded however that the Queen, who knew the integrity of his intentions, would relieve him from his present disgrace. The Marquis de Torcy, as soon as he had received an account of the transaction, returned Lord Lovat his thanks for the zeal and loyalty that had actuated him in the affair.

In the mean time this adventure, which proved the fidelity of Lord Lovat to her Majesty and the Most Christian King, and which was calculated in its own nature to have given him the most unimpeachable claim to the restoration of his liberty, was destined only to accumulate his misfortunes. He was afterwards assured, that the Queen turned this unequivocal proof of his loyalty to his prejudice. She gave the Court of France to understand, that this priest had written her a letter, by which it appeared, that it had really been Lord Lovat who had employed the most dishonourable expressions respecting her and Lord Middleton, and who had endeavoured to escape into England. Upon her representation the wretch was set at liberty unpunished, though he was taken with a false route in his pocket.

The Marquis de Torcy may well recollect the circumstances of this story. It made a considerable noise at Angoulême, and gained Lord Lovat much credit among the inhabitants, at the same time that it was extremely agreable to his friends. Such was all the advantage that he ever reaped from this distinguished instance of his loyalty and zeal.

He had now been two years in prison. The Marquis de la Frezeliere was of all Lord Lovat's advocates the most mortified at this circumstance; and he resolved to do every thing in his power to put an end to so disgraceful a restraint. It is necessary in this place, to give some account of the origin of the Marquis's extreme attachment to Lord Lovat, as well as to present the reader with an idea of a person, who will make so considerable a figure in the future part of this history.

The house of Frezel or Frezeau de la Frezeliere is one of the most ancient houses in France. It ascends by uninterrupted filiation, and without any unequal alliance, to the year 1080. It is able to establish by a regular proof sixty-four quarterings in its armorial bearings, and all noble. It has titles of seven hundred years standing in the abbey of Nôtre Dame de Noyers in Tourraine. And it is certain, that, beside these circumstances of inherent dignity, the house de la Frezeliere is one of the best allied in the kingdom. It numbers among its ancestors on the female side daughters of the families de Montmorenci, de Rieux, de Rohan, de Bretagne, de la Savonniere, de la Tremouille, de la Grandiere, and de St. Germains. Through the houses de Montmorenci, de Rieux, de Rohan, and de la Tremouille, to which the Marquis de la Frezeliere is nearly allied, he can trace his filiation through all the French monarchs, up to Charlemagne, King of France, and Emperor of the West. Down again through the various branches of the illustrious house of France M. de la Frezeliere may without impropriety assert his alliance to all the royal houses, and almost all the principal nobility of Europe.

It is demonstrated by various historians, by the tradition of the two families, and from letters written from time to time from one to the other, that the house of Frezel or Frezeau de la Frezeliere in France, and the house of Frezel or Fraser in Scotland, were of the same origin, and derived from the same blood. The Marquis de la Frezeliere, the head and representative of the Frezels or Frezeaus in France, and Lord Lovat, the representative of the Frezels or Frasers in the north and the Highlands of Scotland, having happily encountered each other at Paris, in the second journey that Lord Lovat made to France for the service of his King,* were therefore both of them highly gratified with the opportunity that offered itself, of renewing their alliance, and declaring their affinity, in a common and authentic act of recognition, drawn up for that purpose.

*1702

This record was executed on the one part by the Marquis de la Frezeliere himself, by the Duke de Luxembourg, the Duke de Châtillon, and the Prince de Tingrie, the three worthy and illustrious children of the late Marshal de Luxembourg Montmorenci, whose heroic exploits are not less glorious and celebrated, than his descent is ancient and august. Several other lords of the house of Montmorenci, the Marquis de Rieux, and many noblemen related by blood and marriage to M. de la Frezeliere, joined with the Marquis in affixing their signatures to this act of recognition. On the other part it was executed by Simon Lord Lovat, Mr. John Fraser his brother, and Mr. George Henry Fraser, major of the Irish regiment of Bourke in the French service, for themselves, in the name of their whole family in Scotland,

By this deed the kindred of the two houses of the Frezels or Frasers is placed out of all possible doubt. Accordingly from the moment in which it was executed the Marquis de la Frezeliere regarded Lord Lovat rather as his brother and his child, than as his remote relation ; and had his re-establishment in Scotland nearer his heart than his own elevation in France.

The house de la Frezeliere has always followed the profession of war; and has served its King and the state with a singular valour, which has successively drawn upon them marks of esteem and distinction from their sovereigns. Many Marquises de la Frezeliere have been decorated with the order of St. Michael and of the Holy Ghost. The Marquis de la Frezeliere, who renewed his kindred with Lord Lovat by the above act of recognition, was the sixth lieutenant-general in the French service in lineal descent, almost all of them having been governors of towns or provinces.

If the father of the Marquis de la Frezeliere, who was one of the oldest lieutenant-generals in the French service, equally celebrated for his bravery and military skill, had lived three months longer than he did, as he was much loved and esteemed by the King, he would have been the first upon the list of marshals of France in the great promotion that was made in 1702. And it is certain, that, if the Marquis de la Frezeliere himself had lived to the age of fifty years, he would have illustrated the antiquity and honours of his house, by obtaining the first dignities of the sword, the duchy and the peerage.

He was an eagle in the concerns of war. His greatest enemies, who loved not his authoritative manners, his hauteur and his rapid advancement, were however forced to acknowledge, that, in regard of the science of artillery and tactical invention, which were particularly his forte, as well as of campaign war, the Marquis de la Frezeliere was one of the most skilful and best informed officers of his age in Europe.

Marshal de Boufflers informed the King particularly of the actions performed by the Marquis, and the brilliant reputation he acquired at the siege of Lisle,* and the battle of Malplaquet.† His Majesty declared publicly, upon more than one occasion, that the Marquis de la Frezeliere appeared at so early an age to be the true son of his father, and would infallibly arrive at the first degree of military excellence.

*1708
†1709

M. de la Frezeliere, upon his return from the present campaign, hastened to solicit the Court of France in behalf of Lord Lovat. He was answered, that the Court was as sorry as he could be, to see Lord Lovat in custody; but that the King was obliged to give this satisfaction to the Queen of England, who had absolutely determined to abandon the affairs of her son, and totally to retire from the world, if she had not obtained the punishment of that nobleman. It was added, that, provided the Queen would consent to his

1707

of release, the King and his ministers would be extremely happy, since they wished for nothing more ardently than to see him at the head of the Scottish project, of which he had been the original author; that therefore M. de la Frezeliere had nothing to do, but to apply to the Court of St. Germains, if he would obtain the liberty of Lord Lovat, persuaded that the Court of France would yield its concurrence.

The Marquis, having received this favourable answer, hastened to St. Germains. He represented to the Queen, that, as bearing the same name, and being derived from the same stock with Lord Lovat, he could not see him languish in prison without intreating her Majesty, either to set him at liberty, or to order his trial: if he were criminal, he would be the first to condemn him; but if he were innocent, it was a most inauspicious cruelty, thus to oppress and persecute him without reason. He added, that, if her Majesty refused him this request, he should be obliged, as the relation of Lord Lovat, to throw himself at the feet of his King, to demand that from his Most Christian Majesty which he had in vain intreated from her.

The Queen was extremely sorry to find herself assailed by a man of so haughty and enterprising a character, and so much esteemed at the Court of France. She demanded a day to consider of his request. On the one hand, she saw herself urged by the untainted loyalty of Lord Lovat, which, after all the calumnies of Lord Middleton and James Murray, she had been obliged to acknowledge to the French King and his ministers. On the other hand, she was still more strongly urged by the desire with which she was animated of revenging herself of Lord Lovat for the pretended disrespect and insolence with which he had treated her. Thus circumstanced, her Majesty thought proper to give her answer to the Marquis de la Frezeliere the next day in writing, signed with her own hand, and countersigned by Lord Caryl one of her principal secretaries of state.

In this answer the Queen declared, that she had nothing to advance against the fidelity of Lord Lovat, that she was equally satisfied of his zeal and of his services, that nevertheless some political reasons respecting Scotland, compelled her Majesty to detain him some time longer in the castle of Angoulême; that, if he had patience, he should speedily be received into favour, and that then the justice done him should be as signal, as the prejudices and partiality of his enemies had been notorious. This written answer is at this day in the hands of the Marchioness de la Frezeliere, among the other important papers of the late Marquis her husband. And Lord Lovat has an authentic copy in the Marquis's hand, who triumphed in it exceedingly.

He carried it to the Marquis de Torcy, and shewed it to all Lord Lovat's friends in the French Court, who were happy to find the Queen obliged to acknowledge

1707 under her hand the loyalty and services of Lord Lovat, after his having been for two years calumniated and maltreated by the Court of St. Germains.

At this incident the Marquis de Torcy intreated M. de la Frezeliere to write to Lord Lovat to take courage; that the King was as resolute as ever to put in execution the Scottish project, that he had the same good opinion of Lord Lovat, and that he was determined to bestow upon him the share he deserved in a scheme, that had originated with him; that for this purpose the King, without communicating his purpose to the Court of St. Germains, would send him his orders to quit the castle of Angoulême, and to come down to the coast, as soon as the expedition should be ready to be executed.

Accordingly, a few months after, the Marquis de la Frezeliere obtained an order, signed by the Most Christian King, and countersigned by the Marquis de Torcy, who signs short 'Colbert.' By this order the King permits Lord Lovat to quit the castle of Angoulême, and to repair to the waters of Bourbon or Pougues, for the restoration of his health. Four days after he received a second order, by which his Majesty commands Lord Lovat, after the restoration of his health by the waters of Bourbon or Pougues, to repair to his town of Saumur, till further orders. At the same time he was permitted to take with him the Chevalier Frezel of Lovat, his brother. Lord Lovat still preserves these orders, signed as above, sealed with the royal seal, and 1707 dated, one on the second of August 1707, the other on the fourteenth of the same month.

It is uncommon, and perhaps unexampled, that a State prisoner should receive an order, signed by the King and his minister, and addressed to himself, either to leave his prison for the restoration of his health, or to go and reside, in a manner in garrison, in a city which is by its situation one of the most agreable in the kingdom. But these orders were distinguishing marks of the sentiments of the Most Christian King and his minister towards Lord Lovat, whom they seemed to regard, more as a general officer in the French service, than as a prisoner, accused of crimes against the State.

I will here assign the reason, that occasioned the brother of Lord Lovat's being mentioned in the King's orders to that nobleman. When Lord Lovat was arrested at Bourges, his brother, who had been placed by him with a doctor of the civil law, in order to learn the French language and the profession of a civilian, was arrested at the same moment. The officers, apparently gained by the enemies of Lord Lovat, would not so much as allow this young man, in spite of his tears, to see his brother, or to take leave of him, at a time that the prevôt carried him off like a pirate, and treated him like a banditti in his route to Angoulême.

Lord Lovat was touched with the most heart-felt concern at leaving his brother behind him, like a

R

criminal, in the hands of these low-bred knaves, when he was in reality young, innocent and inexperienced, and had never had the smallest concern in any affairs of State. Regardless however of his innocence, he was attended by this kind of followers, till the interference of M. de Roujeault, intendant of Bourges, who not only restored him to his liberty, but obtained, from the generosity of the Marquis de Torcy a pension from the government, fixed on his person so long as he resided in France. It was not however till two years and ten months after this, that Lord Lovat obtained as a particular favour from M. de Torcy, permission for his brother to come and reside with him at Angoulême. The Chevalier Fraser had now resided two months at that place, when this nobleman received orders to quit Angoulême and repair to Saumur, in which the Chevalier was of course comprehended.

Behold then Lord Lovat dismissed from his prison with a degree of glory, respectability and triumph; the Queen of England confessing his fidelity and services in spite of the malice of his enemies; and the King of France sending him his orders to approach the coast, in order to his taking a share in the project of Scotland. During the three years that he was imprisoned, in spite of the dungeon into which he was thrust, and in spite of his sufferings, the malice of his enemies dares not assert, that he wrote a word, or received a line from any individual, relation or stranger, in England, Scot-

LIFE OF LORD LOVAT.

land, or Ireland. It seems to me, that he could not have exhibited a more striking proof of his submission and inviolable attachment to his King and to France.

But before we quit Angoulême, it is proper that I should relate an incident of the blackest and most shameful nature, illustrative of the malice of Lord Middleton. Lord Lovat* had resided only a few months in the Castle of Angoulême, when he received advice from one of his intimate friends in the French Court, that Lord Middleton had influenced the Queen, to speak to the Most Christian King to take away his annuity. The Queen observed to his Majesty that the pension, which he was pleased to bestow upon Lord Lovat, amounting to four thousand francs†, was the means of discouraging her subjects, and particularly the loyal nobility residing at St. Germains; that they complained, that they were particularly unhappy, that their pensions amounted to no more than nine hundred francs per annum‡, a sum, so extremely inadequate to the annuity of Lord Lovat, although he were actually imprisoned, and suspected of disloyalty and high treason. The Queen therefore intreated of Louis, to take away this subject of mortification, and to reduce Lord Lovat to the regular prisoner's allowance, which is twenty sous per day§ to the meanest peasant who is arrested by order of the King of France.

Lord Lovat's friends advised him, that the King

* 1704

---

† 166*l*. 13*s*. 4*d*.　　‡ 37*l*. 10*s*.　　§ Eight-pence.

replied in these words: 'The nine hundred francs, madam, that you give to your British nobility at St. Germains, are douceurs that you are pleased to extend to them out of the six hundred thousand francs*, which I allow you every year to dispose of as you think proper. But the four thousand francs which I give Lord Lovat are not deducted from your six hundred thousand francs: they are paid out of my treasury, of which it is right that I should dispose as I please. They are indeed less than what I have promised him, and less than his merits.'

The Queen, mortified at this very generous and dignified answer, never opened her mouth a second time upon the subject. Lord Lovat held his pension, which was regularly paid him for eleven years during his imprisonment and exile, up to the very moment that he left the kingdom of France.

It must however be confessed, that no man ever pushed the spirit of hatred and revenge, further than Lord Middleton did in this instance. He was not contented with having ruined the family, the clan, the property, and, as far as it was in his power, the reputation and good name of Lord Lovat. He was not contented with having thrust his person into a dungeon, and held him imprisoned for three years without the smallest crime. He added to these injuries the further exertion, of endeavouring to deprive him of

---

* 25,000*l.*

daily bread, and to cause him to die of pure hunger, in his present humiliating and cruel situation. Surely we must be a little surprised, that the Queen could stoop to become the instrument of this last instance of his malice. She well knew, that Lord Lovat had expended very large sums in her service without ever having received a farthing in return.

In reality, beside the rents of the estates of which Lord Lovat retained the possession, he was obliged at two several times to call upon his clan for a general contribution, after the manner of his country, for his journey into France: and the last time his poor tenants gave him the half of their little income, which reduced them to considerable distress, and of which Lord Lovat, who had the tenderest attachment to his clan, has always entertained the extremest regret. In the mean time neither Lord Lovat's elder brother, who contributed his whole estate to the support of Lord Dundee and his forces in the north, nor himself, who continually expended large sums in the service of his King, ever received a penny, either from the late King James, or from the Queen regent, or from any person on the part of the Court of St. Germains.

Lord Lovat arrived at the city of Saumur in the month of October 1707, having spent some time upon his journey at the very agreable seat of the Marquis de la Frezeliere, which is nine leagues from Saumur, and at which the reception he met, was such as might have

1707

1707 been expected, if he had been master of the house. It was to give him this pleasure, and in order that he might repair as often as he pleased to the seat of the Marquis, that that nobleman obtained the city of Saumur for his residence in preference to any other place, the Court of France having left that circumstance to the Marquis's choice.

1708 Lord Lovat had not long resided at Saumur, before he received frequent letters from M. de la Frezeliere, informing him, that the Court of France was as much determined as ever upon the Scottish project, and was preparing every thing for its immediate execution. In the mean time his intimate friends at the Courts of France and St. Germains, wrote him regular accounts of all that Mr. Hooke and Mr. John Murray had done in Scotland, and of the magnificent promises with which they were charged to the two Courts, on the part of the Duke of Hamilton and Lord Athol.

Lord Lovat thought himself obliged by this circumstance to write repeatedly from Saumur to the Marquis de Torcy, stating his real sentiments respecting the Scottish project. Only a short time elapsed before he appeared too true a prophet. Indeed the very principles from which he deduced its failure, were the circumstances, that in reality proved its ignominious overthrow and final destruction. He knew full well the timidity, the hypocrisy, the tergiversation of Lord Middleton. He knew that the Duke of Hamilton and Lord Athol, in whom so much confidence was injudiciously placed, 1708 had never appeared favourable to the interests of the King, but with a view of playing upon the fears of the reigning government, in order to swell their pensions and accumulate their civil employments.

On a sudden however it was generally published at the Court and at Paris, that King James was upon the point of setting out for his dominions. The Marquis de la Frezeliere was at that time at Paris, and perceived with regret that Lord Lovat was not thought of in this expedition. He hastened immediately to wait upon the exiled King, to whom he was well known; and the interview took place precisely two days before his Majesty set out from St. Germains to Dunkirk.

The Marquis, having wished the King a happy voyage and success, intreated him in a very earnest manner, to permit Lord Lovat to attend and hazard his life with him in the execution of an enterprise, the first idea of which had originated from his lordship. The King replied, that it was painful to him to think, that he should refuse the first favour the Marquis de la Frezeliere had ever demanded of him; but that he was so far from being ready to permit Lord Lovat to accompany him in the expedition, that, if he were not already in prison, it should be his first request to the King of France to throw him into one.

The Marquis replied, that the King's decision gave him extreme pain, but that he would still take the

1708 liberty to intreat him, since he did not think proper to employ Lord Lovat, that he would at least have the humanity to re-establish him in his property and estates, which he had lost for his service. 'Of that,' said the King, 'I will think when I am in Scotland, and will do what shall seem most conducive to my interests.'

Mr. Gordon O'Neil accompanied the Marquis de la Frezeliere, in order to join with him in soliciting the King of England in favour of Lord Lovat. This gentleman was the head and representative of the illustrious house of O'Neil in the kingdom of Ireland. He was a man of honour and probity, who had lost his estate, and shed his blood for the King his master. The Irish however in general, as appears by the terrible complaints and reiterated remonstrances which they presented as a body to the King and Queen, were extremely ill treated by the Court of St. Germains; and Mr. O'Neil partook in the ingratitude that was extended to his countrymen.

Mr. Gordon O'Neil, commonly called Prince O'Neil, was cousin-german to the present Duke of Gordon, and on that account remotely related to Lord Lovat. A marriage had been proposed, soon after Lord Lovat's arrival in France, between this nobleman and Mademoiselle O'Neil, daughter of this gallant veteran. From that time Mr. O'Neil acted the part of a faithful, an intimate, and a spirited friend to Lord Lovat,

This gentleman, as well as the Marquis de la Freze- 1708
liere, wrote Lord Lovat that very day from St. Germains
the words of the King's refusal. They united to conjure him to set out immediately for his own country;
to think no longer but of restoring the prosperity of his
family and clan; not of destroying himself as he had
done, by a headlong zeal, for a court so unjust, so
ungrateful, and so barbarous. When Lord Lovat read
these letters he was distracted. He worked himself up
to a resolution of setting out without a moment's delay,
of endeavouring at all adventures to gain the coast of
Scotland, and of convincing the King, at the head of
his clan, by dear bought experience, how much he
mistook his true interest, when he refused his service
and trampled upon his conscious integrity.

The same courier however brought him a second
letter from M. de la Frezeliere, which he now opened,
and which was dated from Versailles. In this letter the
Marquis observed, that he sent him life in the evening
from Versailles, after having announced to him death
in the morning from St. Germains. The Marquis de
Torcy he said, had assured him, that the Most Christian
King, together with himself, and the other friends of
Lord Lovat at the Court of France, were still more
offended than Frezeliere could be, that the Queen and
King of England peremptorily refused their consent to
Lord Lovat's being employed. He added, that this
however ought not to give him much pain; and he

1708 intreated M. de la Frezeliere to inform Lord Lovat, on the part of the Most Christian King, that, as soon as the King of England had set his foot upon the Scottish shore, his Majesty would send a second army, larger than the first, to support him; that with this embarkation the King would commission Lord Lovat, as a general officer in the French service, and would thus reduce his own sovereign to an absolute necessity of receiving him in a gracious and honourable manner.

Lord Lovat has all these letters still in his possession, and they should have been inserted verbatim in this place, if such a proceeding would not have had too great a tendency to swell the work, and to make a voluminous performance of what was simply intended for a memoir, or a very cursory history of a few years of the life of Lord Lovat: a work that I thought myself obliged, as his relation and intimate friend, to undertake for his justification.

The letter of the Marquis de la Frezeliere written from Versailles, assuring Lord Lovat of the protection of the Most Christian King, and that he should be sent into Scotland with an early opportunity, as his Majesty's general officer, consoled him extremely under his present adversity. He immediately dispatched his brother post to Paris, in order, that, having first conferred with M. de la Frezeliere, he might set out for Scotland to place himself at the head of his clan, while

Lord Lovat expected at Saumur the orders of the 1708 Court of France. The Chevalier Fraser had however been only four days at Paris, when news arrived, that the King of England was upon his return to Dunkirk, after the entire failure of his unfortunate enterprise.

This event obliged the Marquis to alter his measures. He exerted all his talents to endeavour to mitigate the resentment of the Queen. Finding her as inflexible as ever, he wrote to Lord Lovat, peremptorily advising his return to his own country, in order to make his peace with Queen Anne. Lord Lovat replied, that he was upon the worst terms with that princess, having done every thing in his power to overturn her throne; that the Duke of Hamilton and Lord Athol, his personal and inveterate enemies, were her particular favourites; and that for these reasons he could not hope for justice, either in England or Scotland, during her life.

The Marquis was not satisfied with these reasons. He wrote Lord Lovat continual letters to convince him that his ruin in France was irretrievable; that indeed the Court of France was sufficiently well disposed towards him, but that she would always regulate her conduct in his regard in conformity to the inclinations of the Court of St. Germains, and that, during the life of the Queen and Lord Middleton, he had nothing to look for in that country, but uninterrupted disappointments, and eternal disgrace. 'You ought therefore,' added the Marquis, 'to apply without delay to all your relations and friends, to procure you a favourable reception from the Court of London. In a word, with the permission or without the permission of that Court, you can no longer be excused from throwing yourself at once upon your clan and your family, and living or dying like a brave and an honourable man, and in a manner worthy of your descent; rather than to remain in France with the character of a criminal, and to languish in prison like a traitor. I therefore conjure you, as your relation and friend, to summon a firm resolution, to escape out of the hands of your enemies, and to employ the remainder of your days in restoring the prosperity and credit of a clan and an ancient house, which, both in honour and conscience, you are obliged to support. You have nothing to do but to apply to my steward for any sums of money necessary for the execution of this undertaking.'

Lord Lovat now thought himself obliged to review the objections he had made, and to bestow a deliberate examination upon the proposal of his friend. He knew, that whatever the Marquis de la Frezeliere had the goodness to suggest, was the simple truth, and the pure effect of his affectionate attachment to Lord Lovat and his house, which indeed he considered as his own. He saw the malice of his enemies in the administration of St. Germains, and the ascendancy of the Duke of Hamilton, Lord Athol, and Mackenzie of Prestonhal,

their creature and the usurper of Lord Lovat's estate,* 1708
in that unjust and ungrateful Court. He was in a
manner distracted, when he recollected, that he had
ever hazarded his life, that he had ever sacrificed his
property and estate in the service of that unfortunate
Court, which had treated him with the utmost inhumanity, and as if he had been the basest and most
contemptible of the human race.

From this moment he resolved to exert every
faculty he possessed, in order to effect his return to

---

* The late Marquis of Athol being disappointed in his scheme of marrying the eldest daughter of Hugh Lord Lovat, who by his direction had assumed the title of Baroness Lovat, with Lord Salton's son, proposed to match her with Alexander Mackenzie, son of Lord Prestonhal, then one of the judges in the Court of Session in Scotland. His lordship and his son readily accepted the proposal, and a marriage settlement was executed, by which Mr. Mackenzie was to assume the title of Fraserdale, and the children of the marriage were to bear the name of Fraser. The estate of Lovat was settled upon Fraserdale, during his life, with remainder to the heirs of the marriage; of which there was issue a son, named Hugh Fraser, who in right of his mother claimed the honours and title of Lovat, and several other children. Fraserdale was engaged in the rebellion of 1715; and being attainted and his estate forfeited, Lord Lovat got possession of it by a gift from the crown, during the life of Fraserdale. A suit was now commenced between Simon, the hero of the present memoirs, and Hugh Fraser, Fraserdale's eldest son, who both of them claimed the title of Lord Lovat; the suit was awarded in favour of Simon. A second suit was instituted in order to try the right of Hugh Fraser in the reversion of the Lovat estate. This suit was at length compromised in consideration of a sum of money paid by Lord Lovat; and thus about the year 1732 a termination was put to disputes which had for so long a time subsisted. *Vide Memoirs of the Life of Lord Lovat*, a pamphlet printed in the year 1746; which in matters of heraldry and genealogy is tolerably accurate, but in every other respect exhibits a tissue of the most impudent and ridiculous lies that ever were published.

his own country, and to abandon the interests of a court, which had employed all the artifices that hell could invent, to take from him his life, and what was dearer to him than life, his reputation. The sole object of his attention, and what was nearest to his heart, was now to return to his beloved clan, and to live and die in the midst of them. Thus circumstanced he would not merely have inlisted himself in the party of the House of Hanover, which was called to the crowns of Scotland, England and Ireland by all the states of the kingdom; he would have united himself to any foreign prince in the universe, who would have assisted him in the attainment of his just and laudable design, of re-establishing his family, and proclaiming to all Scotland the barbarous cruelty of the Court of St. Germains.

He was however unwilling to do any thing, which might be construed into ingratitude and disrespect to the Most Christian King, or afford a plausible handle to the Court of St. Germains to ruin him beyond redemption at the Court of France. He contented himself for the present with applying to the Marquis de Torcy, for permission, either to return to his own country, or to serve in the armies of France. He told the minister, that he could no longer passively submit to the calumnies and persecution of the Court of St. Germains; that he must beg leave humbly to demand that an end be put to his disgrace; and that, if this request was not granted, he was unalterably resolved to return into his own country.

To this letter he received no answer. The Marquis de la Frezeliere however wrote him repeatedly, that M. de Torcy had told him, that Lord Lovat would do well to return home; that the Court of France would not be offended at his taking that step, but that she would never act so directly in opposition to the Queen and Court of St. Germains, as to grant him a formal dismission; that his departure was a thing to be done and not to be talked of. This notice was perfectly satisfactory to Lord Lovat; and, being acquainted with the ideas of the Court of France, he thought no longer but of making his escape, and overlooking all the risks of his journey, in order to arrive with his brother at his own estate.

In the interim however a misfortune happened to the Marquis de la Frezeliere, which prevented the execution of his design. The Marquis was a man of the most comprehensive and insatiable ambition. He was already at the head of the artillery, of which he was hereditary first lieutenant-general, and commander in chief, wherever the grand-master of the ordnance was not present. This degree of promotion however did not satisfy him. He believed he could not so soon arrive at the truncheon of marshal of France by that path, as he might do by commanding as a general officer in the line of battle. He was now in the army of Marshal Villars, and being much esteemed by that nobleman, he obtained from him permission to command the artillery of his army, and to take rank in the line of battle at the same time.*

The talents and the superior genius of M. de la Frezeliere had excited against him many enemies in the corps of general officers. They accordingly made their complaint to the King and the Duke de Maine, grand-master of the ordnance, respecting this unusual indulgence. In compliance with their representations the King wrote to Marshal Villars, to prohibit the Marquis from taking rank as a general officer in the line of battle; observing at the same time, that it was unprecedented, and prejudicial to his service, it being impossible for M. de la Frezeliere to be at once at the head of the artillery and in the line of battle, and to give the necessary orders in these different departments. Marshal Villars, notwithstanding his particular friendship and esteem for the Marquis, was obliged to signify to him the orders of the King; and, in consequence of this prohibition, M. de la Frezeliere withdrew to his own estate under pretence of sickness.

This incident happened in the campaign of 1707. The Marquis seemed to intend to have no concern in the ensuing campaign, unless he were permitted to assume rank in the line, as well as in the artillery. To this indulgence the Duke de Maine, grand-master of the ordnance, particularly opposed himself. He was how-

ever perfectly sensible how essential it was to the 1706
service of France, that M. de la Frezeliere should be
employed. He knew, that the artillery had never been
so well served as by the Marquis, who supported the
glory and reputation of the corps, as well by the fertility
of his genius and his extreme skill in the science, as by
the very expensive and magnificent manner in which he
always appeared.

The Duke therefore took some pains to represent to
him that his father had advanced very quickly in the
road of promotion, and that he would infallibly do the
same; that his taking rank in the line would in reality
only obstruct his advancement; that he might depend
upon his good offices; and that he would give him his
word that he would push him forward, and carry his
affair, provided he remained quiet at the head of the
artillery.

The Marquis however, who had once served in the
line, had it too much at heart to give it up. He
believed that the officers would regard him as disgraced, by the affront he would sustain in being driven
from his station by the order of his sovereign. Beside,
M. de la Frezeliere was of a high and elevated spirit.
He did not pretend to be ignorant of the superior
talents he possessed in every part of the science of war.
And he could ill brook the being obliged to receive
orders from a young brigadier, or sometimes a young
colonel, fresh from the mousquetaires or the academy,

1708 to whom he might be subject, as commandant of the artillery, in marches and detachments.

Induced by all these considerations, he intreated the King, and the grand-master, to permit him to serve at the head of the artillery and in the line at the same time. He engaged to forfeit his head if the King's service suffered the smallest disaster in consequence of this permission, or in case he did not perfectly discharge the duties of both departments. If however the King and the Duke were of a different opinion, he solicited them to permit him to serve only in the line of battle, and to bestow the artillery upon any person whom they should think qualified for the command. The Duke de Maine replied positively, on the part of the King, that he would grant neither the one nor the other; but that it was necessary, that he should serve at the head of the artillery, as his father and he had always done.

To this decision the Marquis answered, that he had rather quit the service altogether, and retire to his own estate for the rest of his life, than not continue to serve in the line of battle. The grand-master, stedfast to his purpose, exerted his utmost rhetoric to convince him of his error, and to persuade him to recede; observing, at the same time, that the King would be greatly displeased, if the Marquis talked of retiring in the commencement of a campaign, and in the midst of a most extensive and destructive war. M. de la Frezeliere remained inflexible. He resolved, with somewhat

too haughty a firmness, to abide by his dilemma, and 1708
either renounce the service, or have his post in the line
confirmed to him.

The Duke de Maine, understanding that the equipage of the artillery was ready to march for the Rhine, and perceiving that he gained no ground in his endeavour to subdue the hauteur of the Marquis, became seriously offended. He sent the secretary of the ordnance to tell M. de la Frezeliere, that he allowed him only twenty-four hours to form his resolution, to assume the command of the artillery, or to refuse it, bidding him at the same time take care what he did. The Marquis piqued at an order couched in such precise and menacing language, was lead to an action, bold beyond all example, and bordering upon insanity. By way of answer to the Duke's message, he inclosed in a letter his commission of commandant of the artillery, and sent it by a courier.

The Duke de Maine conceived himself to be insulted by this step, and hastened instantly to complain of it to the King. His Majesty considered the offence as done to himself, and his service treated with contempt by this unheard of proceeding. M. de la Frezeliere was the next day thrown into the Bastile, to the astonishment of the whole kingdom of France.

The court, the ministers, the marshals of France, and in a word every person of distinction at Versailles and at Paris, took part with the Marquis, on account of his birth, his reputation, his own important services, and those of his father and his house. Many persons of the first rank solicited the King and the grand-master for his liberty. But the one and the other appeared inflexible, and the friends of M. de la Frezeliere gave him up for lost. He himself became apprehensive of the worst. The brother of Lord Lovat had resided at the Marquis's house at the arsenal, ever since the King of England had set out for Dunkirk. In his present situation the Marquis thought proper to send for him incognito to his apartment in the Bastile, and spoke to him in the following manner. 'You know, my dear chevalier, that I have extremely pressed my lord your brother, to return to his own country, persuaded that he was irretrievably ruined in France. I have even given you an order upon my steward in Anjou for whatever money Lord Lovat may want for the prosecution of his journey.

'The tables are now turned upon me. You see in what a situation I am. The King is absolute master in France, and there is nothing I have not reason to fear. If then your brother quit France in the present crisis, my enemies will not fail to tell the King, that it is in concert with me, that he is set out to join our enemies. I shall then be ruined without resource. My houses and plantations will be rased, and my family for ever annihilated. For these reasons I must intreat you, my dear chevalier, to set out immediately for your

brother at Saumur, to tell him, if he set any value upon
me as his relation and friend, or if he retain any regard
for my family and children, who bear the same name,
and are derived from one common stock with himself,
that I conjure him, by our mutual intercourse, and all
the engagements between us, not to leave France till
my fate be decided. In the mean time he may use my
seat as his own, and depend upon my sharing with him
every thing I have to the last farthing.'

The brother of Lord Lovat and the Marquis now
took leave of each other, with tears on both sides. The
Chevalier Fraser made all possible diligence to reach his
brother at Saumur, as he knew that he was preparing
for immediate escape.

In reality Lord Lovat had proposed to set out that
very week. There were at that time at Saumur several
Englishmen, who had been taken prisoners at the battle
of Almanza. Among them Lord Lovat had found a
subaltern officer in General Hervey's regiment of horse,
of the name of Jones, a man of good sense, resolution
and enterprise. To this man Lord Lovat communicated
the design he had formed of escaping from France, and
throwing himself at the feet of the Dukes of Marlborough and Argyle, to intreat them to interpose in his
favour with Queen Anne.

Mr. Jones approved of his intention, and promised
to accompany him at the hazard of his life. Apprehensive in the mean time of a discovery, Lord Lovat

1708 feared that every post might bring an order from Court, to throw him once more into the dungeon from which he had been so happily delivered. He therefore concealed himself every post-day in Mr. Jones's apartments in the suburbs, in order to avoid a surprise. At the same time he gained an intimate friend of the lieutenant, to give him early intelligence of the orders the principal received from Versailles.

Lord Lovat was thus upon the eve of setting out for England, and had provided against every hazard that might attend his undertaking. He was therefore extremely astonished, when he saw his brother, whom he expected to join at Paris, arrive at Saumur. Little had he expected such a letter as was now put into his hands from M. de la Frezeliere; dated from the Bastile, acquainting him with the great misfortune that had befallen him, and conjuring him not to quit France, till the King, moved by the intercession of his numerous friends, should grant him his liberty; adding, that, if Lord Lovat pursued his purpose in the present conjuncture, his person and family would be the victims of his unkindness, and the name of Frezel be extinguished in France.

Lord Lovat was extremely affected to learn the very unexpected misfortune of M. de la Frezeliere. He loved him as his brother; his request and his situation led him therefore to the total alteration of his design. He now resolved, rather to encounter all the calamities that could overtake him in France, than by his flight to bring on the ruin of the Marquis and his house. He wrote immediately to the Marquis, intreating him to be perfectly easy on his account, assuring him, that he was resolved rather to die in a dungeon in France, than to attempt to make his escape, till he was restored to his liberty and former situation.

Lord Lovat, being thus obliged to depart from his original plan, when the English prisoners at Saumur were exchanged, gave to his confident Mr. Jones letters for the Duke of Argyle and some other of his relations and friends. He informed them of the persecutions he had experienced on the part of the Court of St. Germains. He declared himself unalterably resolved to abandon the interests of that Court. For these reasons he intreated them to make his peace with Queen Anne; adding, that for the rest of his life it was his firm intention, to live peaceably in his own country, and to demean himself like a good and faithful subject to her Majesty.

Mr. Jones promised to deliver these letters faithfully according to their address, and at the same time to give an account to the Dukes of Marlborough and Argyle, of the essential services Lord Lovat had rendered to the English prisoners, during their residence at Saumur. Such was the first correspondence of any kind, or with any individual, that Lord Lovat had entered into in the British kingdoms since the commencement of his imprisonment and exile.

The Marquis de la Frezeliere remained only three months in the Bastile, when his Most Christian Majesty, and the whole kingdom of France found occasion for his personal services. After the unfortunate day of Oudenarde, the generals of the allies visibly threatened to besiege the rich, beautiful and important city of Lisle. As Marshal Boufflers was governor of French Flanders and the city of Lisle, he resolved to repair in person to the defence of the capital of his province. His intimate friends assured him, that M. de la Frezeliere was the first man in the world for the attack and defence of places, and had even improved in these respects upon the discoveries of Vauban. Marshal Boufflers had himself been the intimate friend of the Marquis's father, and was acquainted with the singular valour and extensive capacity of the son.

Immediately therefore upon the present occurrence, he hastened to wait upon the King, of whom he was the favourite, and who had always shown a very singular esteem for his person. 'Your Majesty,' said M. de Boufflers, 'has favoured me with your permission to have the honour of defending the city of Lisle in person. Permit me then most humbly to intreat you to give me for a second in this enterprise M. de la Frezeliere. He is not only one of the best engineers in France, but also the first man in the universe in the conduct of artillery, and a most brave and excellent officer in the affairs of war in general.'

The King had been importuned by all the marshals of France and almost every person in his court in favour of the Marquis de la Frezeliere. He was himself perfectly acquainted with the reality of his merits. His Majesty was therefore by no means displeased at the present occasion's being offered him to receive him once more into favour. He readily granted Marshal Boufflers's request. A few days after, an order was sent to the Marquis at the Bastile, to repair with all diligence to the city of Lisle, and to discharge his duty under Marshal Boufflers, as first lieutenant-general of the artillery, and major-general in the army.*

This order gave the extremest pleasure to the Marquis; and so much the more, as it had never been seen in France, that any person, whatever were his rank, should be liberated from the Bastile by an order to go and command in the armies or cities of the King's dominions, except in the case of the immortal Marshal Luxembourg, and that of the Marquis de la Frezeliere. Having received the order of the King in the close of the evening, he did not leave the Bastile; but ordered his postchaise to the gate early the next

---

* This is probably a mere expression of form, and implies titular rank, without including actual permission to serve in the line. It appears from what follows, that it did not imply the concession of M. de la Frezeliere's original demand.

morning; and, without once entering his house at the arsenal, which was but a musket-shot from the prison, he set out strait for Lisle, where he arrived in two days.

The day after his arrival he wrote a letter to Lord Lovat acquainting him with the glorious manner, in which he had been liberated from the Bastile, and restored to the good graces of his sovereign. He informed him that the enemy appeared to have the design of investing the place, but that, for himself, he regarded this enterprise as the most rash and inconsiderate that had ever been formed; that by all the rules of war the allies must perish in the attempt. At the same time he observed, that Lord Lovat was now at liberty to resume his design; that however, if he were willing to wait the termination of the siege, he hoped to render such essential services to his King, as should give him a right to expect and to obtain for that nobleman his return to the Court, and the termination of his disgrace. Lord Lovat the more willingly consented to wait the event, as he had yet heard no news of the letters he had intrusted to Mr. Jones for the Duke of Argyle and his other friends.

M. de la Frezeliere acquired immortal glory in this affair. The admirable defence of Lisle turned chiefly upon him, as well in consequence of his extraordinary capacity, as by the great confidence placed in him by M. de Boufflers. The siege being finished, he was promoted to the rank of lieutenant-general in the King's service, previous to his accompanying Marshal Boufflers in entering the citadel for the defence of that excellent fortress.

The citadel being at length, as well as the town, surrendered to the enemy, after the most obstinate and incomparable defence that has ever been made in our days, M. de Boufflers returned to Court to give an account of his trust to the sovereign. He had the goodness to observe to the King that he was entirely indebted for this admirable defence to M. de la Frezeliere, and that now he had the honour to assure his Majesty, that the Marquis was one of the best generals in his service, and that not less in campaign war, than in the attack and defence of fortresses. The King, having so much reason to be satisfied with the character that Marshal Boufflers gave of the Marquis, bestowed upon him, as a mark of his approbation, the favour, for the claim of which he had some months before been thrown into the Bastile. He gave him his orders for the ensuing campaign, to command in chief the artillery in Flanders, and to take actual rank as lieutenant-general in the line of battle.

In this campaign he perfectly did his duty in both departments. This was particularly conspicuous at the battle of Malplaquet, where the artillery was entirely well conducted, at the same time that the Marquis distinguished himself in the most honourable manner, in his post on the left wing in the line of battle. He had the happiness to have under his orders the brigade of Navarre, commanded by M. de Gassion, nephew to the lieutenant-general of that name, and heir to his valour; and the royal regiment of infantry, commanded by the Count d'Aubignè, now inspector-general and governor of Saumur, a young officer, whose courage and merit are not less distinguished than his birth. M. de la Frezeliere, with these five battalions, attacked in so vigorous a manner a large column of the allies, as entirely to defeat it, pursuing them with great carnage far beyond their intrenchments.

The success he obtained would have chained victory to the wheels of the French, if, almost at the same time, the allies had not penetrated into the centre of the line, where the regiment of French guards gave way in a very disgraceful manner. It was this circumstance, which completed in favour of the allies a glorious, though it must be confessed a most destructive victory.

They had already gained a considerable advantage over the right wing of the King's army, commanded by Marshal Villars in person. The brave Duke of Argyle, at the head of the English and Scottish infantry, entirely defeated all the infantry of this wing, driving them back into the woods which covered their flank. Marshal Villars rallied his men several times, always to no purpose; and having exposed himself too much, he received that dangerous wound in his knee, which 1709 decided the fate of the engagement on that side.

The action of M. de la Frezeliere, at the head of the brigade of Navarre, having made a great deal of noise, added considerably to his reputation, and to the esteem which the whole army had for him. The Chevalier de St. George, in order to dissipate the mortification he had experienced in the miscarriage of the Scottish enterprise, and at the same time to learn the science of war, made the campaign of Malplaquet in Villars's army. He was the first to express his respect for the Marquis, and the high opinion he had of his conduct that day. M. de la Frezeliere, on his side, made his court in the most assiduous manner to the Chevalier and his minister, Lord Middleton. He had always kept one of the best tables in the army, and he now entertained these distinguished persons several times in the most sumptuous manner.

His design in all this was to turn the esteem of the Chevalier to the immediate advantage of Lord Lovat. He addressed himself indifferently to Lord Middleton and to his master. But he found both the one and the other perfectly inexorable upon this head. He wrote immediately to Lord Lovat, assuring him that he must at no time expect any thing from the Court of St. Germains, but mortification, unworthy treatment and disgrace; and recommending to him, once more in good earnest to think of bidding a final adieu to France.

1709 Lord Lovat was satisfied, by the intelligence he received from M. de la Frezeliere and his other friends at the Court of St. Germains, that the Chevalier de St. George, the Queen and Lord Middleton had so decided a preference for the Duke of Hamilton and Lord Athol, that he had nothing to hope for from that Court, during the life of these two noblemen, of the Queen or her minister, all of them his declared enemies, but oppression and disgrace. He recurred therefore to the resolution he had formed more than twelve months before, of entirely abandoning, and surely with sufficient reason, the interests of this unjust and ungrateful court, and of returning to his own country at all adventures.

Not that the difficulties were not very great on this side. The enemies of Lord Lovat had much influence at the Court of London, as well as at St. Germains. Their honour was not less engaged than their interest, to prevent by every means in their power the return of this nobleman, their capital and personal enemy. Lord Lovat however was conscious, that his authority and credit in the north of Scotland could scarcely be regarded as an object of contempt. He knew, that he could be useful in times of war to any king or queen of England who should be able to engage his services. In fine, he was resolved to try every possible method to make his peace with Queen Anne, and for that purpose to address himself to the great nobility who directed the affairs of her Government.

Lord Lovat believed that he had met with a happy occasion for this purpose. There were six officers of the regiment of the English guards, by name Messieurs Saubergue, Brady, Bradbury, Pulteney, Hamilton and Fogg, who had been taken prisoner at the battle of Almanza, and were confined at the town of Loudun, seven leagues from Saumur. These officers had the liberty of passing from one of these places to the other, and visiting their privates who were confined at Saumur.

Lord Lovat constantly paid to these gentlemen, every possible degree of attention, and exerted in their behalf a power, which was in many respects by no means useless to them. M. de la Frezeliere's beautiful house of Anglers was only one league from Loudun, and the Marchioness residing there at that time, Lord Lovat was in a manner the child of the house. He engaged this lady, whose manners were by nature extremely polite and affable, frequently to receive these six English officers at her seat, and to entertain them in a very elegant manner.

There happened about this time an accident to these gentlemen, which serves to shew the friendship and generosity of Lord Lovat, at the same time that it was extremely ill requited in the sequel. Mr. Hamilton, for a quarrel of a straw, killed his companion, Captain Bradbury. Some people said he was to blame in the affair; others that he was innocent. Be that as it will,

Mr. Hamilton received a very considerable wound in his arm, the sword having pierced as far as the shoulder. Covered with blood, and pursued by the archers of the prevôt and judges of the town of Loudun, where he had killed Bradbury, he fled directly to Anglers. He had spent the preceding evening there in company with Lord Lovat, whom he called his cousin, being, as he said, the son of Mr. Hamilton of Hussey, and by his mother nearly related to Lord Mar, to whom Lord Lovat was also allied on the mother's side.

As soon as he arrived, he desired Lord Lovat to be called out of the castle to speak with him. Mr. Hamilton now threw himself into his arms, crying, 'My lord, I am come to ask my life of you. I have had the misfortune to kill my comrade, Captain Bradbury; I am myself severely wounded; and I am pursued by the judges and prevôt of Loudun with their archers. If I am taken, I shall infallibly lose my life. Let me beseech you then, my dear lord, to take pity upon me, and protect me in my present distress.' Lord Lovat replied, that he would do for him, as he would for his brother in his situation.

Having said this he vanished in a moment. He flew immediately to the Marchioness, and related to her the melancholy tale. He intreated her, if she had any regard for him, to receive his relation and friend into her house, and to protect him in his present deplorable condition from falling into the hands of his pursuers.

The Marchioness was at first terrified at the proposal, 1709 fearing the laws of France, and the ordinances of the King, which are extremely severe in the case of duels. Her natural temper however overflowed with generosity and compassion. She had a very high friendship for Lord Lovat. She replied, that indeed she risked much in harbouring a man, who had killed his antagonist in a duel; there was nothing however that she could refuse to Lord Lovat; he might therefore introduce Mr. Hamilton, and she would order her people immediately to prepare for him a proper apartment.

Lord Lovat instantly left the Marchioness. He brought Mr. Hamilton into the castle of Anglers. He sent with all diligence for the Sieur de la Tour, surgeon to the family, and a man of great skill in his profession. That gentleman came upon the first summons and dressed Mr. Hamilton; and pronounced his wound to be very dangerous. Lord Lovat obliged him not to leave the house till the convalescence of his patient.

The prevôt and his archers conjectured that Mr. Hamilton had taken refuge with the Marchioness de la Frezeliere, and did not adventure to enter the castle in search of him. They returned to Loudun to draw up a verbal process upon the dead body of Captain Bradbury. Mr. Hamilton in the mean time was sheltered and nursed for two months in the castle of the Marquis de la Frezeliere, as if he had been with his

T

own father. Lord Lovat did not quit him till he was perfectly recovered.

During this period the friends of the Marchioness gave her repeated information, that the prevôt and judges of Loudun threatened to advertise the Court, that she harboured in her castle Mr. Hamilton who had killed his man in a duel. Lord Lovat therefore at the end of this term was obliged to conduct Mr. Hamilton during the night, to the residence of a man of rank of his acquaintance. This person was the Marquis de Borstel, who resided about three leagues from Anglers. He was a man of much politeness and generosity, full of merit and good sense, and extremely partial to foreigners; because his father was descended from a noble house in Germany, and had been ambassador from the Elector Palatine, King of Bohemia.

M. de Borstel was the intimate friend of Lord Lovat, and from affection to him, at the hazard of his life and property, he received Mr. Hamilton, in defiance of the severe laws of France against duelling. Mr. Hamilton resided two months longer with the Marquis as if he had been the child of the house.

The seat of this nobleman was one league from Loudun, where Mr. Hamilton had a mistress. In going frequently to see her without sufficient precaution, he was at last discovered and taken by the prevôt, and thrown into prison at Loudun, where he was in much apprehension for his life. The moment

Lord Lovat had intelligence of his misfortune, he went 1709
to see and console him. He immediately interested his
friends at the Court of France in his behalf, and obtained an order to remove Mr. Hamilton from the
horrible prison of Loudun to the agreable castle of
Saumur.

As Lord Lovat resided in person at Saumur, he was
continually rendering Mr. Hamilton considerable services, not only there, but by his friends at court; till,
contrary to his own hopes, this gentleman was set at
liberty, and exchanged with the other officers of his
regiment.

Mr. Hamilton appeared extremely sensible of the
services Lord Lovat had done him. He often swore
that he should always be ready to hazard his life for the
person and interest of that nobleman; and, as he was
about to set out for England, he earnestly pressed to
be employed in doing some service for him in that
country. Lord Lovat placed an entire confidence in
him, as his relation, and a man who owed to him his
life. He communicated to him his intention, tired out
as he was with the barbarous and unremitted persecutions of the Court of St. Germains, of quitting
France; and gave him letters to the Dukes of Marlborough, Argyle and Queensberry, and to the Earls of
Wemys and Leven, his friends and relations.

In these letters Lord Lovat extolled in high terms
the condescension and goodness of the Court of France

towards him. He bitterly complained of the ingratitude and injustice of the Court of St. Germains. And he most humbly intreated these noblemen to make his peace with Queen Anne, since he desired nothing with more ardour, than to return, to restore his family and clan, and to live peaceably upon his own estate, as her Majesty's most faithful subject.

Lord Lovat delivered these letters open to Mr. Hamilton, and intreated him to communicate them to the Marquis de la Frezeliere, who commanded at that time at Valenciennes, through which Mr. Hamilton's route lay. Lord Lovat was desirous, not to do any thing, without having first taken the advice of the Marquis, who knew the intentions of the Court of France respecting him. Accordingly he requested Mr. Hamilton to leave these letters with M. de la Frezeliere; or to burn them, in case that nobleman disapproved of their being sent to the lords to whom they were addressed.

Mr. Hamilton took his leave with a thousand protestations of friendship and unalterable gratitude. When he arrived in Paris, he waited upon the Marchioness de la Frezeliere, who received him with her usual politeness, and gave him a letter for her husband at Valenciennes. But, in spite of his several promises to the Marchioness and to Lord Lovat, he passed into the conquered Netherlands without seeing M. de la Frezeliere.

Upon his arrival, his friends acquitted him, by a favourable court martial, of the death of Captain Bradbury. He afterwards passed into England; but, in the room of delivering Lord Lovat's letters according to their address, he carried them to the Duke of Hamilton and Lord Athol, his personal and declared enemies. Previously to his arrival the English administration had been changed:* the Duke of Marlborough • 1710 and the friends of Lord Lovat had begun to lose their credit with Queen Anne. The country party had been called into power. The Duke of Hamilton and Lord Athol were already among the greatest favourites. Mr. Hamilton knew that he could not better make his court to these noblemen, than by delivering up Lord Lovat to be ruined by them in France; and he believed, that by this infamous piece of treachery he should make his fortune.

The Duke of Hamilton and Lord Athol, conceiving that they had now met with an opportunity of rendering it impossible for Lord Lovat ever again to become formidable to them, carried his letters to the Earl of Mar, at that time Secretary of State for Scotland. The Earl was assailed with the united solicitations of the Duke of Hamilton, Lord Athol, and Mackenzie of Prestonhal, who enjoyed the estate of Lord Lovat, and who gave himself out for a zealous Jacobite, the better to ruin the interests of Lord Lovat at the Court of St. Germains. In compliance with their intreaties, the Earl of Mar transmitted these letters to the Court of St. Germains, by his near relation, Mr. Erskine.

This measure had nearly its entire effect. The Queen no sooner received the intelligence than she sent it by Lord Middleton to the Marquis de Torcy, by this means to establish the treason of Lord Lovat against his sovereign, and induce the King to consign him to a perpetual imprisonment. It was only, to the credit of the Marquis de la Frezeliere, and to the natural generosity of M. de Torcy, that Lord Lovat was indebted for his not being shut up between four walls for the rest of his life.

Mr. Hamilton had been indebted in a most singular manner for his life to Lord Lovat; he had promised a just return for this service, and an unalterable gratitude. In the instance I have related he did every thing that depended upon him, to destroy Lord Lovat, and to take away the life of the man to whom he owed his own. I leave it to the universe to decide upon the blackness of this treachery, and the character that is due to this monster of ingratitude.

The friends of Lord Lovat saved him from the misfortune of a perpetual imprisonment, upon this occasion. It must not however be imagined that the treachery of Mr. Hamilton had not the most unfavourable effect upon the future events of his story. From that moment the sworn enmity of the Court of St. Germains seemed to acquire new energy, and to kindle

LIFE OF LORD LOVAT.

with new hopes. The Court of France, which till this occurrence had always protected Lord Lovat, after having seen his own letters, began to believe, that there was some truth in the crimes of tergiversation and treason, which the Court of St. Germains had all along charged upon him.

He was now ruined at the Courts of St. Germains and Versailles. For himself he saw more than ever the necessity of escaping as he could, with his honour and his life out of the kingdom of France. Still however he would do nothing without consulting the Marquis de la Frezeliere, whom he regarded as his father in that country. The Marquis found his reputation and credit daily increasing at the Court of France, and he was in a perfectly good understanding with the King of England. He understood from his friends at Versailles, that the design of a Scottish insurrection was revived. Upon these circumstances he took it in his head to build the plan of a new project for Scotland, and to engage the Courts of France and St. Germains to name him commander in chief and generalissimo of the expedition.

Full of this design, he advised Lord Lovat to defer returning to his own country till he had the pleasure of seeing him; adding, that as soon as the campaign was terminated he would come to Saumur expressly for that purpose. Lord Lovat therefore waited his arrival with impatience.

About the latter end of November the Marquis de la

1709 Frezeliere, with his marchioness and family, arrived at Saumur. Lord Lovat went some leagues to meet him, and they encountered each other with marks of inexpressible friendship and tenderness on both sides. The Marquis was received at Saumur with a salute of cannon, and every testimony of honour and celebrity. After having remained some days in this city, he conducted Lord Lovat and his brother to the pleasant castle of Anglers, where all of them passed the winter together.

It was here that M. de la Frezeliere disclosed to Lord Lovat the idea he had indulged. He knew the credit and influence that nobleman possessed in Scotland. He was satisfied, that he was more intimately acquainted with the affairs of that country, and with all that regarded the Court of St. Germains, than those that were most active in its concerns. He therefore endeavoured to engage Lord Lovat to co-operate in digesting a new project for Scotland. But it was not easy to overcome the repugnance of his friend, to lead him to suspend the very different ideas and designs he had formed, and to induce him to take a share in any scheme, that concerned and involved the interests of his persecutors.

To his objections the Marquis answered by protesting, that his grand object was the restoration of Lord Lovat to his clan in the most honourable manner; that, if the King of France approved of his scheme, he

would himself be named to conduct the enterprise; and 1709
that the Court of St. Germains would be well pleased
with the appointment, since he was upon better terms
with the King of England than any lieutenant-general
in the service; that, when the enterprise should be executed, Lord Lovat might depend upon being employed
as a general officer of France, and next to himself in
conducting the expedition, and in all the honours and
advantages that could result from it.

Induced by the representations and the wishes of
M. de la Frezeliere, Lord Lovat consented to lay aside
the disgust and resentment, that had been excited in
his breast by the ill usage of the Court of St. Germains.
He entered afresh upon the detail of the information,
subservient to a Scottish project. He was won over by
his perfect persuasion of the sincerity of the Marquis's
friendship and affection to him, and by the character
he bore with all the world of being one of the ablest
generals existing.

Lord Lovat stated in a very accurate and particular
manner all that might be expected from the Highlanders of Scotland, from the loyal inhabitants of the
Lowlands, and from several districts in the north of
England. He gave a precise description, of the situation and nature of the whole country from the remotest
mountains of Scotland to the Tweed; of the degrees of
subsistence this country could furnish to an army; and
of all the passages and defiles that such an army might

1709 seize, in order to hinder the enemy from entering into their fastnesses, and to guard themselves from the danger of surprise.

Lord Lovat gave a copy of the project he had delineated to M. de la Frezeliere; who had a particular talent at digesting plans for a campaign. He therefore took as much from that nobleman's plan as he judged proper, and formed, from all the documents in his hands, a general project for the enterprise, containing an excellent enumeration of every thing that was necessary for the expedition, what troops, officers, arms, money, ammunition and provisions. He added to this a detail of what the King of England might do after his arrival in the north of Scotland, in spite of the resistance of his enemies; and of the proper routes for an army to pursue, from the Highlands to Edinburgh, and from Edinburgh to London.

1710 This plan, which was extremely beautiful and well digested, the Marquis carried to court; and, it being first approved by the minister, it was afterwards shown to the Most Christian King. His Majesty was much pleased with it. He ordered his servants, to labour incessantly at completing the necessary preparations, which was accordingly done with great diligence. Indeed had the enemy delayed for ten days the siege of Douay, the King of England would have sailed a second time for his dominions.

It seemed however as if this prince had always been

followed by an unfortunate star. Marshal Villars had 1710 consented to spare six thousand men, and 1,600,000 francs*, from what had been stipulated between him and the administration for the ensuing campaign in Flanders; so great was his partiality to the interests of the King of England. In a very short time however before that which was fixed upon for the expedition, he received a courier from the frontiers, with intelligence of the investiture of Douay, which entirely overthrew the project of Scotland. He was now obliged to employ the troops and money destined for this enterprise, in forming an army with all speed in Flanders, to endeavour to raise the siege. And such was the unfortunate success of the arms of his master in this and the following campaign, that the Court of France were no longer able to think of a Scottish insurrection.

At the time that the enemy advanced to form the 1711 siege of Bouchain, the Marquis de la Frezeliere commanded a separate camp of about thirty thousand men. He made a rapid march to arrive before them to the passage of a river a few leagues from Bouchain. Being arrived with his whole army, before the enemy had been able to pass more than a small part of their troops, and conceiving that he had met with a valuable opportunity for cutting them in pieces, he immediately drew up his forces in order of battle, and advanced to attack them. At this moment two *aides de camp* arrived one after the

---
* 66,666*l.*

other from Marshal Villars, with orders to M. de la Frezeliere not to attack the enemy.

The Marquis, who saw victory within his grasp, and was presented with a favourable occasion for annihilating the allied army, instantly dispatched a general officer to Marshal Villars, to tell him, that he could not undertake to answer with his head, as a good servant of the King, the not attacking the enemy with so manifest an advantage. Villars, who was perfectly acquainted with the merit and enterprise of M. de la Frezeliere, and convinced that he would not fail to beat the enemy, came himself upon a full gallop to prevent the encounter.

The Marquis was in the utmost degree enraged at so great a disappointment. He had spent the four preceding days without sleep, almost without food, in a constant march towards the enemy. Being at once oppressed by fatigue and agitated with disappointment, he fell dangerously ill.

Not only the whole army, but all France cried out upon Marshal Villars for having failed to improve so admirable an occasion, of ruining the allied army. They knew not that he had secret orders, not to attack the enemy at whatever advantage, peace being already privately concluded between Louis XIV. and Queen Anne. This indeed appeared in the most indubitable manner in the sequel of the present campaign, and in the campaign of Denain that followed it,

The Marquis de la Frezeliere died of the distemper he contracted in the neighbourhood of Bouchain. He was extremely regretted, not only by the King, who publicly declared that he had lost in him one of the best officers in his service, but also by the whole Court. The marshals of France, the army, and indeed the whole kingdom, were afflicted with the loss of an officer, equally distinguished by his skill in campaign war, by the fertility of his genius, and his knowledge in the science of artillery.

By his death Lord Lovat lost his support, his consolation under misfortunes, and all the hopes he indulged of living either agreably or honourably in the kingdom of France. M. de la Frezeliere indeed bequeathed him as a mark of his affection, his daughter in marriage, with a considerable part of his estate as a portion. But the lady being extremely young, Lord Lovat regarded the marriage as impracticable. He had lost every thing, that had hitherto bound him to France and suspended his resolutions, and he thought no longer but of returning to his own country.

SECT. IV.

1711 IT was the Countess de la Roche Millaye, widow of the cousin-german of M. de la Frezeliere, who announced to him the Marquis's death. In this melancholy letter she had the goodness to offer to Lord Lovat, as he had lost a relation who had loved him with the affection of a brother, to put herself in the place of the Marquis, and to render that nobleman every service in her power, as his good friend and relation by marriage.

Lord Lovat shed many tears when he received this letter, and the death of the Marquis so greatly overwhelmed him, that from sorrow and dejection it almost seemed as if he would not have survived his friend. He was indeed extremely ill for several weeks.

When he recovered, he wrote to Madame de la Roche Millaye to conjure her to grant him her friendship and good offices at the Courts of France and St. Germains; adding, that he had now no longer any other relation in France, and that she was the only person capable of doing him service at Court. Upon the receipt of this letter the Countess assured Lord

Lovat anew, that he might absolutely depend upon her friendship.

In reality from that time the Countess de la Roche acted towards Lord Lovat as if he had been her brother, rather than her friend and relation by marriage. She was indeed extremely capable of rendering him the most essential services. She was not only upon good terms with the ministers, but also with all the princes and princesses of the blood. She had been born and educated at the house of the *grand Condé;* and had served for more than twenty years as lady of honour to the Princess de Conti, daughter of that hero.

Assuredly the Countess de la Roche was perfectly qualified to be near the person of a queen or a princess of the blood. She was endowed by nature with a masculine and spirited character, and was capable of affairs of the first order. She had but one passion: it was that of ambition. And she would have arrived at the greatest honours, if her star had been as happy, as her genius was admirable.

She had an acute and penetrating understanding; she had read much, and was endowed with an astonishing memory. She was particularly acquainted with the conduct of suits at law, and the science of an advocate, in which she did not fall short of those, who had been regularly admitted in the parliament of Paris. It was this circumstance, which made her the heroine of the great suit between the Duke de Bourbon Condé, and his three sisters, the Princess de Conti, and the Duchesses de Vendôme, and de Maine.

To these rare accomplishments she united a disposition, bold, politic and insinuating, which frequently engaged her in the most delicate and hazardous intrigues of the Court. But what rendered her agreable to all the world, was an easy and astonishing eloquence, which captivated all who had the honour to know her, and was the almost infallible instrument of her attaining those points, which she seriously and perseveringly pursued.

1713 Lord Lovat had need of an advocate and friend not less able and sincere than Madam de la Roche. Peace being made public between France and England, the King named the Duke d'Aumont for his ambassador extraordinary to the Court of London: Queen Anne on her side appointed the Duke of Hamilton to represent her to the Most Christian King.

The Duke, as being brother in law to Lord Athol, had become one of the most inveterate enemies of Lord Lovat. He was considered as the leader of the tory party, and was in perfect good understanding with the Court of St. Germains, who believed him strenuous in his exertions for their restoration. Lord Lovat was with reason apprehensive of the arrival of the new ambassador at the Court of Versailles. He believed, that, by uniting his effort to the intrigues of the Court of St. Germains, the Duke would at length obtain of the Court of

France the great object of which his enemies never lost 1712 sight, his imprisonment for life.

Agitated by these apprehensions, Lord Lovat wrote his sentiments upon the subject to the Countess de la Roche, assuring her, that he was resolved to make his escape from France with whatever danger, rather than spend the remainder of his life in a prison; and intreating her to obtain for him certain intelligence of the sentiments of the Court of France in his behalf.

The Countess failed not to sound the administration, and talked very seriously respecting him to the minister. She wrote to Lord Lovat, as the result of her conference, that he had nothing to fear from the arrival of the Duke of Hamilton; that, should the ambassador demand it, the Court of France would never commit Lord Lovat to a close imprisonment; that, on the contrary, the minister had promised to exert the influence he flattered himself he possessed with the Duke of Hamilton, to reconcile him to Lord Lovat; and that neither she nor M. de Torcy entertained any doubt respecting their success. This advice afforded some degree of consolation to Lord Lovat, but his fears were not entirely dissipated, till the public papers announced the fatal duel, fought at London between the Duke of Hamilton and Lord Mohun.

In the person of the Duke of Hamilton Lord Lovat saw the destruction of his most formidable enemy; but he was both touched and afflicted at his death. The

1712 Duke was a man of high courage, and his personal qualities were such, that he might naturally have adorned the annals of his country, and been respected as a person of a superior order to the latest posterity. But his unparalleled avarice debased his character, annihilated all the fine qualities of his mind, and rendered him so unpopular with the whole body of his countrymen, and even with his personal friends, that there was nothing but the tragical manner of his death, which could have rendered his memory lamented in Scotland.

1713 After the death of the Duke of Hamilton, Lord Lovat believed that Athol would have less credit with the Court of St. Germains. He therefore supposed he might easily make his peace with that Court, or at least obtain permission to return to his own country. With this view he made fresh application to the Court of France, in whose breast it was, to detain him in prison, or to set him at full liberty.

He employed in this business a person for whom the Marquis de Torcy, in whose hands he had always been, and who had given him successive proof of his goodness, had much regard and esteem. It was Abbé Pouget, a priest of the oratory, and the favourite and friend of M. Colbert, Bishop of Montpelier and brother of M. de Torcy. The Abbé was a man of extensive learning, but better qualified to correct and new model breviaries, a business in which he met with great success, than to direct and manage intrigues of state. Though he were

a man of integrity, and by his labours very useful to his 1713
fraternity, he was at the same time so full of himself
and his books, that he often preferred the applauses of
those who flattered his publications to his own interests,
always to those of his friends.

Lord Lovat had the misfortune to employ Abbé
Pouget, being drawn in by the boasts that he made of
his extraordinary influence over the Marquis de Torcy.
In the room however of rendering any good offices to
Lord Lovat with that minister, he prejudiced him more
in his good opinion, than the Court of St. Germains had
been able to do in the course of its persevering efforts.
And this happened more from imbecility than malice:
for Lord Lovat has always believed, that the Abbé was
incapable of perpetrating a malicious action. His letters
however, all of which are still in being, proved but too
unquestionably how weakly he conducted himself in this
affair.

Soon after his arrival at Paris M. Pouget wrote to
Lord Lovat, that he had an audience of the Marquis de
Torcy upon his account; that the minister had declared,
he was persuaded of his innocence, and of his good and
faithful services to his own king and to France, that
this had engaged him constantly to enlist himself among
his friends, that his misfortunes originated solely in the
Court of St. Germains, that, if that Court were reconciled to him, the Court of France would be willing and
ready to give him his liberty and promote his interests,

1713 and that M. Pouget ought himself to wait upon the Queen's administration, to learn decidedly what they had to alledge against Lord Lovat; adding, that, if they could not prove something essential against him, he would apply to the King his master, to release him from prison, and recal him to Court.

To this letter Lord Lovat returned an immediate answer. He thanked Abbé Pouget for the favour he had done him in speaking to M. de Torcy; observing at the same time, that he was extremely mortified, that the Marquis had made any thing that he should do in his behalf, turn upon his being first justified by his inveterate enemies at the Court of St. Germains. He told M. Pouget, that he was persuaded of his zeal, and impressed with the warmest sense of his exertions; but he intreated him not to expose himself, by interposing in his behalf with that Court, till Lord Lovat had first endeavoured to soften the aversion of the Queen and her minister, by the Countess de la Roche Millaye, and his other friends at the Court of France.

He observed, that, if this previous step were not taken, he would be obliged to hear an infinity of falshoods and calumnies against him; that indeed he did not fear their making any impression upon a man of his understanding and penetration, but that it might be injudicious, to reduce himself to the necessity of repeating to the Marquis de Torcy, the fictions of Lord Middleton and his creatures.

This reasoning made no impression upon M. Pouget. 1713 He replied, that his visit to the Court of St. Germains would be of the utmost use to Lord Lovat; that for his own part, he did not entertain the smallest doubt of bringing over Lord Middleton and his other enemies, and of making his peace with the Queen; that in all events he had no mischievous consequences to apprehend from this step, since the Marquis de Torcy was already convinced of his loyalty and innocence. He therefore begged pardon of Lord Lovat, for deviating in this instance from his instructions, and resolutely taking a step, which could produce nothing but benefit. The truth is, the good Abbé was so full of his own judgment and penetration, and so impatient of any delay in the pleasure he proposed to himself of presenting his catechism of Montpelier, lately published, and which had so great success in the world, to Lord Perth and Lord Middleton, that all the remonstrances Lord Lovat could make were incapable of diverting him from his purpose.

His visit produced all the ill effects that Lord Lovat expected from it. Such was his agent's imbecility, that he was smitten in the extremest degree with the great compliments and high applauses that Lord Perth and Lord Middleton bestowed upon his performance and abilities. In return, he could not refuse to give implicit credit, to the calumnies they repeated to him against Lord Lovat. Accordingly, he felt himself obliged to take a second step, more simple and more injurious than the former. He hastened to the Marquis de Torcy, to repeat to him, as facts, the evidence of which was undoubted, the detestable fictions that had just been communicated to him. That this was the case, is unquestionably certain from the letter Abbé Pouget wrote to Lord Lovat after his return from St. Germains.

He told his correspondent, that he had been received in the most polite manner by Lord Perth and Lord Middleton; that he had found these two noblemen equally accomplished in science and good breeding; that they had bestowed unbounded commendations upon his performance, and had loaded his person with instances of their condescension. He observed, that in the mean time he was extremely sorry to be obliged to tell Lord Lovat, that he had heard and seen various things relating to him, which condemned him in the most unanswerable manner, but the particulars of which he was not at liberty to discover, as they related to State affairs. He added, that he was still further mortified to be obliged to inform him, that, having waited upon the Marquis de Torcy immediately after his return from St. Germains, he had found the opinion of the minister totally altered; M. de Torcy had assured him, that he was now perfectly satisfied of the guilt of Lord Lovat, and absolutely resolved to have nothing more to do with his affairs,

The Abbé concluded, that he was *au desespoir* to tell him, that, as he now saw him ruined without redemption, and for ever at the two courts, he must beg leave to decline any further concern, either directly or indirectly, in his affairs: that, as his friend, he thought himself obliged to observe that Lord Lovat had no other choice left, than to enter into a convent for life. Upon this subject the Abbé made a sermon, and with this moral wound up his letter.

Lord Lovat preserves this epistle as one of the choicest morsels that all his adventures have afforded him. In the mean time it may be remarked, that fourteen days had not elapsed between the date of this letter, and that which M. Pouget had written, to tell Lord Lovat that the Marquis de Torcy was convinced of his loyalty and innocence. And in this fortnight, in which so great an alteration had taken place in the sentiments of M. de Torcy, it does not appear that any person had spoken to him in relation to Lord Lovat, except Abbé Pouget.

Lord Lovat was extremely afflicted with the ill conduct of the Abbé, and particularly mortified to perceive, that by his blunders he had lost the friendship and good opinion of M. de Torcy. With regret he wrote upon the subject to the Marquis; at the same time addressing a second letter to the Countess de la Roche Millaye, intreating her to endeavour to recover for him the acquittal and approbation, that had hitherto belonged to him in the judgment of M. de Torcy. He observed to the Countess, that she was acquainted with the real state of every part of his conduct, and that the Marquis ought rather to give credit to her representations on the part of Lord Lovat, than to what had been reported to him by the Reverend Father Pouget, who only retailed the accusations of Lord Middleton, his declared enemy.

The Countess in return to this letter blamed Lord Lovat for having trusted his affairs in the hands of an ecclesiastic, who was more fit to superintend the discipline of a convent, than to conduct an intrigue of State. At the same time she intreated him not to be discouraged by his ill success, as she did not doubt that she should be able to restore things to their former condition with respect to the Marquis de Torcy. This assurance afforded some consolation to Lord Lovat; but he was still in the highest degree anxious about his fate, and he longed with the extremest ardour to return to his own country.

About this time the King bestowed the Abbey de St. Florent near Saumur, upon Monseigneur de Crillon, Bishop of Vence, and now Archbishop of Vienne in Dauphiné. His reverence was therefore obliged to take a journey to Saumur, in order to be inducted into his appointment. Lord Lovat profited of this occasion to make his court to this great prelate. He took the liberty to offer him his carriage, the Bishop having come by water to Saumur, and consequently having

brought no equipage along with him. M. de Crillon 1713
received Lord Lovat with all possible politeness, and
manifested great respect for him during some months
that he spent at Saumur.

All who have the honour to be acquainted with the
Archbishop of Vienne, know that he is not less distinguished by his personal merit, than by his illustrious
birth. He is acknowledged by the whole kingdom, not
more for a good theologian, than for an intelligent
politician, and an able courtier. Lord Lovat knew
that this prelate was the intimate friend of the Marquis de Torcy, and of his first secretary, M. Adam.
He had conducted the King's affairs in the states of
Provence for many years, and this province being in
the department of M. de Torcy, that circumstance gave
occasion to a great intimacy between the minister and
the Bishop of Vence.

Lord Lovat, acquainted with these circumstances,
and being offered by this amiable prelate his good
offices with M. de Torcy, earnestly intreated him,
when he returned to Paris, to solicit his recal to
Court, or the minister's permission for him to return
into his own country. The Bishop of Vence promised
to exert himself for that purpose; and indeed, from the
period of his residence at Saumur, he has always continued the sincere and generous friend of Lord Lovat.
He spoke so often, and in so spirited a manner in his
favour to the Marquis de Torcy, that the minister at
length replied, 'If Lord Lovat has property and rela-

tions in Scotland, as he says he has; why, in the devil's name, does he not go thither? He will never experience any thing but disgrace and persecution on the part of the Court of St. Germains, and the Court of France will at no time be able to serve him, in opposition to the King and Queen of England and their minister.'

As the Bishop of Vence did not think proper to write this last reply of M. de Torcy, he commissioned a gentleman of distinction, who lived at Saumur, and was then at Paris, to relate it by word of mouth.

The person intrusted with this commission was M. de Valliere, lieutenant to the marshals of France, and who had a very noble house in Saumur. He had done the King distinguished service, and had been governor of the town and castle of Annecy in Savoy during the last war. His brother, Major-General de Valliere, had been one of the best officers of foot in France, and was commander in chief of the forces in Savoy for many years. Upon his death he left one hundred thousand crowns[*] to the governor of Annecy, and this legacy placed him in a condition to do perfectly well the honours of Saumur. He was extremely hospitable both to Frenchmen and foreigners, and he was the first person that took notice of Lord Lovat upon his arrival. He afterwards rendered him essential services, and continued his sincere and intimate friend during the whole period of his exile.

---
[*] 12,500*l*.

As he was also the friend of the Bishop of Vence, 1713 who knew him for a man of honour and probity, this prelate did not hesitate, to intreat him to persuade Lord Lovat to follow the advice of the Marquis de Torcy. M. de Valliere faithfully discharged his commission, and as he was a man of great sense and ingenuity, and Lord Lovat was well satisfied of his good-will towards him, he was able fully to persuade that nobleman to make a final effort, to escape from France, and be no longer the victim of an unjust and inexorable court.

The Countess de la Roche in the mean time wrote to him to have patience; that she was taking measures to gain over the Queen of England; and that he ought by no means to think of quitting France, without the permission of the Court of St. Germains, at a time when Queen Anne was resolved, and was taking every necessary measure to restore her brother to his throne. She added, that all the world believed, that the King would set out without delay for Scotland, where every thing was prepared to receive him; and that in such a moment to pass into that country without his permission, must certainly produce irretrievable ruin.

In deference to the representations of so respectable a friend, Lord Lovat thought himself obliged to delay his departure for a short time. Meanwhile he resolved to send Mr. John Fraser, his brother, immediately into Scotland, to put himself at the head of his clan, and to act for Lord Lovat's interests, whatever might be the situation of the kingdom.

In pursuance of this determination he wrote an account of his design to the Court of France. His brother at the same time wrote to Lord Perth, that, having been ill treated in France for ten years, he was at length resolved, whatever were the consequences, to return to his own country, and to support the rights of his birth and his family against every one who should oppose them. Lord Lovat received no answer from the Court of France. He therefore embarked his brother on board a vessel bound from the port of Nantes to Edinburgh.

Soon after Mr. John Fraser's departure, the Countess de la Roche advised Lord Lovat, that she intended to pass the winter at her castle of Gigieux near Saumur; that she hoped he would spend some time with her in that place, and that then they would consult together respecting what was proper to be done in his affairs.

At the very time this letter came to Lord Lovat's hands, Cardinal Gualterio, his great friend and patron, arrived from Italy; and a report was propagated, that he had come to France to receive the appointment of prime minister to the Most Christian King. This intelligence gave new life to the hopes of Lord Lovat. Sure he was, that, if Cardinal Gualterio, his intimate friend and most unfailing protector, were declared prime minister of the kingdom, his recal to Court would speedily follow, and he should infallibly make a 1713 brilliant fortune in France.

Animated by these hopes, he dispatched memorials stating the innocence of his conduct, and the barbarity of his enemies, to the Countess de la Roche and the Marquis de Callieres, intreating these two generous friends to address the Cardinal in his favour, and to put into his own hands a copy of his memorial.

In this paper Lord Lovat took Cardinal Gualterio himself to witness the rectitude of his most essential actions, from the day that he co-operated with his Eminence in the project of Scotland, to the period of his disgrace and imprisonment; and concluded with intreating the Cardinal to obtain for him one of three things; his reconciliation with the Court of St. Germains, the consent of the King of France to his serving in one of his armies, or, lastly, permission to return into his own country and make his peace with the reigning government.

M. de Callieres, who was indisputably the best friend in the world, spoke in a very earnest manner to Cardinal Gualterio in favour of Lord Lovat. He wrote by Madame de la Roche, who came into Anjou, that his Eminence had promised him, to go to Bar-le-duc, and to make a strong representation to the King of England, in order to obtain the recal of his lordship.

The Countess de la Roche Millaye no sooner arrived at her castle of Gigieux, than Lord Lovat

1713 hastened to pay his respects to her; and she received him as if she had been his sister, rather than his friend. As she had an infinite deal of wit and good sense, her company was the greatest consolation Lord Lovat could experience in the melancholy situation of his affairs.

Madame de la Roche now acquainted him in detail with her efforts in his favour at the Court of St. Germains. She had engaged her friend, Father Chamillard of the Society of Jesus, to gain over Father Ruga, confessor to the Queen, to exert himself to restore Lord Lovat to her Majesty's favour. At the same time she employed Father Chamillard, to give a copy of Lord Lovat's memorial to Father Ruga, in order to have it presented to the Queen, and to learn her Majesty's sentiments respecting it.

Father Chamillard, indeed, who was cousin-german to the minister of that name, and a man of perfect politeness and good breeding, had written to Lord Lovat, that he was extremely happy to have had this opportunity of showing his esteem for him; that he had given his memorial to Father Ruga, with a proper recommendation and explanations, and that a few days after, that father told him, he had perfectly discharged his commission in the affair. He added, that her Majesty had answered, that Lord Lovat need only to have a little patience, that he was detained merely for political reasons, and that every thing should shortly be done for him that he could possibly wish.

This answer afforded but slender consolation to 1713 Lord Lovat, the Queen having employed nearly the same words in writing to the Marquis de la Frezeliere six years before, without Lord Lovat's having ever experienced any good effects from it.

To the account of her very friendly exertions in this affair, the Countess de la Roche added a long and clear explanation of the designs of Queen Anne and her ministers, and above all of Harley Earl of Oxford, to restore the young King of England to his throne. She observed that no person doubted of the auspiciousness of the event, unless some sudden misfortune should happen to Queen Anne, or her minister: and that therefore Lord Lovat would be an idiot to declare himself against this prince, at a time when all the world regarded his restoration as certain.

It was nearly certain at the same time that Lord Lovat received many letters from a gentleman of his clan in London, to inform him, that, though his enemies were very powerful in the Court of Queen Anne, yet if he were willing to distribute a thousand crowns * among the secretaries of the Earl of Oxford and Lord Bolingbroke, he might, by their means, and by the management and intrigues of one Bromfield, a famous quaker, who had followed King James into France, and who was in a perfect understanding with Lords Oxford and Bolingbroke, obtain his pardon. He

* 125*l*.

asserted, that these ministers were endeavouring to enlist in their party the most powerful nobility in Scotland, to support the great design they had in hand; and that they would, of consequence, be extremely glad to engage Lord Lovat in their favour, who was the head of one of the most considerable clans in Scotland.

Lord Lovat replied, that, however favourable the situation of affairs might appear, he was well assured, that his enemies were so powerful in the Court of Queen Anne, that it would be vain to attempt any thing of the kind. In the mean time he added, that, if his relation thought money would effect the business, he was ready to give, not one, but two or three thousand crowns, whenever it should be completed, in order to convince his clan that he spared nothing, to return to his country, and to put himself at their head.

Some time after Lord Lovat's relation advised him, that Mr. Bromfield had spoken in an urgent manner to Lord Bolingbroke; that the minister had replied, that Lord Lovat was considered as so ill disposed towards the Court of St. Germains, that he could not be trusted; but that, if he were desirous of obtaining his pardon and the friendship of the English ministry, he could not do better than to put himself without delay at the head of his clan, and be the first to appear for his young sovereign, in which case justice would infallibly be done him.

LIFE OF LORD LOVAT. 805

During this petty transaction Lord Lovat received 1714 information from Mr. John Fraser his brother in the north of Scotland, that the lairds of the Highland clans, and the other friends of the Pretender, were holding various meetings; that they had received, and distributed among them arms and ammunition; that they were preparing to embody themselves; and that they expected with impatience the arrival of the Pretender in the north, in order to range themselves under his standard. He related, that his clan had earnestly pressed him to inform Lord Lovat, that they were extremely alarmed at all these movements in their neighbours, while they were yet uninstructed what party to take; and that they most earnestly besought him to come and place himself at their head, now that they were upon the eve of a period when the whole kingdom would be full of war and confusion.

Till Lord Lovat should arrive, his brother intreated his directions in regard to the conduct he should hold, since he found that the Duke of Gordon, Lord Athol, Lord Mar, and other noblemen of the party of the Pretender, and who had much influence at the Court of Queen Anne, had declared themselves his enemies, and had given orders to all the troops in Scotland to take him, dead or alive, believing that he was inlisted in the party of Hanover, and had been sent thither to support that interest.

Lord Lovat advised his brother, since these noble-

x

1714 men persecuted him in so cruel and unjust a manner, to throw himself immediately upon the Duke of Argyle. There had been, he observed, from the earliest periods of history, a strict alliance between the houses of Argyle and Lovat: the only conduct therefore that was proper in the present situation, was to call upon the Duke of Argyle to protect him and his clan; assuring him, in the name of their chieftain, that they would at all times be ready to hazard their lives with him, as their ancestors had so often done with his. He declared, he was well satisfied, that the Duke of Argyle, who was a nobleman of strong understanding, great bravery and acknowledged merit, would not refuse, in consideration of the essential services, which they had rendered to his ancestors, and were capable of rendering to himself in this dangerous conjuncture, to take the family of Lovat and the clan of the Frasers under his protection.

He concluded, that his brother ought not to be discouraged, that the time would soon be most favourable for them, that he would without fail hasten to join him, as soon as he could do it with the least appearance of safety, and that he therefore earnestly intreated him, to defend with firmness and resolution his country and his clan till his arrival.

While Lord Lovat was in this extreme agitation, he employed an officer of the Royal Light Horse, his intimate friend, and to whom he had been first introduced by the Countess de la Roche, to watch the return of

Cardinal Gualterio from Bar-le-duc, and to put into his 1714 hands a letter from Lord Lovat, intreating his Eminence to communicate to the bearer the final decision of that Court respecting him. The name of this officer was M. de Grange Rouge, a man of courage and good sense.

As soon as this gentleman knew that the Cardinal was returning to Court, and was assured that he would immediately set out for Italy, he repaired without delay to the royal apartments at Fontainebleau. Having found the Cardinal, he took the liberty to request a moment's audience. His Eminence going aside with him, M. de Grange Rouge put into his hands Lord Lovat's letter, and said as much as the short time would permit in his favour.

The Cardinal whispered the officer, that he must beg of him to assure Lord Lovat, that he was as much his friend as ever, that no man knew better than he the injustice that was done him, that he had spoken in strong terms to the King of England at Bar-le-duc in his favour, but that things were not yet ripe for the reconciliation he so ardently desired. He observed, that he was extremely sorry not to be able to write to Lord Lovat, but that the Queen of England had pressed and obliged him to promise that he would not. He however intreated the officer to give Lord Lovat a verbal assurance, that his Eminence would not forget him, that he begged him to have patience, that he would not fail to protect him, and that he would make his peace with the King and Queen of England, when things should be sufficiently ripe for that purpose.

The officer replied, that he was told, his Eminence was upon the point of setting out for Italy, and that then he would be at too great a distance to be able to serve Lord Lovat. The Cardinal said, it was true he was going to Rome, but that he should be equally, in Italy and in France, the minister of the King of England; and that it would not be less easy for him to restore the affairs of Lord Lovat when absent, than when present. His Eminence then intreated him to make him a thousand compliments on his part, and took leave of the officer with that complacent and affable manner which was natural to him.

M. de Grange Rouge, having received this answer from Cardinal Gualterio, came by an ordinary leave of absence to the estate in Tourraine. From thence he hastened to wait upon the Countess de la Roche at her castle of Gigieux, where he met Lord Lovat and the Marquis de Saché, the Countess's son, who was upon a visit to his own estates in Anjou and Tourraine.

This gentleman had no sooner given an account of his commission, than Lord Lovat was perfectly convinced, that, since Cardinal Gualterio had not been able to effect his restoration, he had nothing hereafter to hope from the Courts of France, St. Germains and Bar-le-duc. He therefore endeavoured to persuade

Madame de la Roche, that there was nothing left for him, but to return immediately into the Highlands, whatever were the consequence. The Countess, who had much affection and regard for Lord Lovat, set herself to oppose this design with much energy. She said, with some heat, that it would be the extreme of madness to precipitate himself into Scotland in the midst of danger, without having first obtained the consent, either of the Court of France, or the King of England.

M. de Callieres now wrote to Madame de la Roche, that, notwithstanding his sincere efforts, he was not able at this time to obtain for Lord Lovat, either his reconciliation with the Court of St. Germains, permission to serve in the armies of the King of France, or leave to return into his own country; that there was therefore no other part for him to take, but to wait with patience the decision of the fate of the King of England.

The Countess put this letter into the hands of Lord Lovat, and, considering it as a new reinforcement of her own sentiments, she repeated, that it was impossible to think of any other conduct, at a time when nobody doubted of His Majesty's speedy restoration; adding, that, if he would yet remain a short time in France, she was persuaded that she should be able completely to restore him to the favour of both Courts.

Lord Lovat permitted himself to be influenced by

the reasoning, and governed by the counsels of Madame de la Roche. He spent a great part of his time at her seat till she set out upon her return to Paris, in Easter week, 1714. Some days after her arrival, apprehensive perhaps that Lord Lovat might recur to his own ideas, she urged upon him by letter to have patience, and that she had no doubt but every thing would terminate in the most auspicious manner.

Lord Lovat was still agitated by the most tragical apprehensions on the side of Scotland, and with very feeble and glimmering hopes on the part of the two Courts of France and St. Germains. In this situation he was most agreably surprised to see one of the principal gentlemen of his clan, with a Fraser, his attendant, arrive at Saumur about the beginning of July 1714. To have with him a man of courage and understanding, who had been constantly with the Frasers from the beginning of their troubles, and who could give him an exact and particular account of every thing that respected them, was a circumstance, as happy, as it had been totally unforeseen by him.

The gentleman in question was James Fraser of Castle Lader, son of Malcolm Fraser of Culduthel, the head of a very considerable branch of the house of Lovat, which was composed of some of the bravest gentlemen in the world, and had uniformly distinguished itself, during the whole period of their present adversity, by a zeal for the person and interest of Lord Lovat. In this cause they had lost their property, and were continually 1714 in danger of their lives. In spite however of these discouragements, and of the rigorous and unremitted ill treatment of Lord Athol and Mackenzie of Prestonhal, the usurper of their clanship, they uniformly persevered in their original sentiments.

Mr. James Fraser brought Lord Lovat a letter from Mr. John Fraser his brother, and the principal gentlemen of his clan; repeating anew their consternation at his absence, the fierce threats that were thrown out against them by the Highland lairds of the Jacobite party, and their daily expectation of the arrival of their King from France.

James Fraser observed to Lord Lovat, that it was the opinion of the principal persons of his clan, and of his other relations and friends, that he should join himself to the Duke of Argyle, in consideration of the ancient friendship between their houses; since, as the Duke of Argyle was one of the first nobility in Scotland, and a general of high courage and reputation, there was no doubt he would always have a strong party with him, and would be able to make good conditions for himself and his followers, whatever might be the resolutions of the government of the two kingdoms.

James Fraser added, that in passing through London he had seen Sir James Campbel of Arkinglass and Mr. John Forbes of Culloden, both of them members of

1714 the parliament of Great-Britain, and most affectionately attached to Lord Lovat and his house. They protested to James Fraser, that his chief had not in the world any other measure to adopt, than that of coming into that country without delay, to hold himself and his clan ready for the service of the Duke of Argyle, who was the only man in Great Britain, capable of supporting him against all his enemies. They proposed to him to wait upon the Duke: to which James Fraser replied, that, though he had no instructions for that purpose, he should be happy to pay his duty to his Grace, or to receive from their mouth his Grace's sentiments on the subject of his chief, previous to his journey into France to attend him.

Sir James Campbel and Mr. Forbes of Culloden accordingly spoke to the Duke of Argyle. They reported to James Fraser the words of this nobleman, who intreated him to assure Lord Lovat, that he was perfectly disposed to render service to him and his clan; that, the enemies of Lord Lovat and the house of Argyle being the same, he could not do better than join himself to his party; and that, if he were willing seriously to resolve to hazard his life and fortune with him, he protested upon the honour of a gentleman, that he would be equally faithful in return. Sir James Campbel and Mr. Forbes desired Mr. Fraser to report this message to his chief, and warmly pressed him to persuade Lord Lovat to take that party.

LIFE OF LORD LOVAT.

Lord Lovat replied to the long and accurate detail 1714 of his cousin, that he was satisfied, the measure recommended to him by his clan, by his friends in Scotland, and at London, was the best he could adopt. He observed, however, that the execution was extremely difficult; that he was a prisoner in France, and could not leave it but at the imminent risk of his life; that the Court of St. Germains was inexorable towards him; and that the Court of France would never grant him permission to return, without the consent of St. Germains.

Mr. Fraser observed to this, that he had found numbers, both English and Scots, who were continually going into Britain by order of the Court of St. Germains and with the consent of Queen Anne; that Lord Lovat ought therefore to try that Court for the last time, and know, whether, after fourteen years exile and imprisonment, he might not at length be permitted to return to his own country. He added, that, if he pleased, he would carry his letters for that purpose to Lord Perth, and his other friends and relations in France.

Lord Lovat consented to the proposal. He was willing, that his clan and his relations might have nothing with which to reproach him. He however begged his cousin to have patience, till he had previously acquainted with his intention the Marquis de Torcy, the Countess de la Roche Millaye, the Marquis

1714 de Callieres, secretary of the closet to the Most Christian King, and M. de Roujeault, intendant of Rouen, his intimate friends, who were all at that time at Paris. He accordingly wrote by the first post after the arrival of Mr. Fraser, informing them of that event, and that he was going to send him immediately to Court to acquaint the administration with the state of affairs in Scotland, and to endeavour to obtain leave to return to his clan, who demanded him with groans and tears.

In ten days, the Countess de la Roche dispatched M. de Grange Rouge post to Saumur, not daring to commit her sentiments to paper. She desired this officer to prevail on Lord Lovat, by no means to send his relation to Court: to represent to him, that the good understanding between the King of France and Queen Anne was now at so high a pitch, that, if the Court found any individual, that dared to move a finger to the injury of this harmony, or to excite troubles in Scotland, they would ruin that individual without redemption; that, if he had any regard for his life, his liberty or the repose of his friends, he must by all means keep himself easy and quiet, and send back his relation to Scotland without visiting the Courts of France and St. Germains; that, if he ventured upon a step so pregnant with calamity, she must from that moment drop all correspondence with him, and beg him to return all her letters.

Lord Lovat was greatly alarmed at this message.

He saw himself in palpable danger on whatever side 1714 he turned. Since however he had advertised the Marquis de Torcy and his other friends, that he was upon the point of sending to them his relation just arrived from Scotland, he resolved at all events not to fail of his purpose. Nor was this his only motive. He was willing, that his relation should be an eye-witness of the barbarous injustice of the Court of St. Germains, and should be able to give an exact account and an unquestionable testimony upon the subject, when he should return to Scotland. He therefore prepared the necessary letters, and immediately dispatched Mr. James Fraser to Paris.

Mr. Fraser waited according to his instructions upon the Marquis de Callieres, and delivered his dispatches. At the same time he thanked him, in the name of the whole clan of the Frasers, for the generous and persevering services that the Marquis had rendered to their chief during his disgrace, imprisonment and exile. M. de Callieres replied, that he was, and always had been the faithful friend of Lord Lovat; that he perfectly knew his innocence, and the services he had rendered to his King and the Court of France; and that nothing but opportunity had been wanting, to show the sincerity of his affection by the most essential services.

Having perused Lord Lovat's dispatches, he added, that nothing could be done for his chief but by the motion and consent of St. Germains; but that he

1714 would give him a letter to his friend Lord Perth, desiring that nobleman to write to the Queen, who was at this time in the convent of Chaillot, and upon whom every thing depended for the release and re-establishment of Lord Lovat.

Mr. Fraser having received this letter, repaired to St. Germains, where he was extremely well received by the nobleman to whom it was addressed. Lord Perth, having read the letters of Lord Lovat and M. de Callieres, protested that he had at all times been Lord Lovat's friend; that he had suffered a great deal upon his account; but that that lord had taken such accumulated steps against the interests of the King his master, that it was now too late, to think of undertaking to justify him.

Mr. Fraser replied, that Lord Perth ought by no means to give credit to the enemies of Lord Lovat, that nothing was more easy than to invent a thousand calumnies against him, and that it was not very difficult to gain them a pretty general belief, while that nobleman was out of a condition to reply to them. 'All this is true,' said Lord Perth, 'but the proofs I speak of, so unquestionably establish his uniform treachery to his King, and his rooted attachment to the party of Hanover, that no loyal subject acquainted with them, will ever dare to say a word in his favour. But I will make yourself the judge.'

At these words, he turned to a bureau, and took out

LIFE OF LORD LOVAT. 817

of one of the drawers two or three letters. Holding 1714 them in his hand, 'Mr. Fraser,' said he, 'we have had but too many proofs of the determination of Lord Lovat to desert the party of the King. Here is the last, and the most unanswerable. It is a letter that his best friend and near relation, the Earl of Leven, who married his cousin, the sister of the Earl of Wemys, has thought himself obliged to send me, signed by his own hand, with advice of the tergiversation of your chief; in order that, by giving notice of it to the King, I might prevent its fatal consequences.

'Lord Leven has foreseen every objection; and has therefore inclosed a copy, word for word, in French and English, and written with his own hand, of the letter Lord Lovat sent him by his brother, conceiving Lord Leven to be still attached to the interests of Hanover, as he was when he left Britain.* In this letter he

---

* The following is an extract of Macpherson's Original Papers. The letter of Lord Lovat's corresponds in so many circumstances, that it has been thought proper to insert it. It is there said to have been 'intercepted and returned to St. Germains.'

'*The Earl of Middleton to the Marquis de Torcy.*'

(TRANSLATION.)

March the 8th, 1711.

'It is long since my sentiments of the pretended Lord Lovat were known to you. An original letter, written by him to Lord Leven, is come back to us from England. We have compared the hand-writing with that which we have from him; there is an exact resemblance, and the subject and style do not belie their author. I send you a literal translation of it. Balgony is my Lord Leven's son; the young man in the highland dress, is Lord Lovat's brother, who I believe was

informs Lord Leven, that, perceiving that the Pretender was resolved to go into Scotland, and that it was not possible for himself to escape out of France, he had sent to him his brother, whom he calls the young Highlander, that he had dispatched to Lord Leven about twelve years before with twelve attendants in Highland dresses to demand of him a paper of consequence. He adds, that he had ordered his brother to place himself at the head of his clan to join the Hanover interest, and he begged Lord Leven to protect him till his own arrival, concluding, that in the mean time he would send him from time to time, as he had already done, every information respecting the designs of the Court of St. Germains.

in France. Here, sir, is a spy of consequence unmasked, and we know very well the means of preventing this correspondence for the future.

'*Lord Lovat to the Earl of Leven.*

August 20th, N.S. 1709.
'My most dear Lord,

'Though you neglect me very much, and that you never send me any answer to my letters, yet the love I have for your person and interest makes me embrace all the occasions I can find to serve you. As I told you last year to take care of your affairs in Scotland, so I tell you now not to be less diligent. I am informed by several persons, that there is a design of going to see you towards the latter end of the campaign; but I believe that depends upon the peace. If it is done, you will see nobody; but if the war continues, you will most surely have the visit that you missed last year. If that happens, be fully persuaded, that you will see me soon after, to live and die with you, at the head of some brave fellows, that will follow me in spite of all mankind. I wrote, two months ago, to your lordship by a French officer of the English guards. This letter is only to acquaint you of the design in hand. If I have entire certainty of the time it should

'What after this,' added Lord Perth, 'can be said in favour of Lord Lovat? Read yourself the English copy of Lord Lovat's letter, and the original letter of the Earl of Leven. Let your own eyes convince you. Here are French copies of these letters which have been shewn to the Court of France.'

Mr. Fraser, having cast his eyes over the letters, replied, that it was easy for Lord Leven to make his court to the King at the expence of Lord Lovat, whom he knew to be disgraced and in prison; that his enemies might fabricate a hundred letters against him, without his being able to defend himself; and that for

---

be executed, I will send off the young lad to acquaint you, who was seven years ago in your house, with a belted plaid, with whom you left my dear Lord Balgony to keep company to, till you came home. I think my letter will be plain enough to your lordship; and I beg you may believe me your faithful servant, and that I will be still ready to venture, to the last drop of my blood, for you.

'In France.
'20th August, 1709, N.S.

The reader will probably observe that Lord Lovat has stated that the letter said to have been written by him to Lord Leven, was a copy, but that in the Earl of Middleton's billet it is asserted to have been an original; a circumstance, which, if completely established, would tend to undermine the general credit of Lord Lovat's narrative. To this point it may be worth observing, that it was not probable, that the Marquis de Torcy, to whom a translation was sent, would ever call for the original and compare the hands. James Fraser was not thus to be imposed upon, and Lord Perth was too honest a man to attempt it. If Lord Middleton deserved the character that is given him in these memoirs, he would not probably have scrupled the imposition: and perhaps Lord Lovat could not desire to have the veracity of any particular fact brought to a more favourable test, than that of the general openness and sincerity of himself and his antagonist.

1714 his own part, he was persuaded the letter in question had never originated with his chief. Lord Leven believed that the King was going to be immediately restored. What was more natural for him, than to endeavour to gain Lord Athol, who boasted that he was at the head of the royal affairs, by ruining Lord Lovat, who was his capital and declared enemy? But this calumny was an action perfectly inconsistent with the character of a man of sincerity and a man of honour. Mr. Fraser therefore intreated Lord Perth, to give no credit to an imputation, unsupported by the shadow of a proof, and brought against a man who had been persecuted and oppressed for so many years; at the same time humbly intreating his lordship, to have the goodness to write to the Queen in favour of his old friend, who had never done any thing to forfeit that title.

Here I must beg leave to stop my narration for a moment, to remind the reader, that the Earl of Leven could not possibly have any honourable motive for so strange a conduct. Let us suppose for argument sake that Lord Lovat's letter was genuine. It must still be granted, that Lord Leven was one of the vilest hypocrites upon the face of the earth, to endeavour, by betraying in so base a manner the most sacred confidence, not only to ruin the reputation of a nobleman, a near relation of his countess and children, and his intimate friend; but even to expose his life to the most imminent danger. This very letter had been a principal 1714 instrument in the hands of the Court of St. Germains, in their endeavours to prevail upon the government of France, to throw Lord Lovat into perpetual imprisonment.

Indeed, notwithstanding the circumstantial manner in which Mr. James Fraser related this incident, it was very long before he could convince his chief, that Lord Leven was capable of so base a conduct. He recollected all that had ever passed between them. He called to mind the sincere and eternal friendship, that had been a thousand times mutually sworn to by both of them. And he was satisfied, that in no instance had he ever in the minutest point infringed upon so sacred a vow.

To the request that Mr. Fraser still urged upon Lord Perth, his lordship replied, 'I am satisfied that every thing I can either write or do will be of no service to your chief; and that the King and Queen are both resolved never to listen to a syllable that shall be said in his behalf. But since you assure me, that your clan of the Frasers, which has rendered so important services to their King and country, will be totally ruined, if Lord Lovat be not at their head, I will write in his favour to the Queen mother, to the King, to Sir Thomas Higgins, Secretary of State,* and to Mr.

---

* Sir Thomas Higgins succeeded Lord Middleton in that office. The Earl resigned in the beginning of December, 1713, but he appears for some time to have retained his connections and influence with his Court.

Y

1714 Innes, the almoner, who has great ascendancy over the King. You may depend upon my rendering every service in my power to the family of Lovat, and the clan of the Frasers.'

Mr. James Fraser expressed himself in terms of gratitude to Lord Perth for his kindness, and took leave of him. As he was quitting the apartment Lord Perth added, 'Perhaps you may have more success in your affair than I was apt to imagine. We have this morning received intelligence of the death of Queen Anne; and, if the news be confirmed, the King will feel how useful Lord Lovat may be to him in Scotland, and this consideration may engage him to grant him his liberty.' Mr. Fraser answered, that, if Queen Anne were dead, the King would find it his interest to recal Lord Lovat to Court, to do him ample justice, and to fix him in his party.

From Lord Perth Mr. Fraser went immediately to the Queen at Chaillot, who without hesitation granted him audience, and gave him her hand to kiss. When her Majesty had read Lord Perth's letter, she said, 'Lord Perth, I find, has shown you Lord Leven's letter, and has told you the reasons I have to complain of Lord Lovat, and how few motives to put any confidence in him.'

Mr. Fraser took the liberty of observing to the Queen, that her Majesty ought not to believe what the declared enemies of Lord Lovat had invented

against him; that nothing was more easy than to
write or speak against his chief, when he was disabled
from defending himself, or justifying his conduct to her
Majesty; that in fine, whatever fault Lord Lovat might
have formerly committed, her Majesty ought not to
lose a man, so necessary to the King's interests in
Scotland, at a time when he had need of all his loyal
subjects.

At length the Queen conceded, that, since the
service of the King demanded the release of Lord
Lovat, she would forget the many accusations and
complaints she had to make against him, and would
write to the King in his favour. At the same time
she commanded Mr. Fraser to set out immediately for
Bar-le-duc, as she had just received a confirmation of
the death of Queen Anne, and it was probable the King
would soon be obliged to quit Lorraine. This gentleman
now took leave of the Queen, who dismissed him
in the most obliging manner, wishing him every success
he desired in the affair of Lord Lovat, and telling him,
that she would have a letter at Bar-le-duc before him
in his favour.

Mr. Fraser left the Queen, well pleased with his
audience. He wrote that very evening to Lord Lovat
at Saumur, congratulating him, that the Queen was at
length perfectly reconciled to him; that she had written
to the King her son in his favour, and that there was no
longer any doubt of his obtaining his liberty in a very

1714 short time. Lord Lovat was too much surprised with this good news to be able to give much credit to it.

Next morning Mr. Fraser set out for Bar-le-duc; Mr. Hugh Campbel, son of Sir Archibald Campbel of Calder, doing him the honour to escort him a little way. About a league and a half from Paris they met a running footman, whom Mr. Campbel recollected to be in the Queen's service. At a short distance behind were two gentlemen on horseback; and after these followed a post-chaise, with the curtains drawn, and at full gallop. Mr. Fraser observed to his companion, that it was possibly the King, who was travelling with all expedition for England, on account of the death of Queen Anne. Mr. Campbel replied, that that was impossible, that he could not have been so soon advertised of that event, and that, if the Queen mother had known that the King was so near Paris, she would have told it to Mr. Fraser, and saved him his journey.

Mr. Fraser and his companion soon after separated. And the former remained ignorant till he was within ten leagues of Bar-le-duc, that it was really the King of England whom he had met a league and a half from Paris. He now encountered a great number of gentlemen of his suite, who followed him in much confusion; and who told him, that the King was set out for England, and that he might depend upon it that he would never return to Bar-le-duc.

Upon this intelligence Mr. Fraser immediately returned. Near Paris he met several gentlemen, who 1714 assured him, that the King had held secret conferences with the Marquis de Torcy; that his Most Christian Majesty had refused him either assistance or permission to pass into England; and that, after having spent two days with the Queen his mother, he was upon his return for Bar-le-duc, to remain there till circumstances should be a little better prepared.

Mr. Fraser was now convinced, that the Queen had imposed upon him, in bidding him set out for Lorraine, at a time that she knew, the King her son was upon the point of arriving at Paris in his way to England. He went however to Bar-le-duc, in order to obtain the last answer of the prince respecting Lord Lovat, whatever it might cost him.

After enduring great fatigue he arrived at that place: but the King was not there. He had just set out for Luneville, the residence of the Duke of Lorraine. Mr. Fraser, although mortified at this disappointment, proceeded immediately for Luneville, to have his audience of the Chevalier de St. George; for this was the appelation the young prince had assumed in order to go incognito to the waters of Plombieres.

At Bar-le-duc, Mr. Fraser found Doctor Innes, almoner to the King, Doctor Lesly, a clergyman of the Church of England, and Colonel Scott, a Scotsman. He had letters for these three persons, to engage them to solicit his affair. All three assured him, that he

1714 would have no success in his enterprise, that the King could not bear so much as to hear Lord Lovat named, and he was determined never to receive him into favour, unless he was solicited to it by Lord Athol.

This information was not sufficient to divert Mr. Fraser from his purpose. He went strait to Luneville, where he found the King, to whom the Duke of Lorraine and all his Court paid the same honours, as if he had been in actual possession of the three crowns. Mr. Fraser having delivered his letters to Sir Thomas Higgins, the Secretary of State, that gentleman introduced him to the King, who was walking in the gardens. The King received Mr. Fraser in a most condescending manner. He gave him his hand to kiss. He asked him many questions respecting his journey; and particularly how he had been able to find his way so far without speaking a word of French.

They now entered the Duke's palace: and the King having retired to his closet, Sir Thomas Higgins followed, and desired Mr. Fraser to accompany him. As soon as he appeared, the King, having read Lord Perth's letter, said, 'I understand you have been at Saumur to visit Lord Lovat.' 'Yes, sire.' 'I am sorry for it,' said the King. 'I do not wish any of my subjects to have any concern with the man; and for my own part I cannot bear so much as to hear his name.'

Mr. Fraser answered, that he was in extreme pain to hear the King speak in this manner of the head of his family; and that he most humbly intreated his Majesty not to give credit to the calumnies, which his enemies had invented for the express purpose of depriving him of the King's good opinion. His Majesty ought to recollect the services Lord Lovat had from his earliest youth rendered to his father. He ought to call to mind the loyal and illustrious actions of his ancestors for more than twenty generations.

But this was not all. He would intreat the King, to attend to the services which Lord Lovat and his clan were in a condition actually to render him in the present situation of his affairs. He assured his Majesty, that Lord Lovat was a nobleman the most capable of advancing his interests in the north, where, in all appearance, the King would first think of forming an army. He observed, that Lord Lovat was not only cousin-german to the greatest chiefs in the Highlands, but related to and beloved by almost every clan in Scotland; that his own clan had always been regarded as surpassed by no other in courage; that its situation was so favourable, that it might be assembled in four and twenty or thirty hours, while almost every other clan was so scattered, that it could scarcely be assembled and conducted to the low country near Inverness, in less than a month; that on the contrary, the clan of Lord Lovat surrounded the lake; and that, if his Majesty lost Lord Lovat and his clan, he would lose the key to the whole north of Scotland.

1714 The King replied, he was determined never to grant Lord Lovat any share in his confidence; nor on this account, would he lose the clan of the Frasers; he was well and authentically informed, that the Frasers would pay much respect to the recommendations of Lord Athol, and that they would assemble under the orders of Mr. Mackenzie of Prestonhal (who, in compensation for pretended debts, had held the estates of Lord Lovat since his residence in France), and join the standard of that nobleman.

Mr. Fraser rejoined, that people were much to blame to deceive his Majesty in so gross a manner; that the clan of the Frasers would never take the field but under the command of Lord Lovat; and that, if Prestonhal were mad enough to put himself at their head, he would be so saluted with musket bullets, that light would be seen through every part of his body: that the Scottish clans were so much attached to their natural chiefs that they were not only ready to obey them in opposition to the lairds their neighbours, but in defiance of all the kings upon the face of the earth. This remark was confirmed by Sir Thomas Higgins, who observed, that it was well known, the clans would never follow any person but their natural heads.

Upon this the King flew into a passion, and told Mr. Fraser that he would give the clan of the Frasers any other head, any other commander they pleased; but that he would never be reconciled to Lord Lovat, nor admit him into his favour. Mr. Fraser replied, 1714 that he was then very sorry to say, that he thought it his duty to observe, that, unless he first gave liberty to Lord Lovat, and sent him among them, his Majesty must never hope to have the Frasers under his standard.

To this the King answered with an air of indignation; 'Talk to me no more of the man. When I come into Scotland, I will head the Frasers myself, and I am very sure they will follow me. In the mean time I command you, to return directly to Scotland with all the speed in your power, without going near Lord Lovat or the city of Saumur; and to assure the Frasers of my friendship and protection, and that I myself will be their chief.'

He afterwards asked several questions, respecting the nature of the country in the north of Scotland, the best season for landing there, and the quantity of provisions the country could furnish for the subsistence of an army. He commanded Mr. Fraser to tell his loyal subjects, that he expected to have been among them before this time; that it was not his fault, that he had not passed into Britain immediately upon the death of his sister, the Princess of Denmark; but that the King of France had refused him the necessary succours. 'You may however assure them, that I will be in the midst of them at a time when they least think of it.' He then gave Mr. Fraser different messages for persons whom it is of no consequence to name in this place.

1714 Afterwards he presented him his hand to kiss, and Mr. Fraser took his leave.

Having left the closet, Mr. Fraser waited in the antichamber for Sir Thomas Higgins, who remained a little time with the King after that gentleman had left him. When they joined, Mr. Fraser said, 'I am obliged, sir, to tell you, who are the King's Secretary of State, that his Majesty is ill advised; and that he will one day curse the counsellors, that engaged him to treat Lord Lovat, who was capable of rendering him more essential services than Lord Athol and all his connections, in so unworthy a manner. The King is extremely mistaken in imagining, that the Frasers will follow him, at a time when he holds their chief in prison. He may remain assured, that the Frasers will follow Lord Lovat against all the princes upon earth; and he will find no more reason to doubt, that in losing them, he has lost the best feather in his wing.'

In order however to obtain the liberty of his chief, Mr. Fraser proposed one expedient more. He said he was ready to return into Scotland, and would undertake at the peril of his head, in less than two months, to bring over to the King an engagement, signed by the most potent chiefs in the Highlands, by which they would stake their lives, and all that they had for the loyalty and good services of Lord Lovat, in case his Majesty would have the goodness, to release and receive him into favour. At the same time he added, that for himself, he dared not set foot in his own country, till he had seen his chief, and communicated to him the result of the present negociations.

Sir Thomas Higgins admitted that the proposal was extremely reasonable, and offered immediately to mention it to the King. Saying this, he opened the door, and returned into the royal closet. He remonstrated to his Majesty in a very strong manner upon Mr. Fraser's proposal. But the King instantly replied, that if every nobleman in Scotland would engage himself for Lord Lovat, he would never receive him into favour, till Lord Athol desired it. To this Sir Thomas Higgins observed, that Lord Athol could never be expected to solicit the King for a man whom he considered as his declared enemy. Being thus closely pressed, the King turned suddenly upon his heel, crying to Sir Thomas, 'Tell me no more of the man.'

Mr. Fraser, who during this interval stood opposite to the door, saw the King turn his back upon Sir Thomas. When the minister came out, and related the King's answer, he therefore asked pardon of Sir Thomas for the embarrassment he had occasioned; adding, that he would not attempt to open his mouth farther upon the subject, and was resolved to quit Luneville early the next morning. Sir Thomas desired him, in the mean time, to step with him to his apartment.

The Duke of Lorraine, having understood, that

1714 there was a gentleman from the Highlands of Scotland arrived at his Court to speak to the King, begged his Majesty to order this Highlander to dine with them the next day. The King immediately sent to desire Sir Thomas Higgins to stop Mr. Fraser, who received the order with all the respect and submission that was due to it, and dined next day with his Majesty and the Duke of Lorraine.

The Duke, being informed, that the Highlander had come from Scotland to Luneville on foot, and that he preferred that mode of travelling to riding on horseback, presumed that he did not know how to mount a horse. The Highlander offered, if his Royal Highness would permit him, to mount the best blooded horse in his stables. Said the Duke, 'We are going a hunting after dinner, and I will provide you with a horse, in order to see an exhibition of your skill.'

The King, the Duke and Duchess of Lorraine, and the ladies of the Court now prepared for the chace. They gave Mr. Fraser the most vigorous horse in their stables, and luckily Sir Thomas Higgins at the same time provided him with a very heavy and substantial pair of boots. Scarcely was he mounted, when the beast, who was perfectly savage and unbroken, made such furious curvets, that he expected every moment to be crushed to death against the walls of the court. He had however been brought up a very good horseman, and therefore kept his seat in a firm manner in spite of the viciousness of his horse, till the dogs had turned 1714 out the hare.

Then Mr. Fraser put spurs to his horse, and presently outstripped the harriers. He turned the hare three or four times, and struck him with a large whip that he carried in his hand. He leaped every hedge and ditch that came in his way; lost his hat and his wig; and excited infinite laughter in all the Court, who expected every moment that he would break his neck. The ladies however had not the pleasure of seeing much of the hare, Mr. Fraser having killed it in the beginning of the chase.

Upon their return the Duke of Lorraine observed to the Highlander, that, since he was so good a horseman, it would be pity that he should return again into Scotland on foot: he would give him a horse that should enable him to perform his journey in a more agreable manner. The Highlander made a profound bow for his Highness's generosity. Mean while the Duchess of Lorraine, having observed that he had smoked tobacco, had the goodness to make him a present of a very fine Hungary pipe.

Next day he set out with his horse and his pipe, highly charmed with the gracious manners of the Duke and Duchess of Lorraine, and the honours that had been paid him at their Court, which is indeed an extremely polite one. Mr. Fraser rode in two days from Luneville to Paris, and was two days more in travelling

14 from Paris to Saumur, which together amounted to one hundred and forty leagues. He was however almost disabled with the expedition he had made.

He had not judged proper to return to the Courts either of France or St. Germains, being anxious to make his report to Lord Lovat at soon as possible. He told him, that, so far from having been able to obtain his release, he had found him to be ruined for ever with the King of England, insomuch that all his friends in Scotland united would not be able to make his peace for him. He related what had passed in that business between him, Lord Perth, the Queen Dowager, and the King. He observed, that as he understood from Sir Thomas Higgins, the King was resolved to set out for Scotland in the following month, which was October, and that, if he did not make his escape before that time, he must expect to be confined for life, and consequently ruined without resource, while his clan was dispersed, lost and annihilated for ever.

From this moment Lord Lovat thought no longer of any thing but quitting France as soon as possible. He considered however, that he had given his parole of honour in writing to the Marquis de Torcy, that he would not leave the kingdom without the consent of the Most Christian King. He knew that M. de Torcy, as his friend, had long wished his return to his own country, as he was unable to obtain any kind of justice from the Court of St. Germains. Lord Lovat therefore thought proper to write to the Marquis, to acquaint 1714 him with the last act of cruelty and injustice of the Court of St. Germains, and the King of England.

In his letter he observed, that he no longer thought even his life secure in France, while that prince, his mother or Lord Middleton had any influence in it. He most humbly intreated M. de Torcy, not to regard his departure as a breach of his parole. He reminded him, that he had remained nine years before, and one year since the peace, a prisoner; that during this period he had every year demanded his liberty; or, if that were refused, to be brought to his trial in form for the treason, of which without the shadow of foundation he had been accused; but that he had been unable to obtain either the one or the other. He therefore added, that he was resolved to go and hazard his life at the head of his clan, for the restoration of a house that he had ruined in the service of the two Courts; that he had nothing further to look for in France but a perpetual imprisonment; and that he would therefore take the silence of his Excellency for a tacit permission to return to the Highlands.

Having dispatched this letter, Lord Lovat prepared in the best manner he could for his journey. Since however he was proscribed in England and in Scotland, and a price set upon his head, he determined, before he exposed himself by going into Britain, to learn what the Duke of Argyle, his brother the Earl of Ilay, and his other friends, were willing to do for him. For this purpose he dispatched one of his servants into England, with letters for the Duke of Argyle, the Earl of Ilay, and Brigadier General Grant, his relation and neighbour. He requested to know, whether by their interest he could obtain his pardon from King George; promising, in that case, to return to his own province, to serve the government with all possible fidelity, and to live and die in their party. All that he desired was to escape from the tyranny of the Court of St. Germains, to find a quiet retreat in his own country, and to obtain the protection of the reigning prince against his enemies in Scotland.

After having spent ten days in London, his servant returned post to Saumur without bringing any dispatches in writing. He however assured Lord Lovat, that he had seen the Earl of Ilay; Brigadier General Grant; the two Secretaries of State for England, Lord Townshend and General Stanhope; and Mr. Smith, father in law to Brigadier Grant: that they had all directed him to assure Lord Lovat that he had nothing to do, but to set out for England without loss of time, and that as soon as he arrived his affair would be accomplished without difficulty: he had but one danger to guard against, that of being surprised upon the road; since, if he fell into the hands of government in his escape from France, he would be thrown into perpetual imprisonment, and ruined without redemption.

Mr. John Fraser, his lordship's brother, at that time 1714 in London, and Mr. Alexander Fraser, who solicited his affairs in that place, wrote him by post the same things that his servant had told him verbally, adding, that they had been particularly confirmed to them by Brigadier General Grant. They therefore pressed him to pass into England without delay, for that nothing but his presence was necessary to his success.

Being also extremely urged by his cousin James Fraser who was with him, and by his servant who had been in England, to set out without delay, for fear of being surprised and imprisoned for life, Lord Lovat at length resolved to bid adieu to France. He left his furniture, and his other little property, in the confusion that is inevitable in such a conjuncture. About the twelfth of October 1714, under pretence of going to Rouen to pay a visit to his intimate and venerable friend M. de Roujeault, intendant of that generality, he took leave of Saumur, attended by Mr. James Fraser and two servants.

Since however he took with him the most valuable of his portable effects, packed in military chests and loaded upon horses, it was suspected by several persons, that he was going to pass into England, though there were only a very few of his most intimate friends that were privy to his design. The King's lieutenant at Saumur was upon a hunting party at some leagues distance, when Lord Lovat left that place. At his

1714 return he was extremely alarmed at this event, though that nobleman had some time before spoken to him of his intention. It is said, that he was so extremely apprehensive of a reprimand from the Court, that he dispatched several persons to arrest Lord Lovat upon the road. It is certain, that he wrote immediately to the Marquis de Torcy, to acquaint him with Lord Lovat's having escaped in his absence; and to inform him, that it was assured he was about to pass into England; that he had left Saumur with an intention to proceed to the house of M. de Roujeault at Rouen, and that therefore his excellency might take such measures in the affair as he judged to be proper.

Lord Lovat knew nothing of what passed at Saumur after his departure. He had however originally been upon his guard against all sorts of dangers. He travelled almost day and night all the way to Rouen, as if his enemies had been close at his heels. Upon his arrival at that place, extremely fatigued with the bad roads of the province of Normandy, he repaired immediately to the house of his friend M. de Roujeault, of whose generous attachment he had too large and uniform an experience to conceal from him any part of his conduct.

Accordingly he made to him a faithful relation of the last instances of injustice and inveteracy of the Court of St. Germains; adding, that he could no longer consider himself as secure, either of his liberty,

or his life in France. He communicated to him the 1714
promises that had been made by the Duke of Argyle,
the Earl of Ilay his brother, and his other friends at
London, that they would obtain for him the pardon
and protection of King George upon his arrival, and
his consequent design of proceeding to that place. He
intreated M. de Roujeault, to have the generosity to
procure for him the means of passing from some part of
the coast of Normandy into England; as the journey
from Rouen to Calais was long and dangerous, especially
on account of the baggage he had with him.

M. de Roujeault replied, that he was sorry Lord
Lovat was about to leave France in this manner, but
that he could not blame him after the accumulated
instances of ill treatment he had received from the
Court of St. Germains. He observed, that it was impossible for him to take any active concern in his
escape; and that he could not avoid writing to M. de
Torcy, to acquaint him with his having been with him
at Rouen. He therefore advised him to leave his
baggage at that place, to be sent to London in some
English vessel, and to make all the speed he could,
unincumbered, lest he should be arrested before he had
left the kingdom.

M. de Roujeault further recommended to him to go
immediately to Dieppe; where he might possibly find
an English vessel ready to sail, or if not there, at some
other port upon the coast between Dieppe and Calais,

He wished him a safe voyage, and assured him of his unalterable friendship; but added, that he considered the undertaking as extremely hazardous, and was very anxious upon his account. Lord Lovat now took leave of M. de Roujeault, with tears in his eyes, destitute of all hope ever to see again this most generous friend. He conjured him however still to continue to him a small share in his memory and good wishes.

Lord Lovat's servant, who was a Scotsman, found by chance the master of an English vessel, who told him that he should sail for London in five or six days. In pursuance of M. de Roujeault's plan, he proposed to this captain, to take on board the baggage of his master, who was an Englishman of quality; and, as he added, having found the captain in all appearance extremely zealous for the house of Hanover, a relation of the Duke of Argyle, and a faithful adherent of King George.

The captain replied, that, since his master was a friend to King George, he would serve him upon his knees. Satisfied therefore with his success, the servant conducted him to Lord Lovat's *auberge*. No sooner was the man introduced to Lord Lovat, than he began to pray God to bless him, as he was a friend to the great King George, his valiant sovereign. Persuaded by the warm and enthusiastic manners of the captain, Lord Lovat made him drink a health to the King and to the Duke of Argyle, and without hesitation intrusted

to him his baggage, not suffering himself in his haste to 1714
take out of it a little box, containing a number of rings
and other jewels of value.

The captain now added that he had on board his
vessel several tons of wine, addressed to the Earl of
Halifax, and sent by Mr. Arbuthnot, brother to Doctor
Arbuthnot, late physician to Queen Anne. Lord Lovat
was well informed, that Mr. Arbuthnot, who resided at
Rouen, was the confident of the Court of St. Germains,
and the man of his rank in all France, the most employed for the late King James and the Chevalier de
St. George. He therefore intreated the captain by no
means to tell Mr. Arbuthnot, that a relation of the Duke
of Argyle had shipped his baggage on board his vessel.

Having addressed his military chests to Brigadier
General Grant, and in his absence to the Duke of
Argyle, he caused them to be put on board the vessel;
and, taking a receipt for them, he set out an hour after
with all diligence for Dieppe.

Mr. Arbuthnot received information from the honest
captain and an Irish factor of the name of Ross, his interpreter, that Lord Lovat had shipped his baggage on
board their vessel. He immediately sent this intelligence to the Court of St. Germains, who obtained
without delay an order from the Court of France to
arrest Lord Lovat and seize upon his baggage. The
order was forwarded by the Marquis de Torcy to the
Duke de Luxembourg, governor of Normandy; who,

1714 as soon as he received it, dispatched men different ways to take Lord Lovat, and to secure his effects.

Lord Lovat had happily passed into England before it was possible for these people to overtake him. His two military chests however were seized and conveyed to the castle of the Duke de Luxembourg, where they were opened before his secretary; but there was not found in them any paper against the State, as the Court of St. Germains had given out. The Duke de Luxembourg ordered them therefore to be immediately sealed, and delivered over to Ross, the Irish interpreter, to be forwarded with all safety according to their address at London.

This wretch, who had probably no other means of subsistence than his villainy, broke open the seals of the Duke of Luxembourg and the locks of the chests, and completely stripped them of their most valuable contents, together with the little casket of jewels. Two months after, the chests were sent by another vessel and almost empty, so that Lord Lovat received of all his baggage only a few suits of clothes.

Lord Lovat, knowing the danger to which he was exposed, and finding no ship at Dieppe, left that place immediately; and travelled along the coast of Normandy, and from thence through Picardy, as far as Boulogne. During this journey he met with no opportunity of passing into England; and, not daring to go to Calais, he determined to sail from Boulogne, what-

LIFE OF LORD LOVAT. 843

ever it cost him. For this purpose he employed a man, 1714 to whom he had been recommended at Boulogne, to hire a small smack to carry him to any part of England which it could first make.

This gentleman brought to him a seaman, who was accustomed to pass and repass from England without being suspected, because he was by profession a fisherman. Lord Lovat agreed with him to sail immediately. This was accordingly done, and, after having been exposed to a rough sea during the whole night, he gained Dover with considerable trouble about ten in the morning, November the first, 1714.

Lord Lovat met upon the quay with his cousin, Mr. Alexander Fraser, who solicited his affairs in London, and whom he had requested to meet him at this place. Having spent one night at Dover on account of his extreme fatigue, they set out next morning for London, where they arrived in two days.

Immediately upon his arrival Lord Lovat dispatched Mr. James and Mr. Alexander Fraser to the Earl of Ilay and Brigadier General Grant. Brigadier Grant was delighted at Lord Lovat's being arrived in good health, and hastened immediately to wait upon him, and to assure him of every good office in his power. The Earl of Ilay was very far from being equally pleased with the intelligence. It gave him much affliction and regret, to see this nobleman once more in England without being yet in safety, even in respect to his life. He expressed the sincerest regret for his having quitted a regular pension in France, at a time that he had nothing to depend upon in Britain. He however promised to speak in Lord Lovat's behalf that very evening to the King and the Prince; and he desired the gentleman, who had waited upon him, to return next day to learn his Majesty's answer.

When Lord Lovat received this message, he began to repent having precipitated himself into so imminent a danger; there being a sentence of death in force against him in Scotland, and a price fixed upon his head, without having any thing to rely upon for his pardon, but a precarious promise from his friends. He was however too deeply embarked, to be able to draw back; and he finally determined, regardless of the consequences, to throw himself upon the protection of the Duke of Argyle and the Earl of Ilay, to live and die in their service, and to take no step in his affairs, but by their concurrence and direction.

The day following he received intelligence by the same persons, that Lord Ilay had spoken to the King and the Prince, that both of them were well disposed towards Lord Lovat, but they had observed, that prudence demanded, that they should require from that nobleman security for his future loyalty, before they granted him his pardon. Lord Ilay said, that to comply with this requisition, it was necessary to present an address to the King in behalf of Lord Lovat, signed by all his friends, who were well affected towards the present Government; and that in this address they should enter into an engagement for the loyalty of Lord Lovat, in any sum the King pleased. He added, that he would draw up a sketch of such an address as would be proper, which he accordingly did two days after. 1714

With this address Lord Lovat dispatched his cousin James into Scotland, to collect the signatures of his friends. No sooner had he arrived in the county of Inverness where the estates of Lord Lovat are situated, and declared his errand, than all the lairds, and in a word all the nobility, who were well affected to the government, not only of the county of Inverness, but of the county of Murray, the county of Nairn, the county of Ross, and the county of Sutherland, vied with each other in giving in their subscriptions.

Mr. James Fraser carried the address signed by the counties of Inverness, Murray and Nairn, and gave it into the hands of the Earl of Ilay, who was then at Edinburgh. On the other hand, Mr. Monro, laird of Foulis, and colonel of the regiment of the Scottish Guards, tendered it to the Earl of Sutherland, Lord Strathnaver, and the nobility of the counties of Ross and Sutherland; and, after they had signed it, carried his copy to Edinburgh. Lord Ilay took with him these two addresses to London, where he arrived March the first, 1715. 1715

From this moment Lord Lovat believed, that his

affair would be immediately expedited. But a new and unforeseen obstacle arose. The Duke of Montrose, Secretary of State for Scotland, was gained, as it is said, by the influence of the house of Athol and the money of Mackenzie of Prestonhal. He therefore earnestly opposed himself to the pardon, and represented Lord Lovat to the King as unworthy of his clemency.

Lord Ilay was the greatest and most refined politician in the island of Great Britain. Finding the Secretary of State for Scotland in his way, he thought proper to defer Lord Lovat's affair, till, by his own influence, and that of the Duke of Argyle, whose credit at the Court of London was extremely high, he had gained the English ministers, and by their means was able to set at defiance the Duke of Montrose and his interest.

Lord Lovat however was extremely mortified at this event. He had expected, that his affair would be completed the moment he set foot in England. Far from this, by the opposition of the Duke of Montrose, he was obliged to wait in London, from the close of the month of October 1714, to the close of the month of July 1715, with his brother, his two kinsmen and three servants, a circumstance attended with great expence, and with not less anxiety and uneasiness.

In the mean time, about the fifteenth of July 1715, the Court of London received intelligence from the Earl of Stair, their ambassador to the Court of France, that the Pretender was upon the point of invading the three kingdoms, with the French fleet which had been employed for the reduction of Majorca. This alarm roused the diligence of Lord Lovat's friends. They applied to the English ministers; and, having obtained from them a promise that they would exert themselves in the affair of Lord Lovat, Lord Ilay intreated Lord Sutherland and Brigadier General Grant, to present to the King the two addresses he had brought up from Scotland.

They were presented on Sunday the twenty-fourth of July. The Earl of Orkney, who was the Lord in Waiting, held out his hand to receive them from the King, according to custom. The King however drew them back, folded them up, and, as if he had been pre-advised of their contents, put them in his pocket.

* * * * * * * *

FINIS.

CPSIA information can be obtained
at www.ICGtesting.com
Printed in the USA
LVHW081904271121
704614LV00002B/46

9 781340 691370